IMAGES
*of America*

# ESCALON

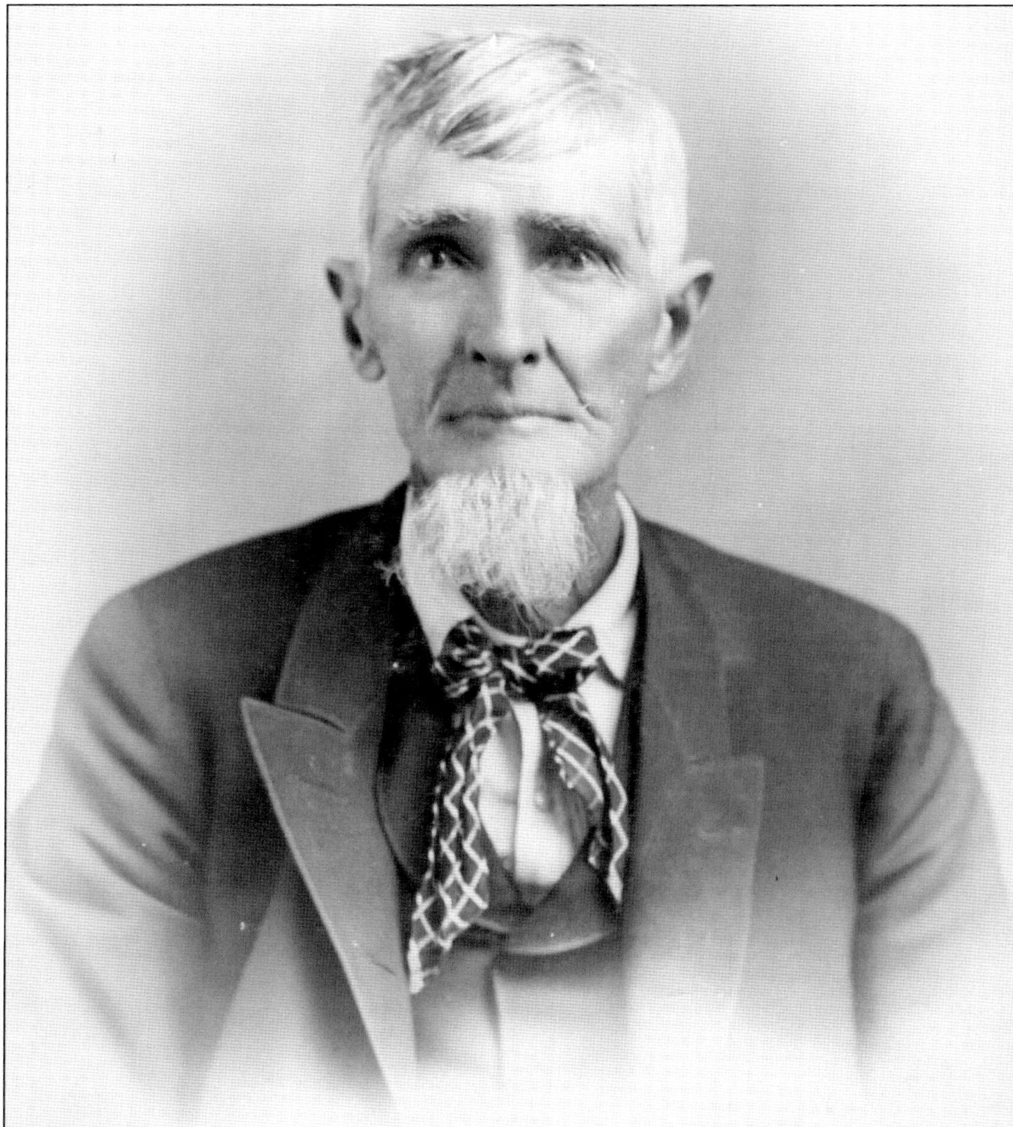

In the 1850s, John Wheeler Jones was the first settler on the land that was to become Escalon. Having arrived in the area with his family, he eventually amassed more than 8,000 acres, on which he operated a large grain farm. He died in 1893, leaving his son, James Wesley Jones, a part of his farm. James began laying out the town of Escalon on this land in 1894 to serve the newly arriving railroad and to be a center for the growing farming community. He chose the name Escalon, Spanish for step or stepping stone, after seeing the word in a publication in the Stockton Free Library. (Courtesy of the Escalon Historical Society.)

**ON THE COVER:** Hugh Litzenberg, proudly advertising Litzenberg's (Litz) Meat Market, then a downtown business, is leading this section of the Armistice Day parade southeast down Main Street in 1934 or 1935. Other downtown businesses from that time, visible in the photograph, include the Escalon Bakery Fountain and a Ford garage. The Escalon banner was proudly hung across Main Street at Second Street when festive events such as this took place. Note the vintage automobiles and the photographer using a camera on a tripod. (Courtesy of Angelo Dugo.)

IMAGES
*of America*

# ESCALON

Barbara Willis and the Escalon Historical Society

ARCADIA
PUBLISHING

ISBN 978-0-7385-5903-2

Published by Arcadia Publishing
Charleston, South Carolina

Printed in the United States of America

Library of Congress Catalog Card Number: 2008924119

For all general information contact Arcadia Publishing at:
Telephone 843-853-2070
Fax 843-853-0044
E-mail sales@arcadiapublishing.com
For customer service and orders:
Toll-Free 1-888-313-2665

Visit us on the Internet at www.arcadiapublishing.com

*This book—a compilation of images, memories, facts, and reminiscences—is dedicated to Angelo Dugo. Because of his interest and love of photography, Mr. Dugo made photography his vocation and accumulated many photographs of Escalon and the surrounding area over a period of many years. Without Mr. Dugo's experiences and recollections, this book might not have been undertaken, nor even have been possible.*

# Contents

# ACKNOWLEDGMENTS

Many people provided me with encouragement and support when this task seemed daunting; knowledge and memories when solicited or prompted; and advice when this project became theirs. Assistance was given by historical society members in general and by some others in particular. Help was also given by a few who joined the society when moved to do so. Many thanks to Irma Bailey, Bill Gonzales, Jeff Gonzales, Sam Jones, John Largent, Minnie Laugero, Palmer Little, Mary Loumena, Vickie Mello, Esther Payne, Jim Payne, Leonard Pereira, Annie Santini, Adice Schuchterman, Chuck Van Gorkum, Marianne Weerts, Mary Rose Wheeler, and John Wright. The Escalon Historical Museum proved to be a treasure trove of caption material based on the efforts of history buffs both past and present, and the myriad reports by Arthur Sanguinetti's high school history students on people, buildings, and businesses in and around Escalon. Relied on for their research were Elsie Alfieri's "Unforgettable Atlanta" and Frank S. Thornton's "History of the Escalon Community in California." Most of all, Angelo Dugo's efforts to preserve the history of Escalon in photographs and his fervent desire to share this history with future generations are appreciated. All the photographs included in this book belong to the Escalon Historical Museum or to Angelo Dugo. Credit is given to the original photographer if other than Dugo and when the name is known.

# INTRODUCTION

Escalon came into being in the late 1800s because of the agricultural production in the immediate area and the need to get the products of that agriculture to market by railroad. John Wheeler Jones settled here with his family in the 1850s, and his son, James Wesley Jones, laid out the community of Escalon 40-plus years later. Although Escalon was incorporated in 1957, celebrating its 50-year anniversary in 2007 by proclamation of Escalon's city council, 1994 was officially acknowledged as the year to celebrate the Escalon centennial. Citizens of Escalon concerned about preserving the rich history of their community formed the Escalon Historical Society in 1989, which, in turn, founded the Escalon Historical Museum later that same year. Today in its fourth location, the museum has on display many artifacts, photographs, and memorabilia that bring to life the history of Escalon and provide fodder to many amusing and entertaining reminiscences on the part of museum volunteers and visitors alike. Monthly society meetings and old-timer gatherings at the museum are spirited and lively. Many additional items pledged to the museum by Escalon residents await space for their display.

In Escalon's days as a fledgling community, when downtown businesses were beginning to thrive, there occurred a series of fires (in 1912, 1916, 1917, and 1920) constituting setbacks to many. Buildings were built and rebuilt, and now stand in tribute to the strength and determination of those committed to Escalon's future. Many original structures were lost, but in many cases, photographic records remain of a life remembered now by only a few.

Angelo Dugo was a photographer by vocation and took most of the photographs on display in the museum. He was instrumental in bringing about the start of the museum by selling much of his photographic collection to the Escalon Historical Society for a symbolic fee of $1, with the stipulation that it be on display at the yet-to-be-established museum and not be reproduced for anyone else's profit. His private collection supplements that of the museum's and together comprise the images in this book.

The pioneer spirit that spawned Escalon and brought people here from around the globe has led to the diversity in agriculture, religion, and life that makes Escalon the unique community it was, is, and will continue to be.

# *One*

# Early Agriculture

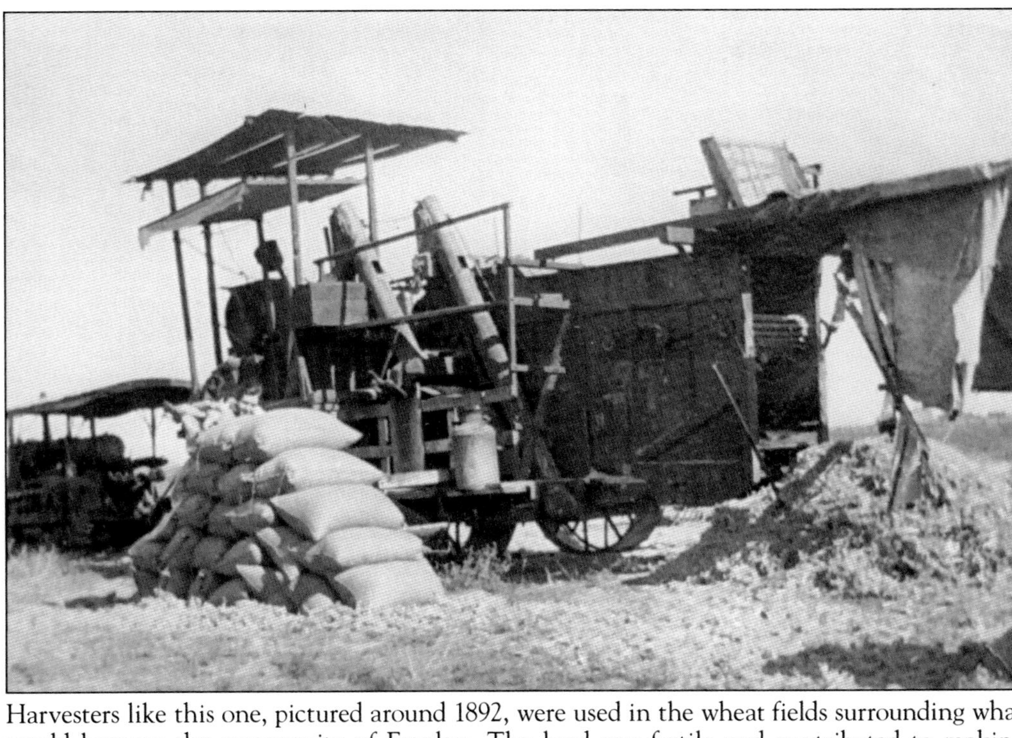

Harvesters like this one, pictured around 1892, were used in the wheat fields surrounding what would become the community of Escalon. The land was fertile and contributed to making California one of the highest-ranking states in wheat production in the late 1800s.

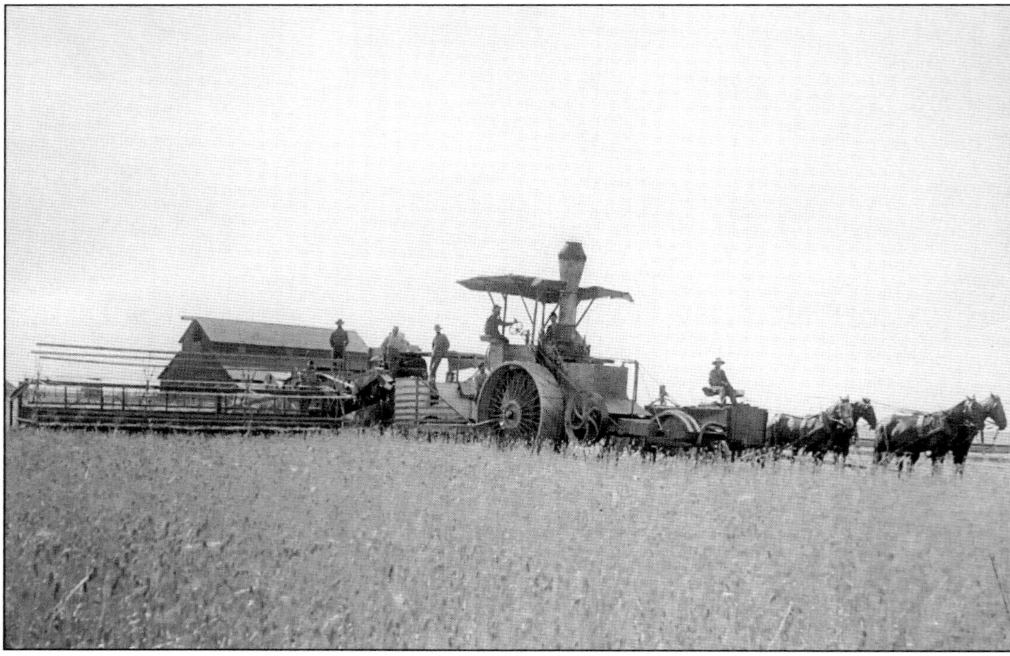

This horse-drawn harvester was also a type used in the wheat fields surrounding what would become the community of Escalon. The first grain crops grown in this area were planted by hand. Wheat was one of the major crops in this central part of California because it could survive and produce a crop on very little water.

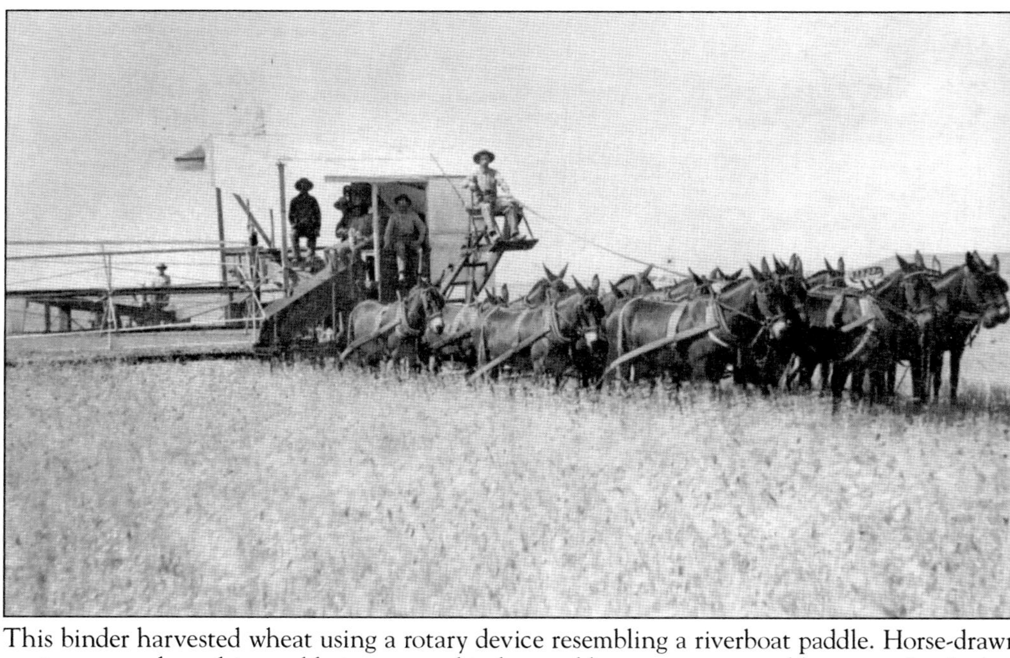

This binder harvested wheat using a rotary device resembling a riverboat paddle. Horse-drawn equipment such as this would give way to binders and harvesters powered by steam. In the late 1800s, a team of horses and/or mules and several men would accomplish in several days what today can be done in minutes.

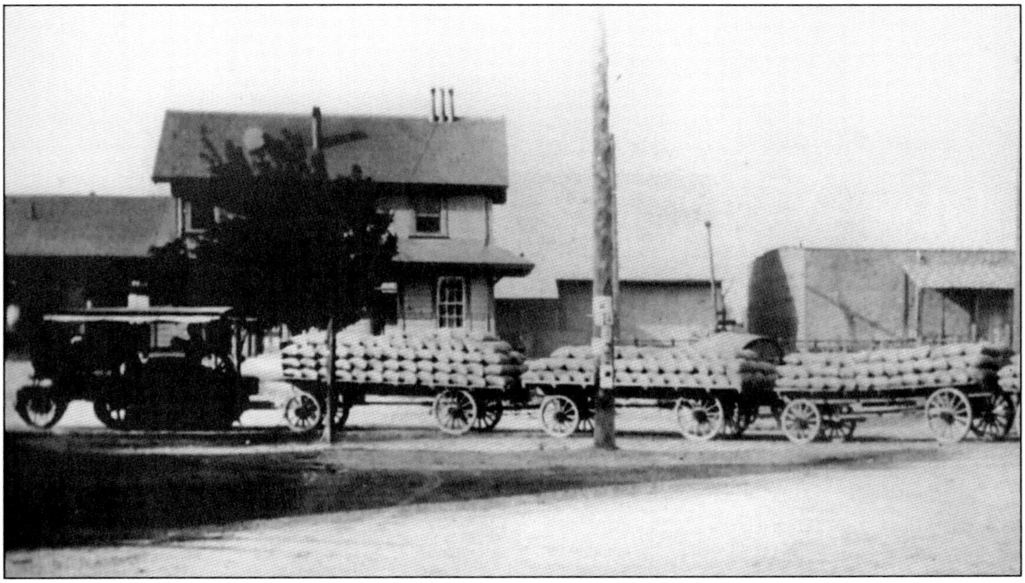

Grain was delivered to the Farmington depot in the early days of the 1890s. With the arrival of the railroad in Escalon in the late 1890s and the development of a good network of roads crisscrossing in and around Escalon, Farmington would be eclipsed as the hub for the shipping of agricultural products. This photograph was donated to the Escalon Historical Museum by Tom Erle.

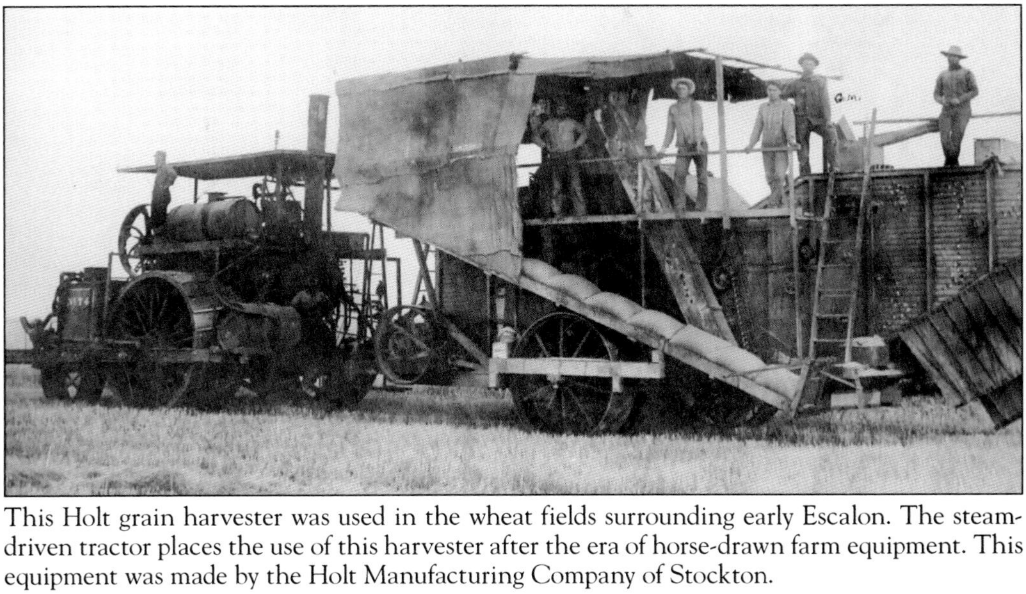

This Holt grain harvester was used in the wheat fields surrounding early Escalon. The steam-driven tractor places the use of this harvester after the era of horse-drawn farm equipment. This equipment was made by the Holt Manufacturing Company of Stockton.

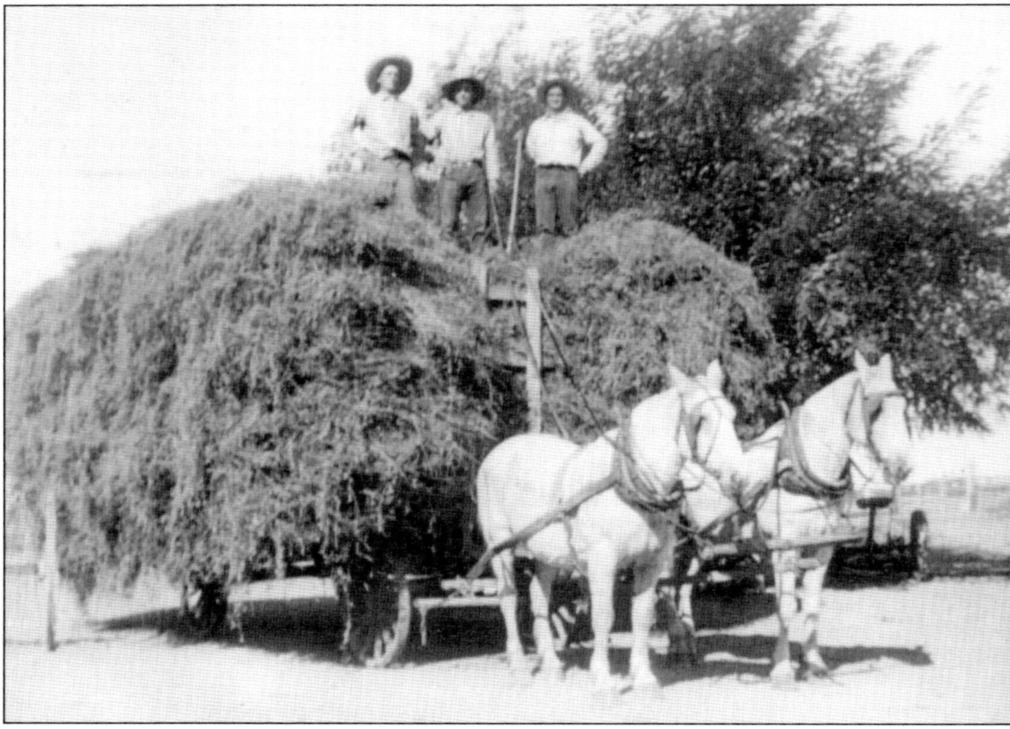

From left to right, dairy farmers Joe Pereira, Manuel Gomes, and Manuel Pereira transport hay to the barn after the harvest. Dairy farms became numerous in the early 1900s because of the influx of Swedish immigrants to the area.

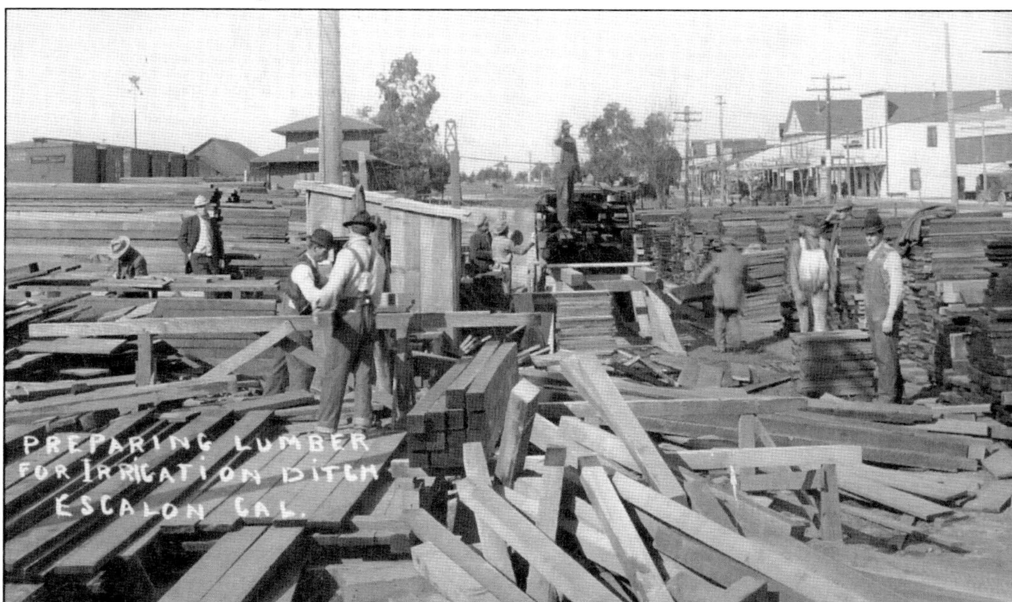


These men are preparing lumber for an irrigation ditch around 1912. Escalon's Santa Fe Depot is visible in the background just left of center. Early downtown structures are visible on the right. With the advent of irrigation, crops other than wheat could be cultivated in greater quantity, and farms became smaller and more numerous.

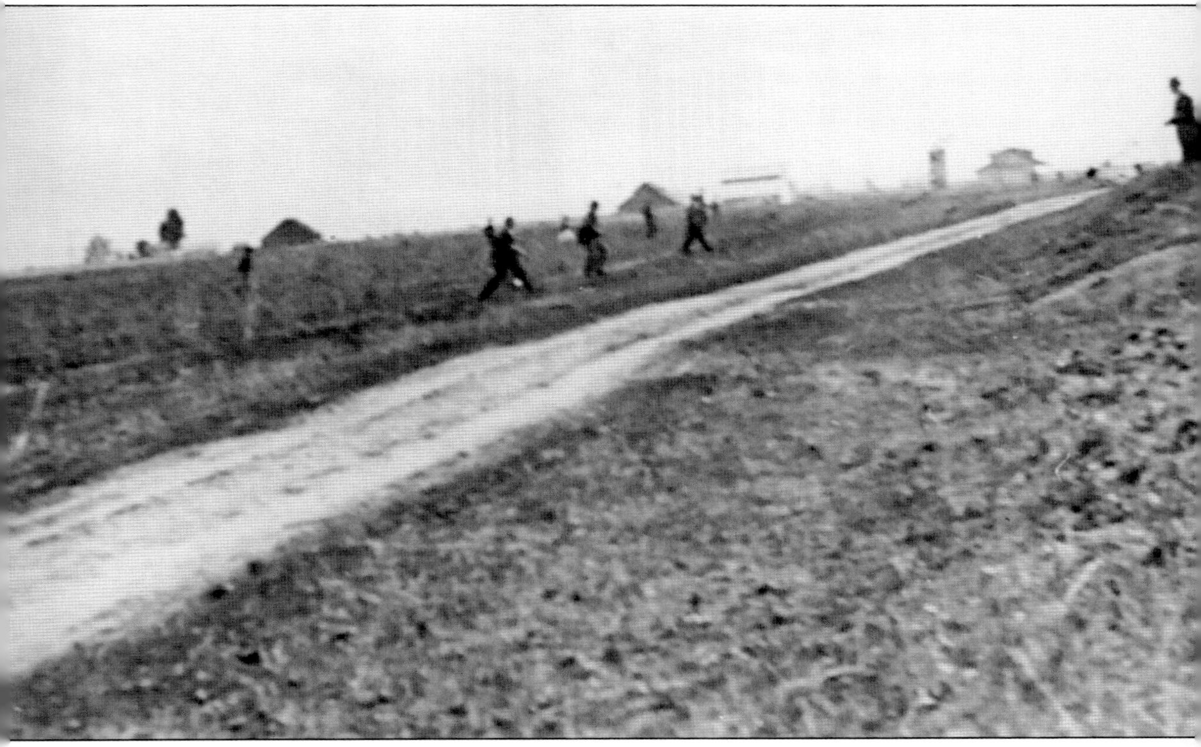

These hunters participated in the rabbit drive on March 12, 1917, and are seen crossing Clough Avenue, south of town. Jackrabbits harmed agriculture, consuming newly sprouted plants, and quickly multiplied. Drives were held periodically with hundreds of hunters spaced out in a line covering a grid, driving the rabbits toward the Stanislaus River. These drives had been conducted previously by Native Americans for food. They continued into the 1930s, carried out by early settlers, farmers, and sportsmen. The drives covered different terrain each year they were held, which was not always annually. The later drives were conducted while riding in jeeps and were held by property owners on their own farms or ranches.

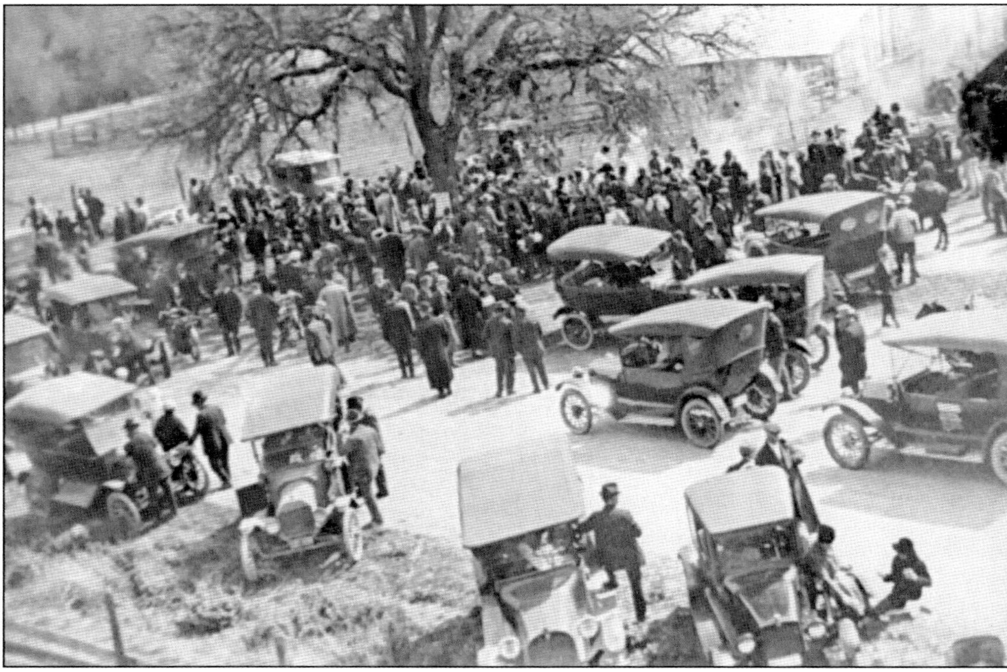

After a rabbit drive, a picnic would be held, such as this one at Meyer's Place on River Road in 1917. Thousands of people would be fed, including the hunters and their families. Participants came from near and far in these now-vintage automobiles. Today this property is the site of the Escalon Sportsmen's Club, and the stump of the oak tree still stands today.

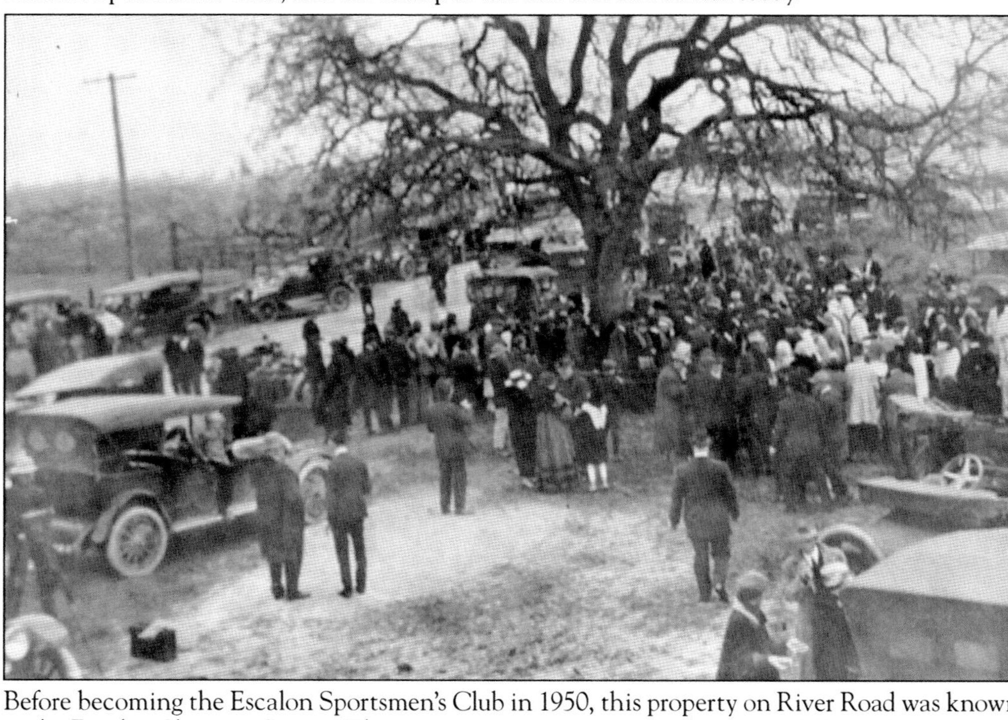

Before becoming the Escalon Sportsmen's Club in 1950, this property on River Road was known as the Escalon Shooting Range. This organization got its start in 1937 at a different location and moved to this property in 1946.

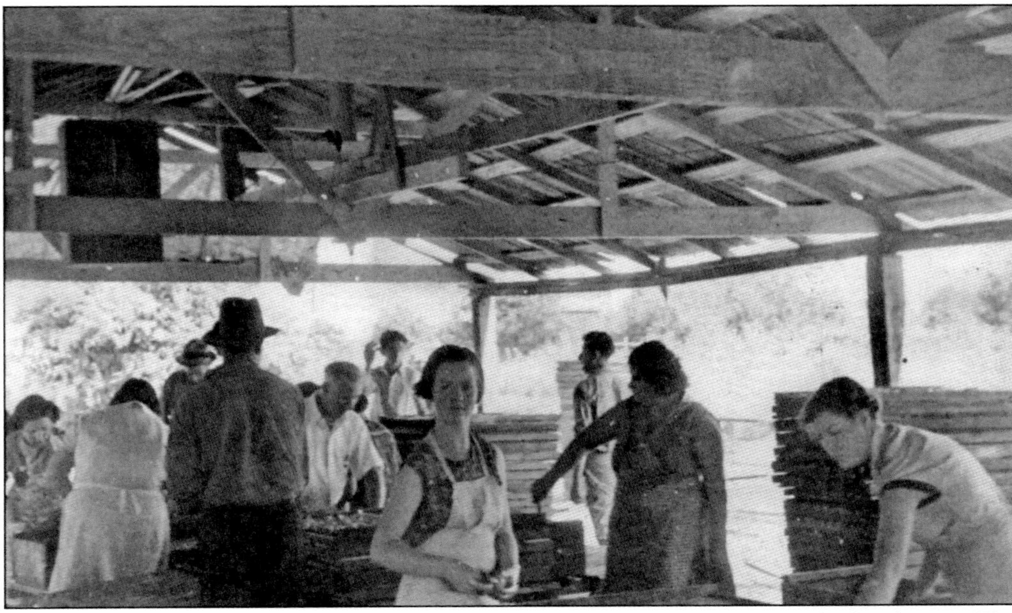

In the Escalon area in the 1930s, peaches and apricots were grown mostly for drying. This cutting shed was used to shelter the fruit being cut for drying, as well as the workers doing the cutting. The cut fruit was put on trays, loaded onto a flatcar, and taken by rail to a sulfur house, where burning sulphur was used as an agent to retard browning. Next the flatcar laden with fruit trays rode the rails to the dry yard, where the trays would be laid out on the ground for between several days and up to a week before being shipped to market. Dry yards employed men, women, and children. The tasks of cutting the fruit and stacking the trays were not highly looked upon. Some workers opted to pick the fruit, thereby earning three times the wage of a cutter.

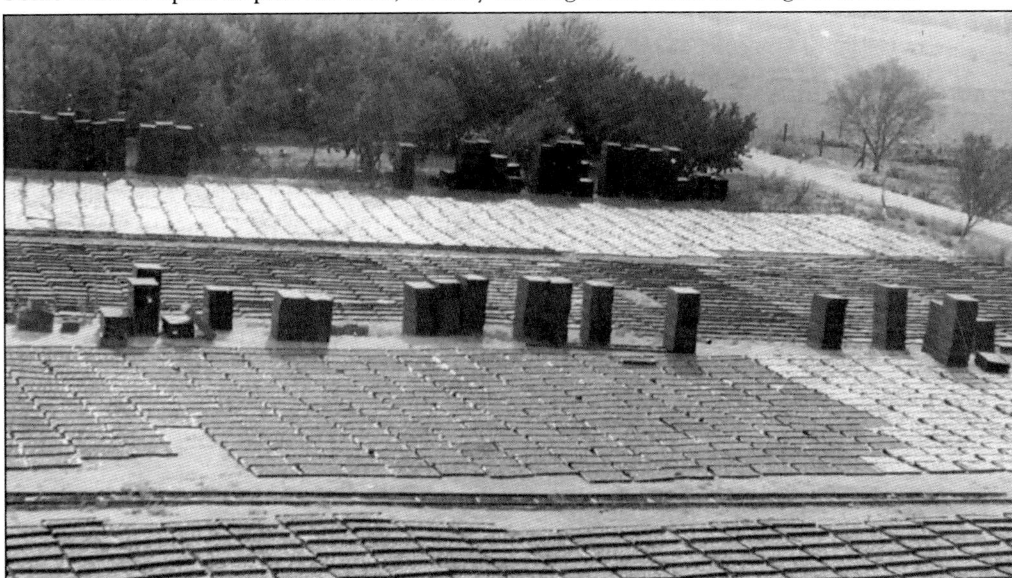

This dry yard, pictured around 1933, was one of several in the Escalon area in the 1930s. When the demand for dried fruit decreased and health regulations became more stringent, dry yards such as these disappeared. Note the rails running from left to right between the trays of drying fruit.

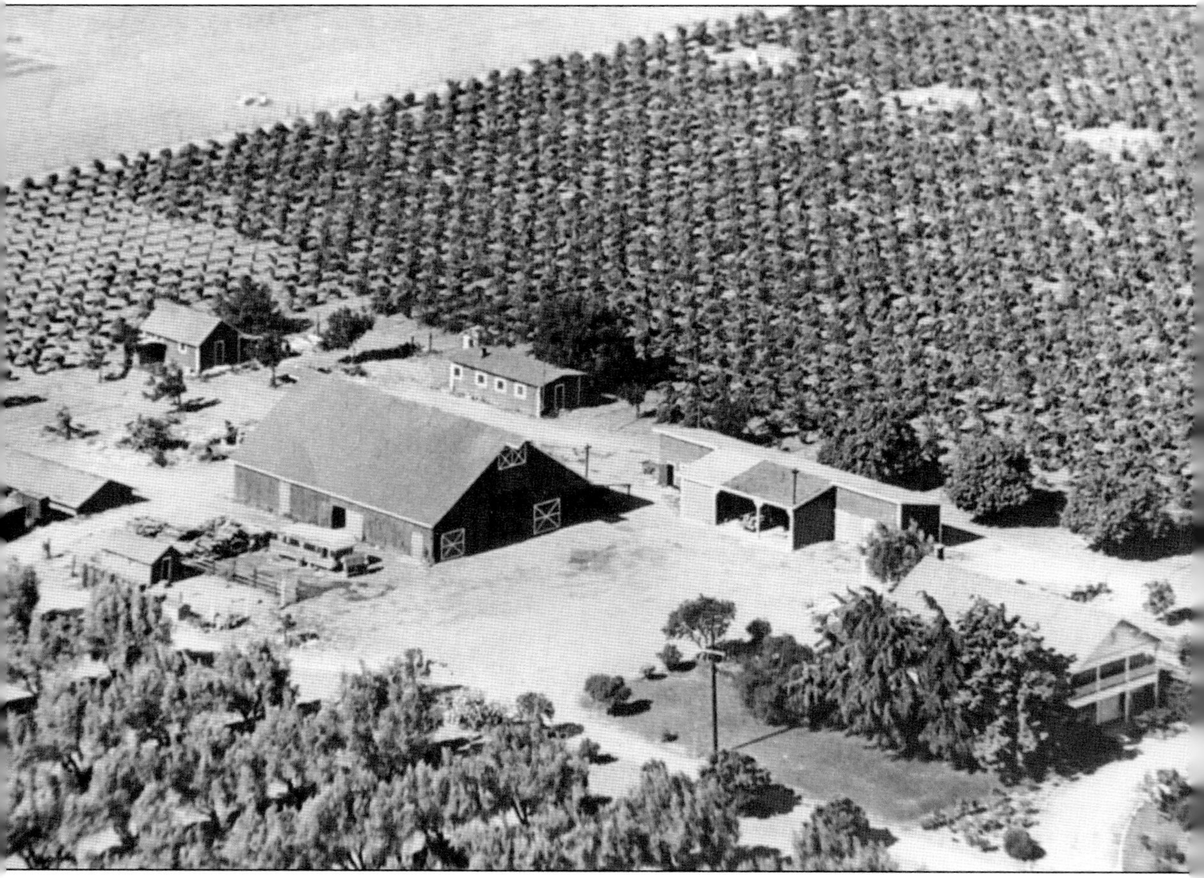

This property was originally part of the Jones Ranch, the building in the right foreground being the bunkhouse. John Wheeler Jones left this portion of his ranch to his granddaughters, whose father, Anthony Byrd Humphrey, developed it. Humphrey was considered to have one of the finest Guernsey cattle and Berkshire hog farms in the west. He propagated the first lady finger grapes in California, planting about 100 acres of them on his ranch in the 1920s. The ranch was eventually taken over by the Stockton Savings and Loan during the Depression, was purchased by Jake Baumbach, and was then purchased by Fred, Charlie, and Frank Sanchez in 1951. The property was located between Brennan and Oklahoma Avenues and between First Street and Ullrey Avenue. El Portal Middle School and the Vintage Estates subdivision now occupy this spot. This picture was taken between 1957 and 1960.

# *Two*

# By Rail, By Rail

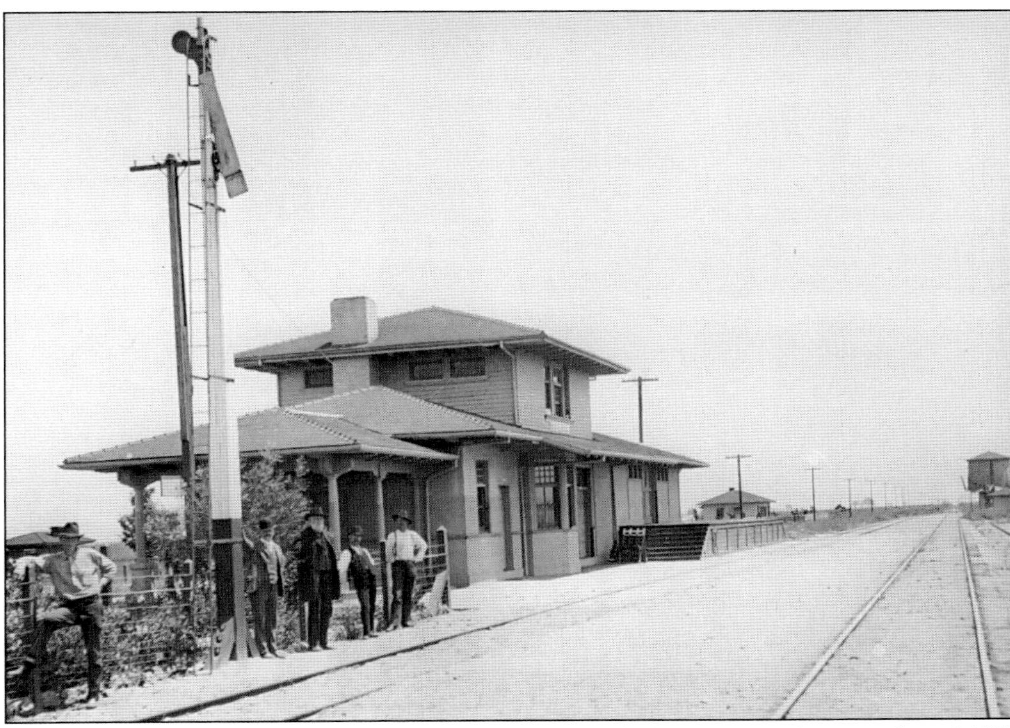

The Santa Fe Railroad Depot, pictured around 1910, was built in 1898 and operated until 1970. It was located alongside the Santa Fe Railroad tracks that bisect the heart of Escalon near Main Street's intersection with Second Street. The upper floor of the train station served as the residence for the agent who worked there. Two of the pillars from this train depot are on display in the Escalon Historical Museum, as well as switchmen's lanterns, a switch lock, and date nails used in the railroad ties. The Escalon station sign was salvaged, refurbished, and placed in the downtown park near the depot's former location.

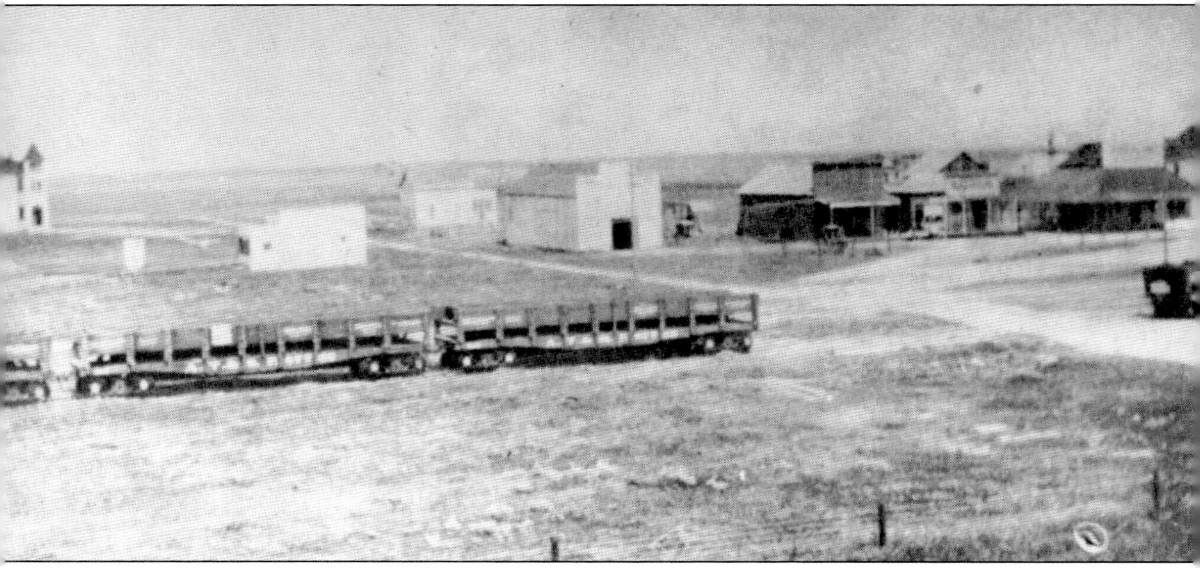

The railroad was constructed through Escalon in the late 1890s. This *c.* 1907 view looking eastward at the intersection of what would become First and Main Streets shows the first schoolhouse in Escalon (built in 1904) on the far left and various other downtown structures that would be destroyed by the fires in the early 1900s. Before being named First Street, this east-west route was French Camp Road, part of French Camp Trail. Its base was sandier than other roads used by horse-drawn vehicles and so was easier to travel upon during the rainy, muddy winter months. The use of this road, in addition to the construction of the railroad in Escalon, provided more reliable, less arduous, and shorter routes for the shipping of goods, and the community of Escalon began to flourish.

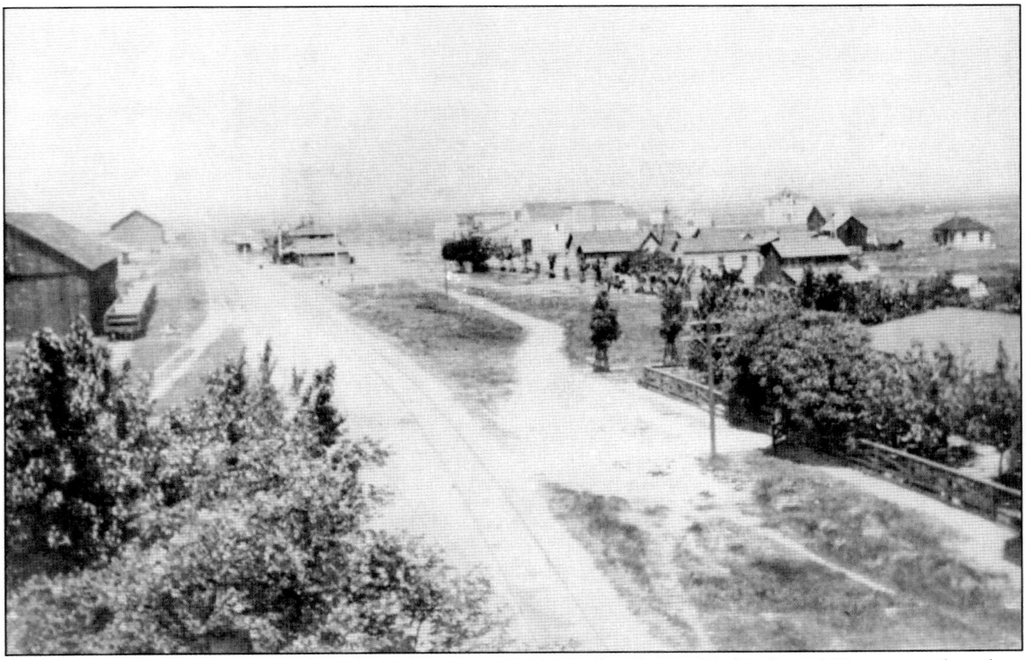

Looking north along the railroad tracks around 1908, the Santa Fe Railroad Depot is ahead to the right of the tracks. To the left are sheds and warehouses. Downtown structures are to the right of the depot. James Wesley Jones, son of founding pioneer John Wheeler Jones, had granted the right-of-way to the railroad in the 1890s.

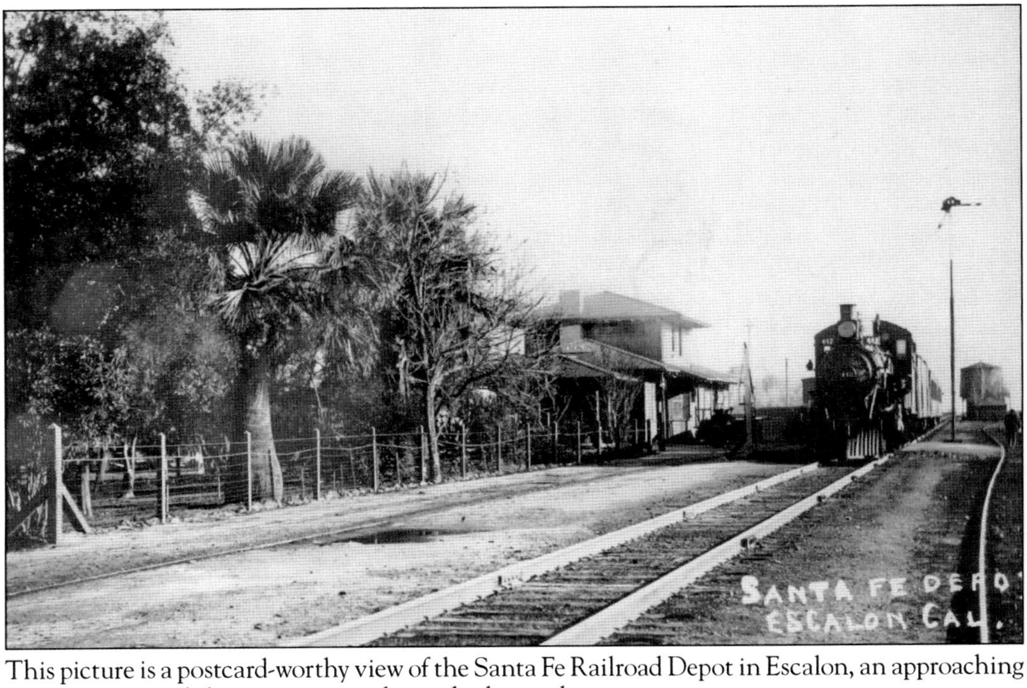


This picture is a postcard-worthy view of the Santa Fe Railroad Depot in Escalon, an approaching train engine, and the water tower alongside the tracks.

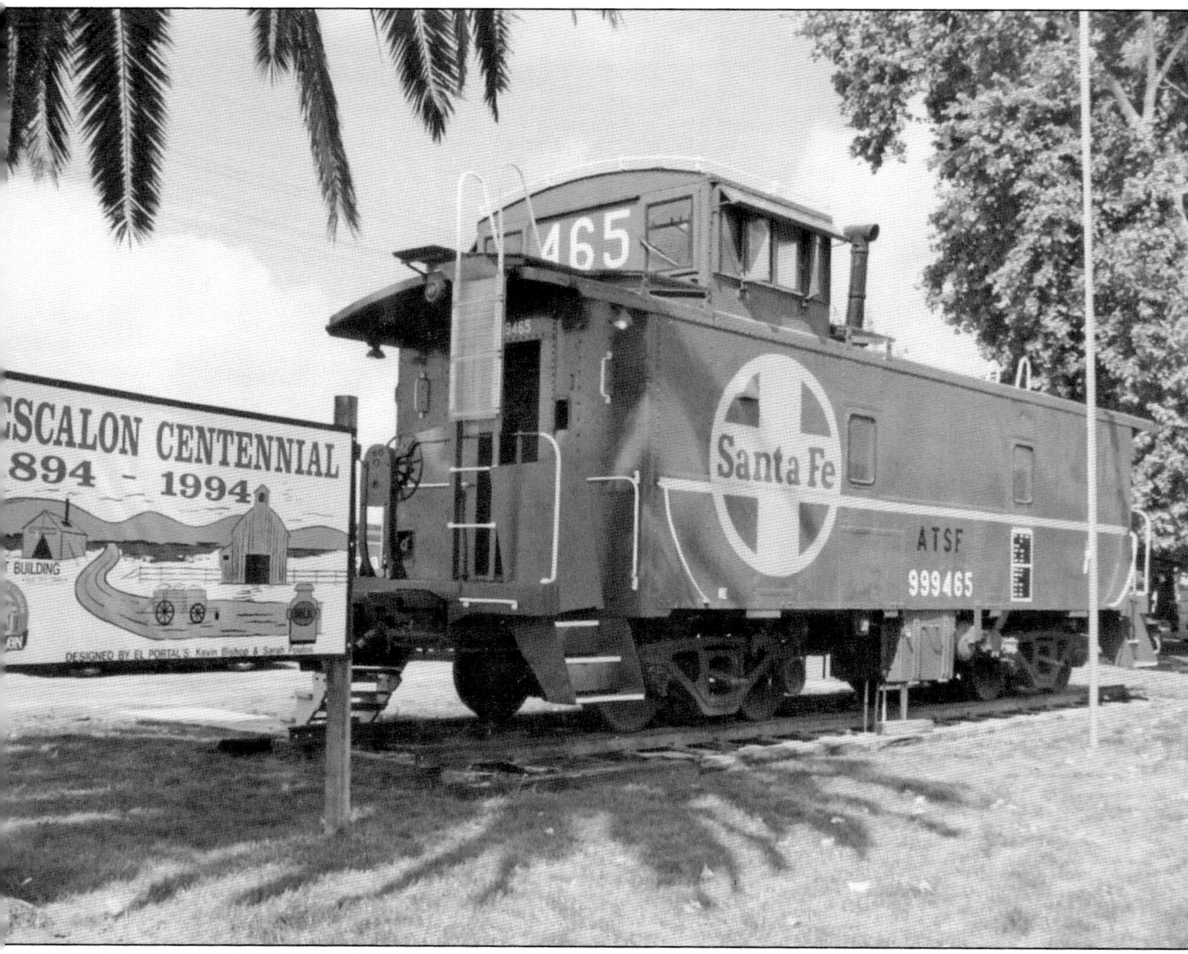


This Santa Fe Railroad caboose is the property of the Escalon Historical Society and sits near the intersection of Main and Second Streets, near where the depot stood until it was torn down in 1970. This caboose may have made several runs through Escalon before the use of cabooses was discontinued. This picture was taken during the celebration of Escalon's centennial in 1994, the anniversary of the laying out of the town by James Wesley Jones on the family's ranch property. The centennial sign near the caboose has a rendering of the Blue Tent Tavern, a wayside establishment that had been owned by John Wheeler Jones east of town. Ownership of this tavern was later shared with William A. Campbell, a retired mule driver and Pony Express rider, who settled for a short time in Escalon in 1900.

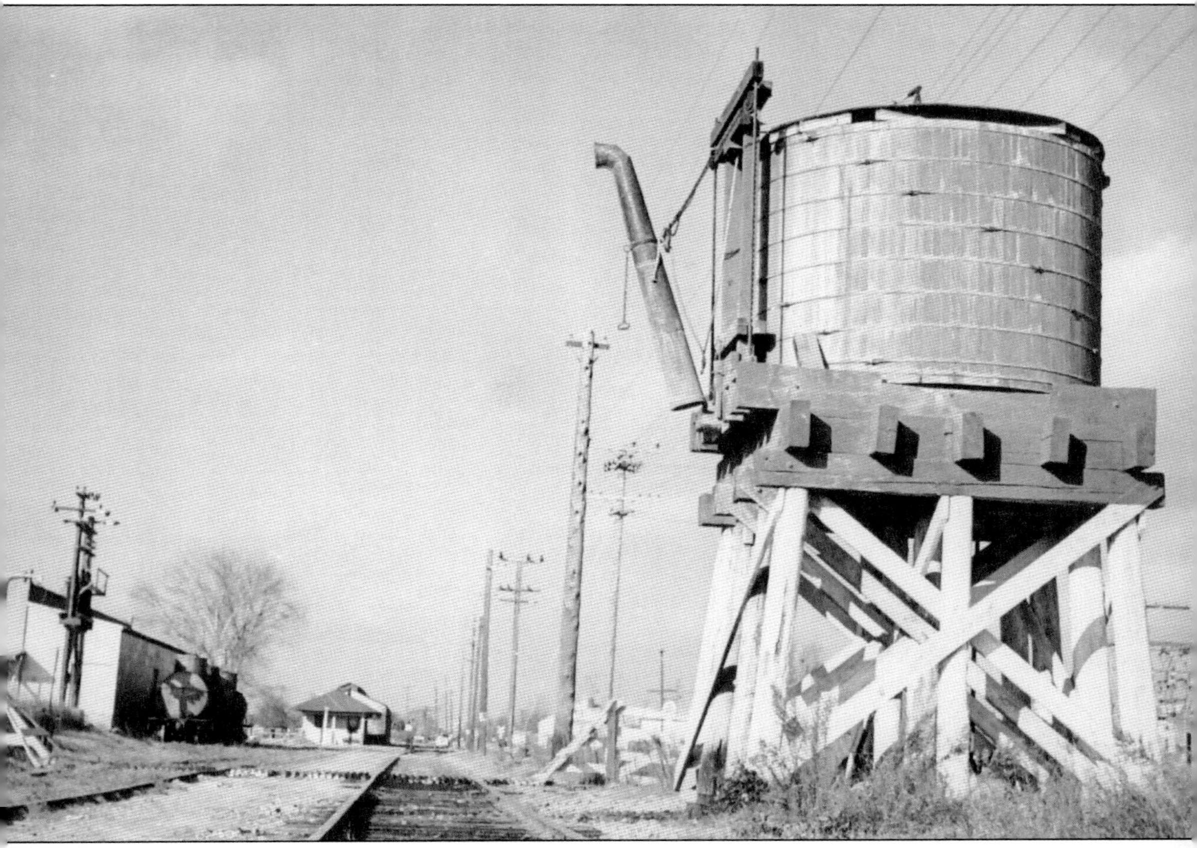

This water tower stood alongside what is now McHenry Avenue, south of First Street, on the east side of the Tidewater Southern Railway tracks, a second rail system serving Escalon. The Tidewater Depot in the background (built in 1913) and the sheds and warehouses to the left (west side) of the tracks were destroyed by fire in the 1950s. The fire caused several explosions, propelling a number of 55-gallon drums through the air. This view is from around 1934, looking northward.

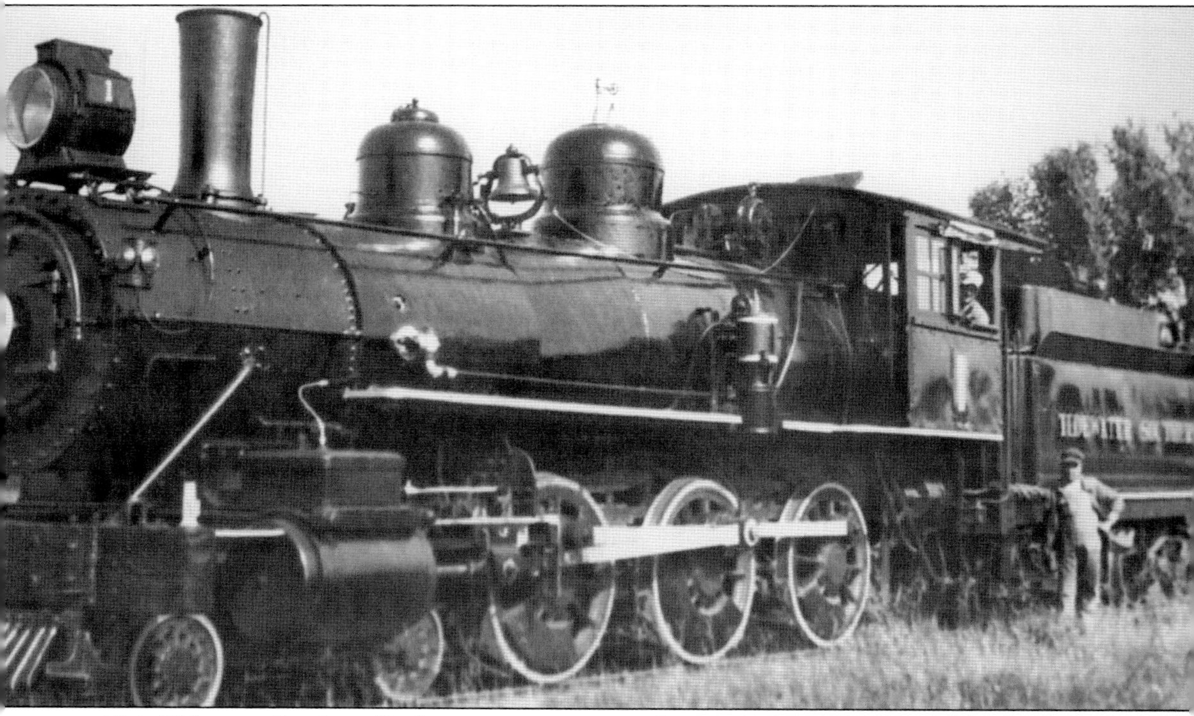

This Tidewater Southern Railway steam engine was known as a 4-6-0 because of the four smaller wheels in front, the six larger wheels in the center, and the absence of wheels under the cab. Steam locomotive engines used to ply the rails between Escalon, Modesto, and Stockton. In the late 1950s, the steam boiler at Escalon Packers (a food processing plant) broke down and could not be immediately repaired. A steam locomotive like this one sat running next to the plant to power the machinery inside so operations could continue, and the produce was not lost.

# *Three*

# A Fledgling Downtown

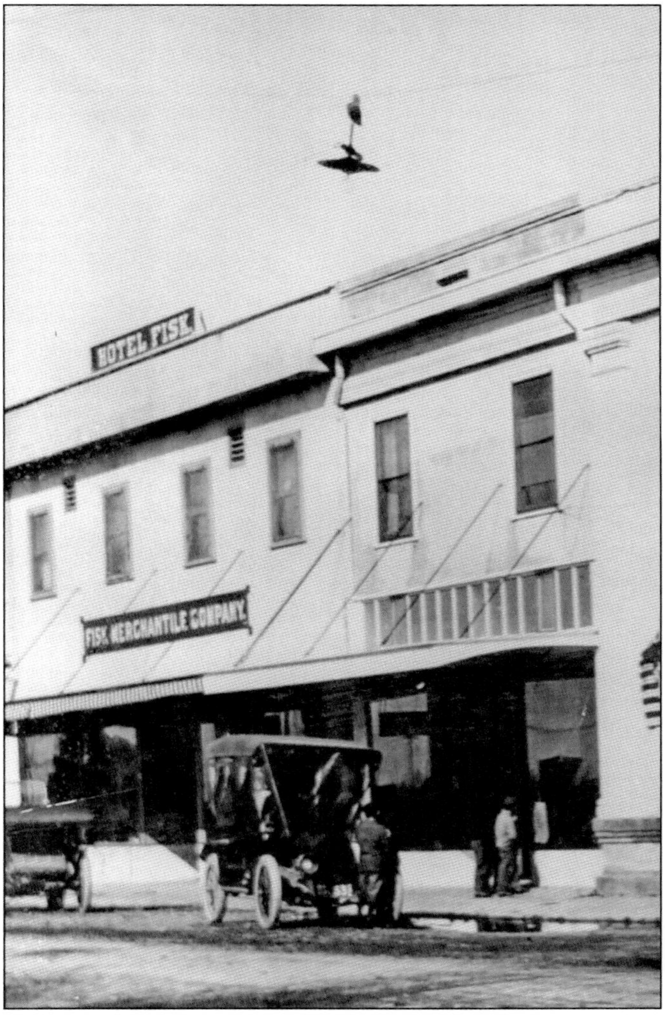


In 1909, Oliver A. Fisk began construction on the Fisk Building, completing it in 1911. This building is still located at the corner of Main and First Streets in its modified form. The first to occupy this building was the Escalon State Bank, the first bank in town, in 1912. The bank was established by S. J. Irwin, the owner of the Irwin Lumber Company. In 1943, the bank was sold to the Central Valley National Bank and then moved across Main Street in 1964. The Bank of the West bought Central Valley in 1990 and now occupies the corner opposite from the Fisk Building. The Fisk Mercantile Company was also housed in the Fisk Building, as was the Fisk Hotel (or Hotel Fisk), both in what was considered an addition to the original building, as seen in the left half of this photograph. According to a sign in the window, a Dr. Lewis had an office on the second floor above the bank. Later the upstairs would contain rented apartments.

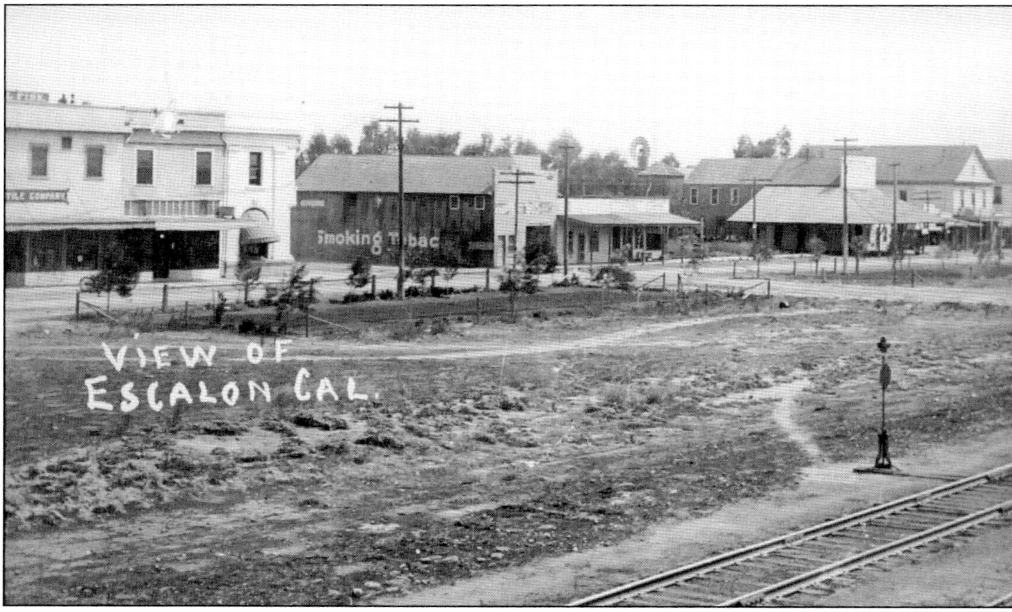


This view of downtown Escalon around 1911 shows the Fisk Building and, across First Street, J. W. Ridley General Blacksmithing and Horseshoeing. The Santa Fe Railroad tracks cut across the lower right corner.

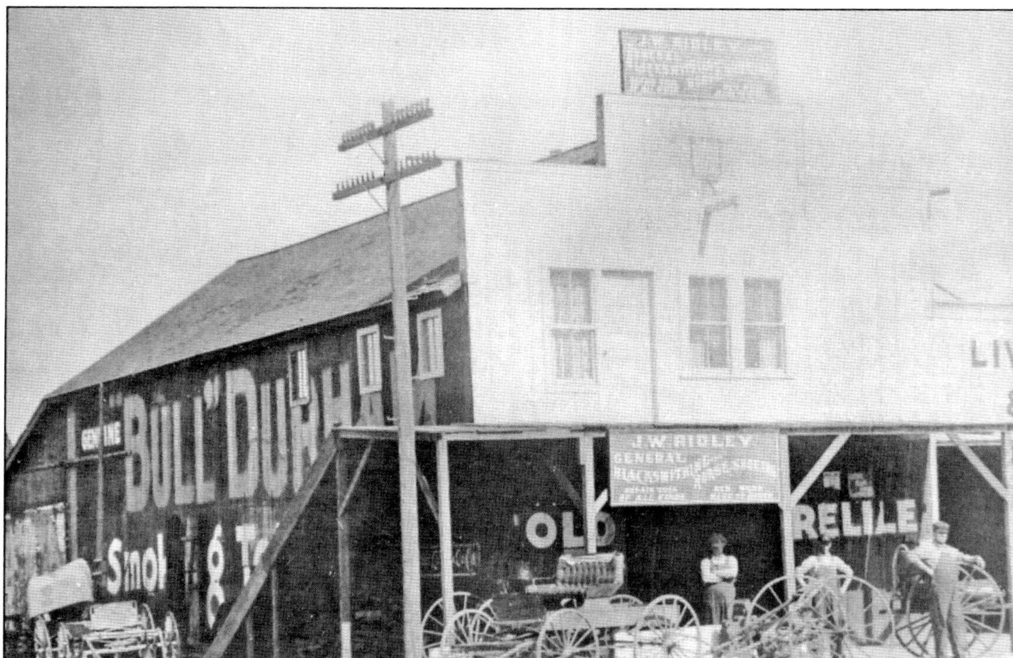


J. W. Ridley General Blacksmithing and Horseshoeing was located at the corner of First and Main Streets, across from the corner the Fisk Building would occupy. The side of the building advertised "Genuine 'Bull' Durham Smoking Tobacco," and the business sign touted "repair work of all kinds" and "new work made to order." Upstairs were living quarters; next door was a livery stable. This building was destroyed in the fire of 1920.

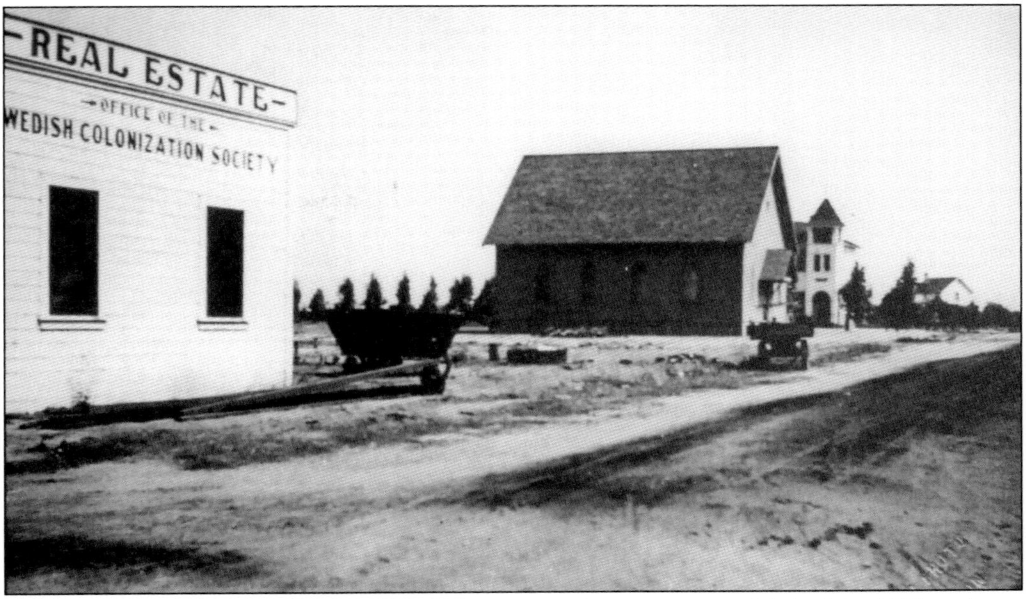


The real estate office of the Swedish Colonization Society was established in 1903 and was located on First Street, east of Main Street. Beyond is the Swedish Church and the first elementary school in Escalon. Swedish immigrants to the Escalon area made up a large part of the population for several decades.

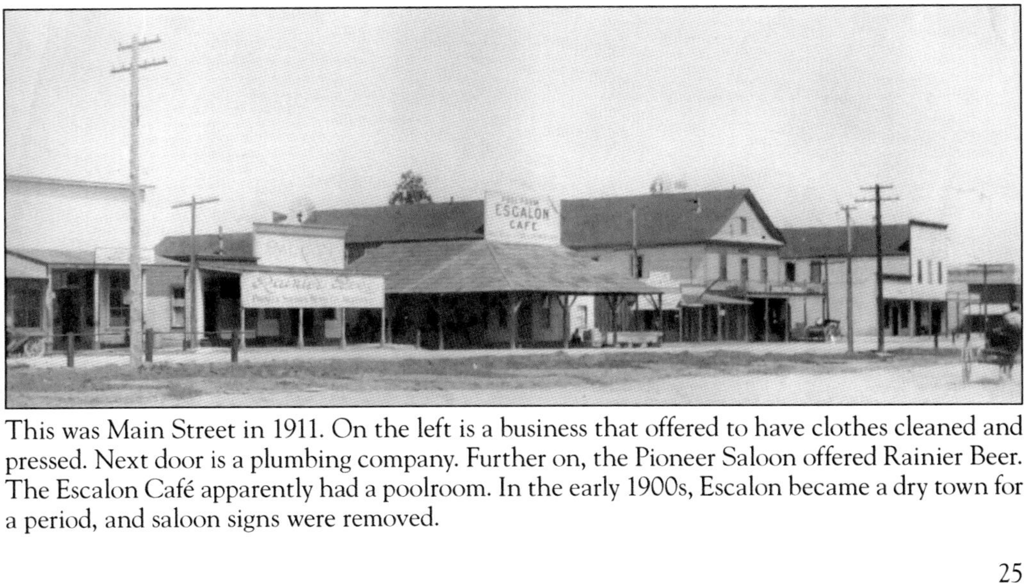


This was Main Street in 1911. On the left is a business that offered to have clothes cleaned and pressed. Next door is a plumbing company. Further on, the Pioneer Saloon offered Rainier Beer. The Escalon Café apparently had a poolroom. In the early 1900s, Escalon became a dry town for a period, and saloon signs were removed.

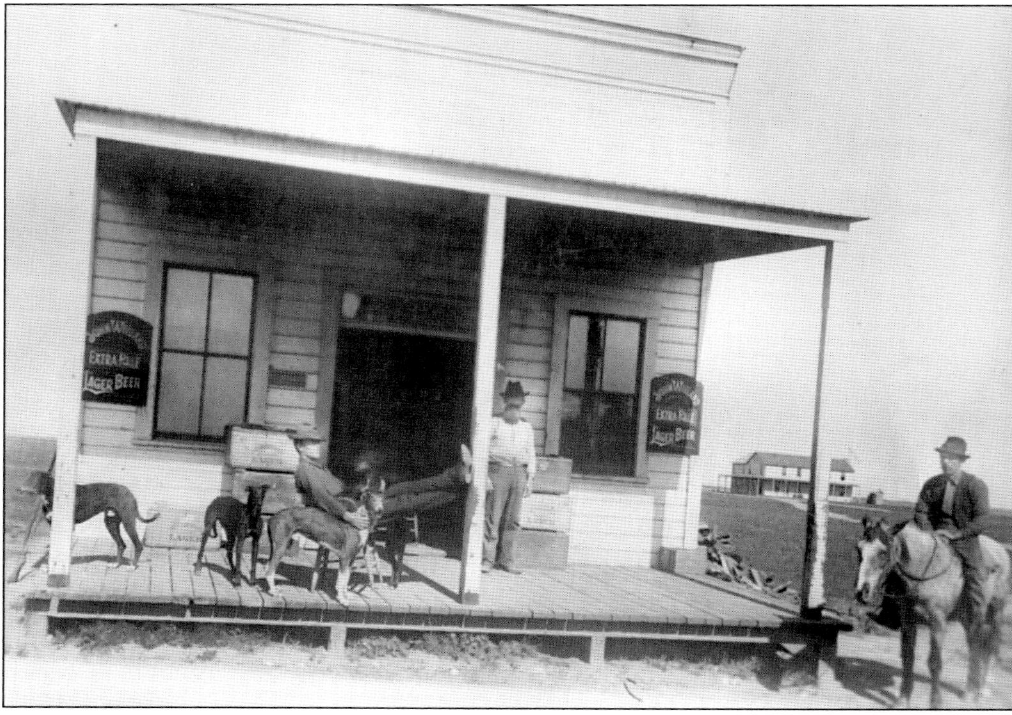


The first saloon in Escalon was owned by James H. Jackson. It was built in the late 1800s and was located on Main Street between First and Second Streets. Jackson is seated on the porch, with Charley Lancaster standing. Escalon's first hotel is in the background on the right. The man on horseback is unidentified.

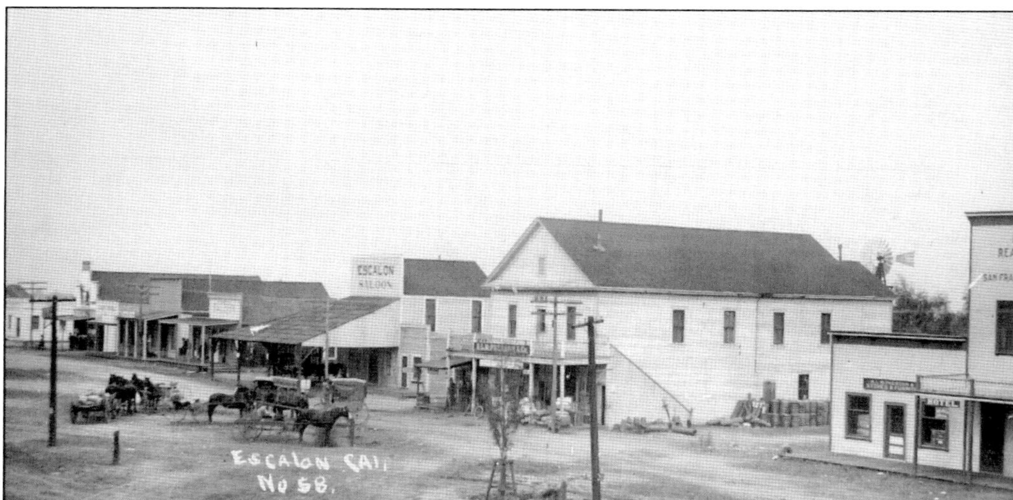


This 1910 view of Main Street looking toward the northwest shows several horse-drawn vehicles parked between First and Second Streets. Perhaps the occupants were in the Escalon Saloon, in the nearer business purchasing a stove or some furniture, or in the hotel. The building in the center is the Leighton Building. It contained the post office for a short time (J. N. Leighton was the postmaster in 1902), a general merchandise store, and a hall on the second floor, which was used for dances and other social functions. The Jackson Saloon and the blacksmith shop and livery stable round out the block.

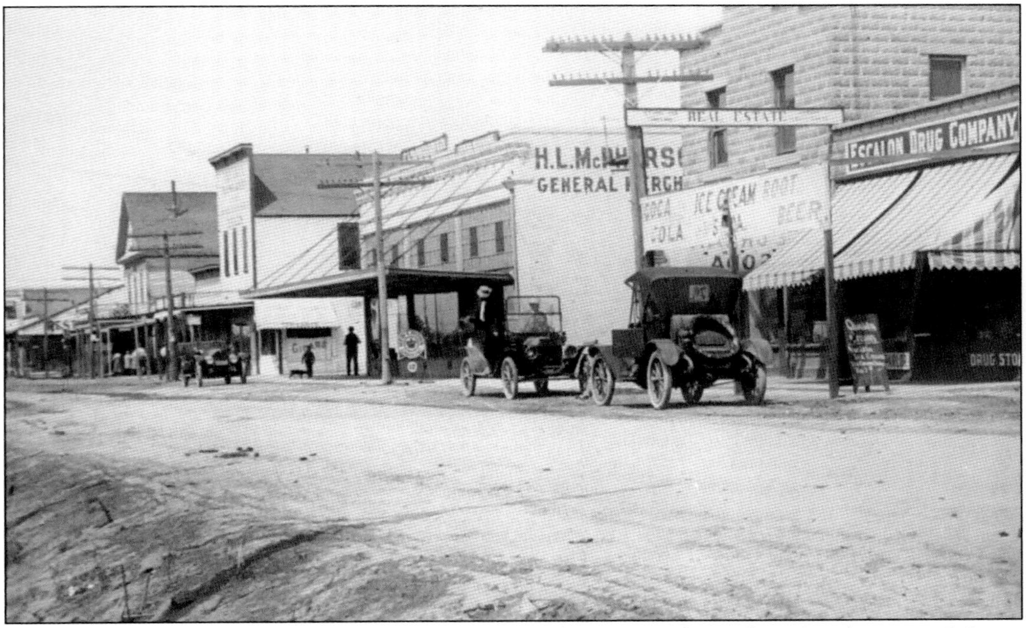


This view of Main Street's intersection with Second Street in the early 1900s depicts a definite lack of parking restrictions. Visible on the far left is the Fisk Building. Downtown Escalon businesses at this time included a restaurant, Leighton Mercantile, John Wieland's saloon and hotel, the H. L. McPherson and Company General Merchandise store, a real estate office, and the Escalon Drug Company. In 1909, the post office was in the McPherson Building, and H. L. McPherson was the postmaster.

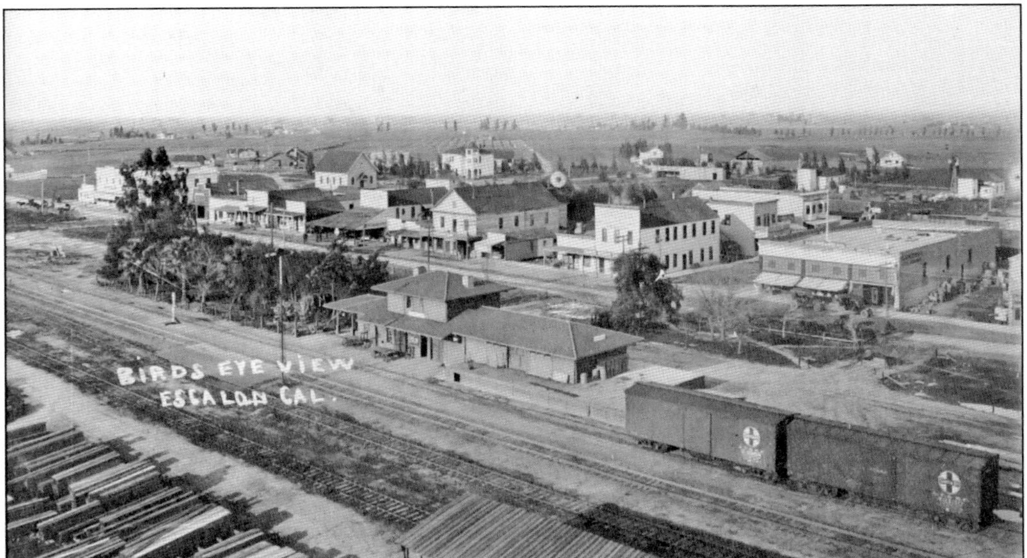


This is a bird's-eye view of downtown Escalon between 1908 and 1915. In the center is the Santa Fe Railroad Depot. Beyond are Main Street and its intersection with Second Street. The H. L. McPherson Building, built between 1900 and 1910, is on the right, and the Fisk Building is barely visible behind the trees on the left. In the center distance is the first elementary school in Escalon, located at the corner of First Street and what is now Highway 120, where the Escalon Presbyterian Church now stands.

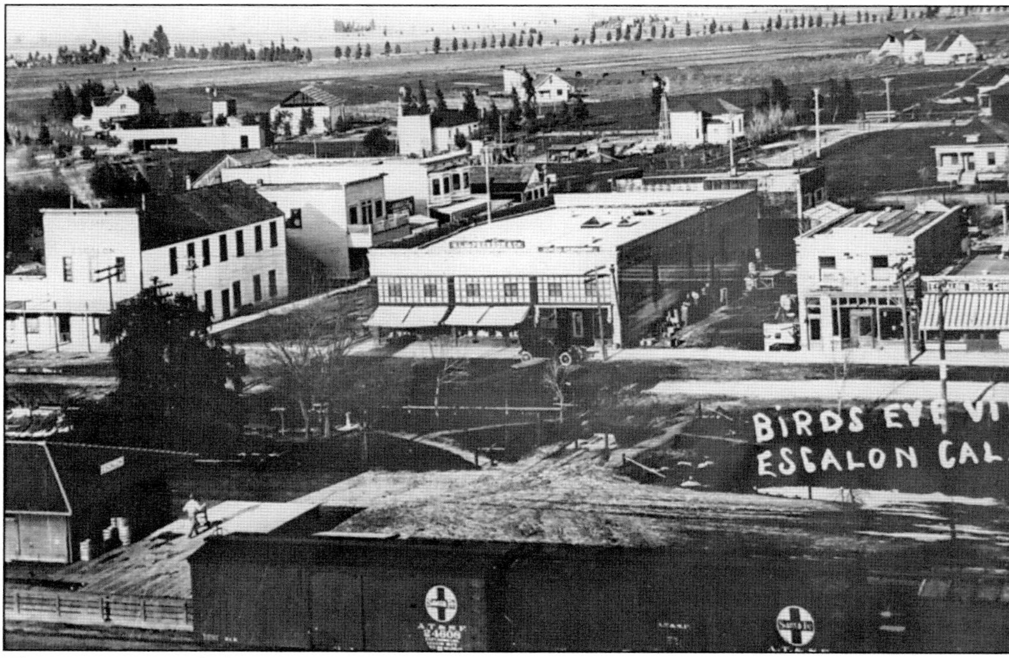


This is a view of the intersection of Main and Second Streets looking northeast around 1912, apparently taken from the elevated height of the town's water tank. In the center is H. L. McPherson and Company General Merchandise store. On the left, across Second Street, is the Escalon Hotel. Part of the Santa Fe Railroad Depot is visible on the left.

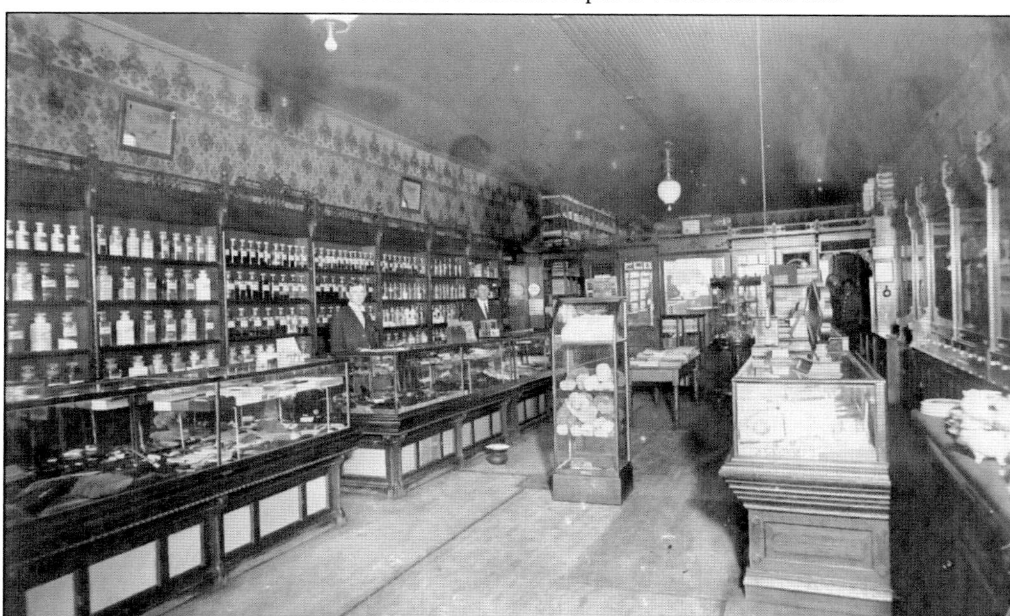

Peck's Candy Store, owned by Wray Milan Peck, was located on Main Street between First and Second Streets. Sadly, it was one of several Main Street businesses destroyed by fire in the early 1900s.

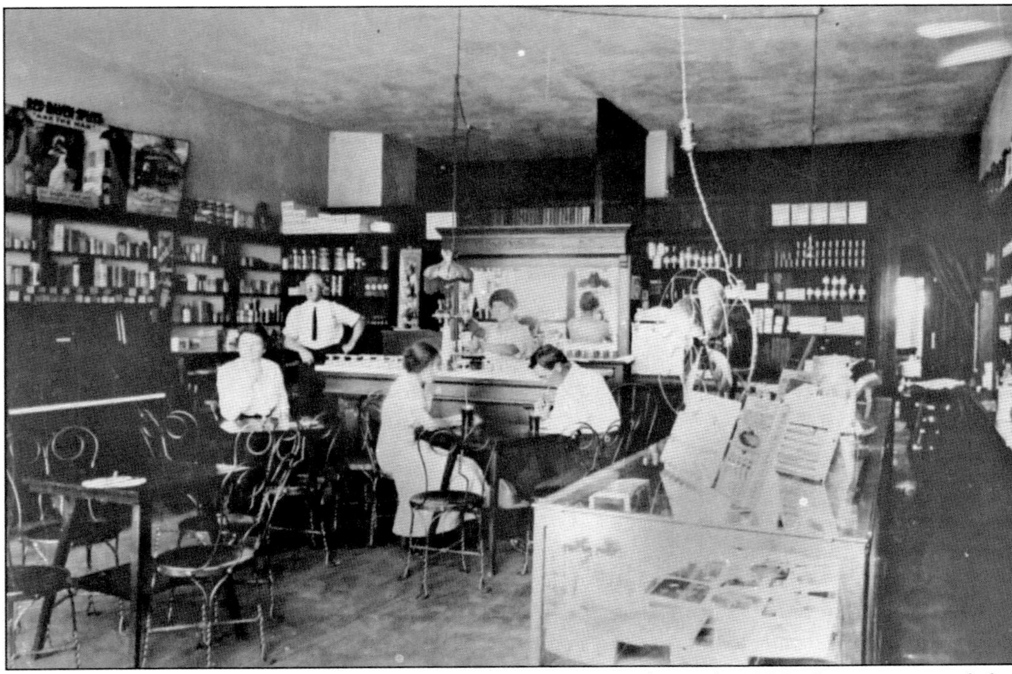

Herzinger's ice cream parlor was located on Main Street in the early 1900s. It was rumored that the fire of 1920 was caused by a still that was in operation in the rear of this building. However, newspaper accounts credited the initial blaze to the explosion of a gasoline stove in the bakery owned by Arno Bender. This address on Main Street would later belong to the Escalon Club and then Escalon Pet Grooming. Mr. Herzinger is standing second from the left.

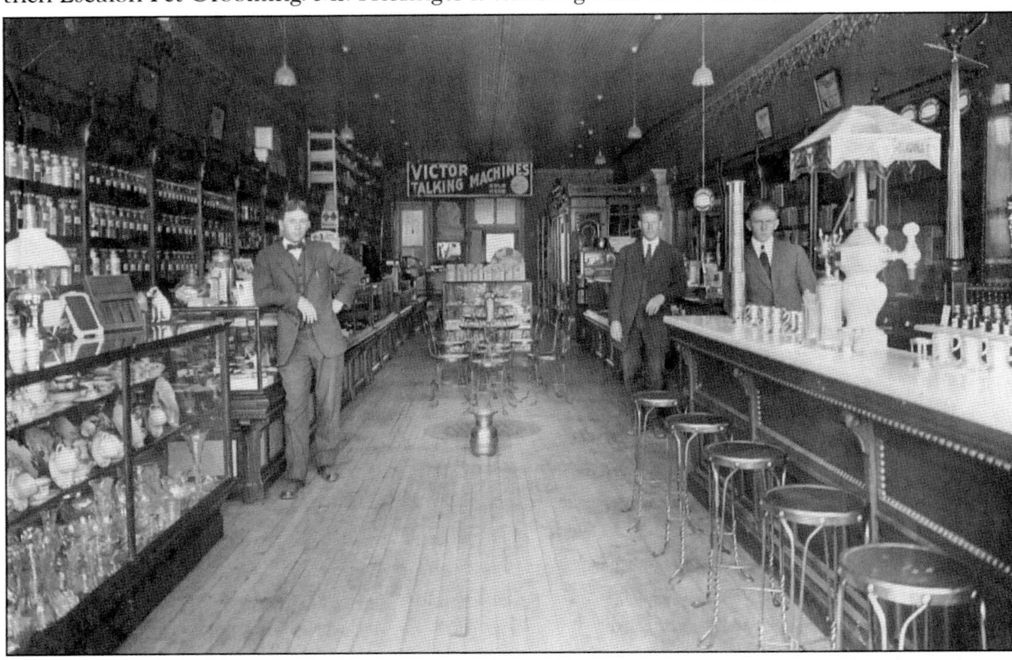


Escalon Drug was located on Main Street between Second and Third Streets. On the right was the marble counter where fountain customers were served. The pharmacy was located in the rear. This building was destroyed by fire in the early 1900s.

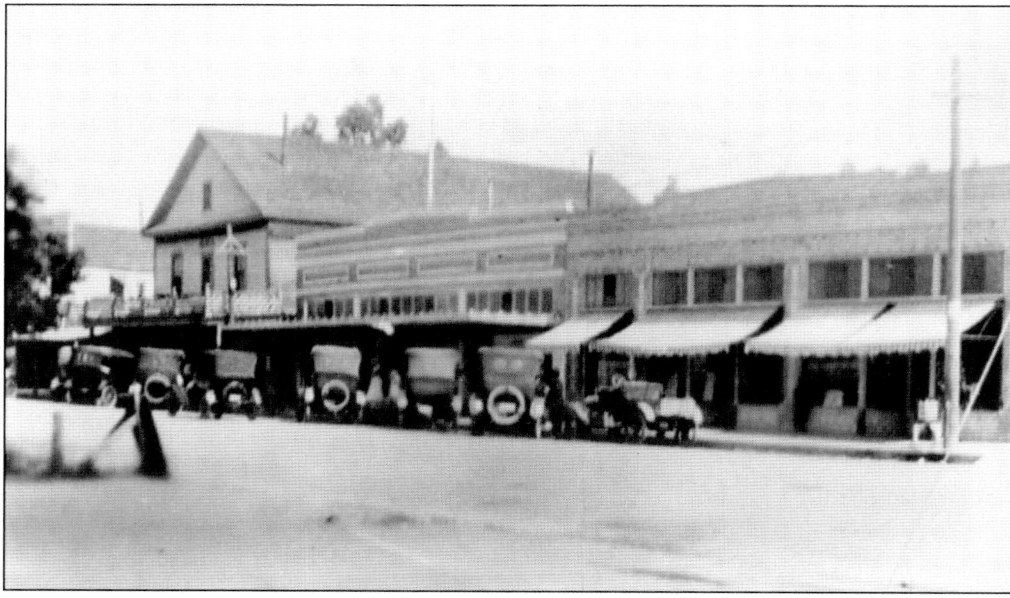

These vintage automobiles are parked on Main Street in front of the Leighton Building and its neighboring businesses sometime before 1919.

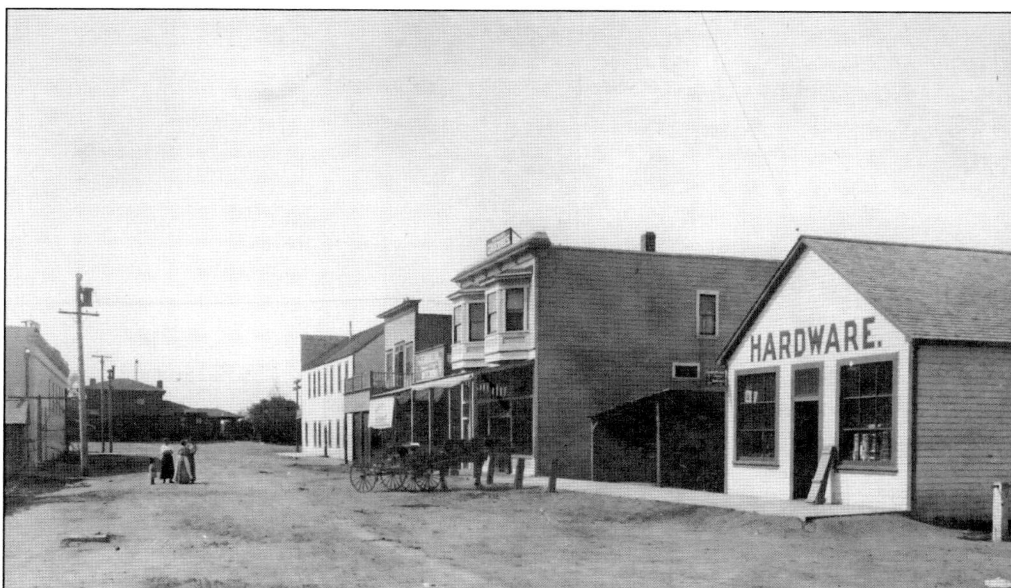


This westward-looking view of Second Street around 1912 shows the Santa Fe Railroad Depot in the distance. Businesses on the north side of Second Street, from left to right, included John Wieland's saloon and hotel, with living quarters above; Bender's Bakery; A. Ridel Company, a butcher; the H. J. Alley Grocery Store; a shed; and Haines Hardware on the corner of Coley Avenue. These buildings on Second Street were destroyed by the fire of 1917.

# *Four*

# Downtown after the Fires

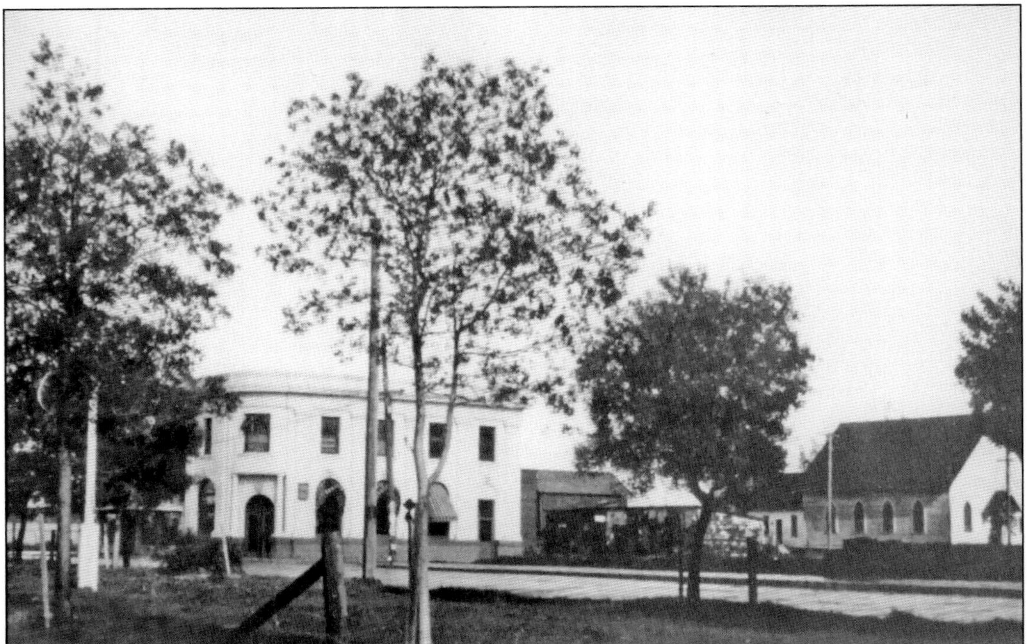

To the right of the Fisk Building on First Street is the Swedish Lutheran Church, pictured before the addition of its steeple. Since no building stands across First Street from the Fisk Building, this picture was probably taken soon after the fire in 1920 that destroyed many of downtown's wooden structures.

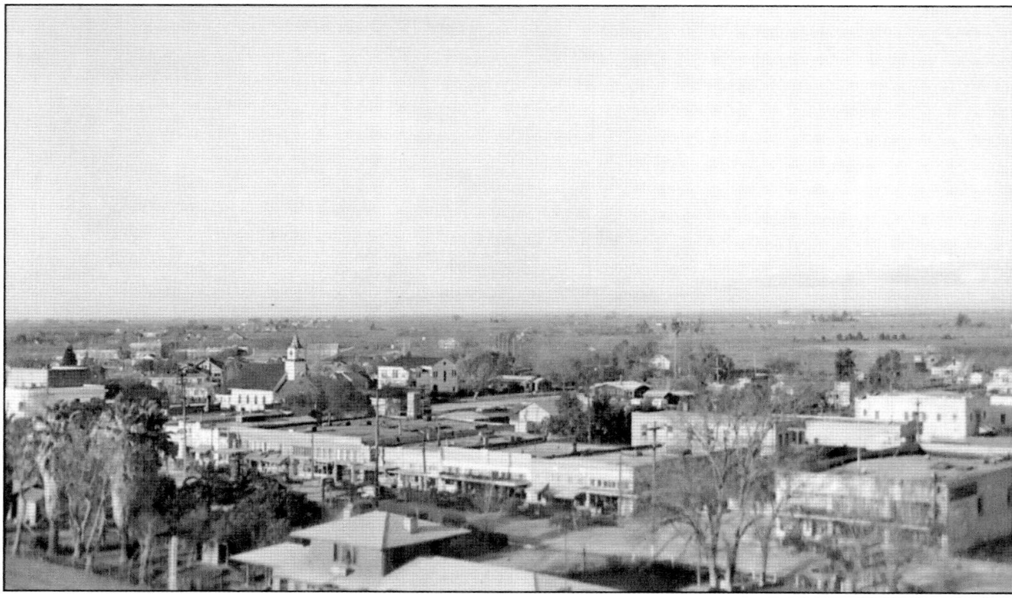

Beyond the Santa Fe Railroad Depot in the foreground, Main Street stretches from the H. L. McPherson Building on the right to the Fisk Building on the left. By the time of this photograph, the Swedish Church had acquired a steeple, and the wooden structures on Main Street that had been destroyed by fire had been replaced with buildings made of stone and brick, many of which are still standing today.

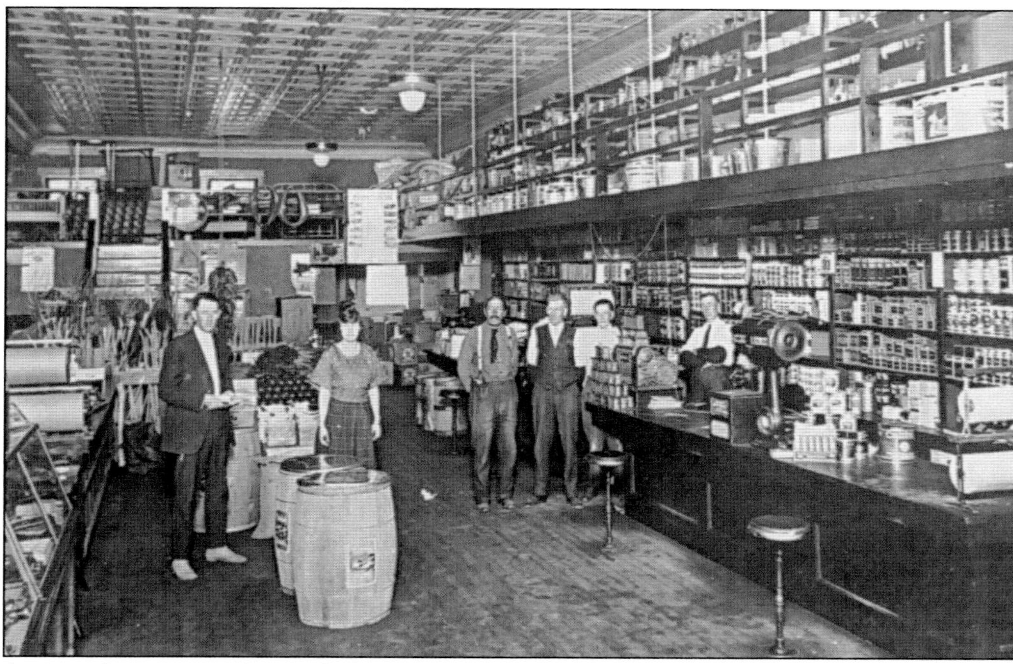

Among those pictured are Clarence and Richard Blackmore in their store about 1925. This part of the Fisk Building, once the home of Fisk Mercantile, had been sold to the Blackmores. They operated Blackmore Grocery in one half and Blackmore Dry Goods in the other. After Blackmore's, the building was home to J. Anderson Dry Goods and then B&L Market, which was owned by Bob Bookwalter and Leroy Shaw.

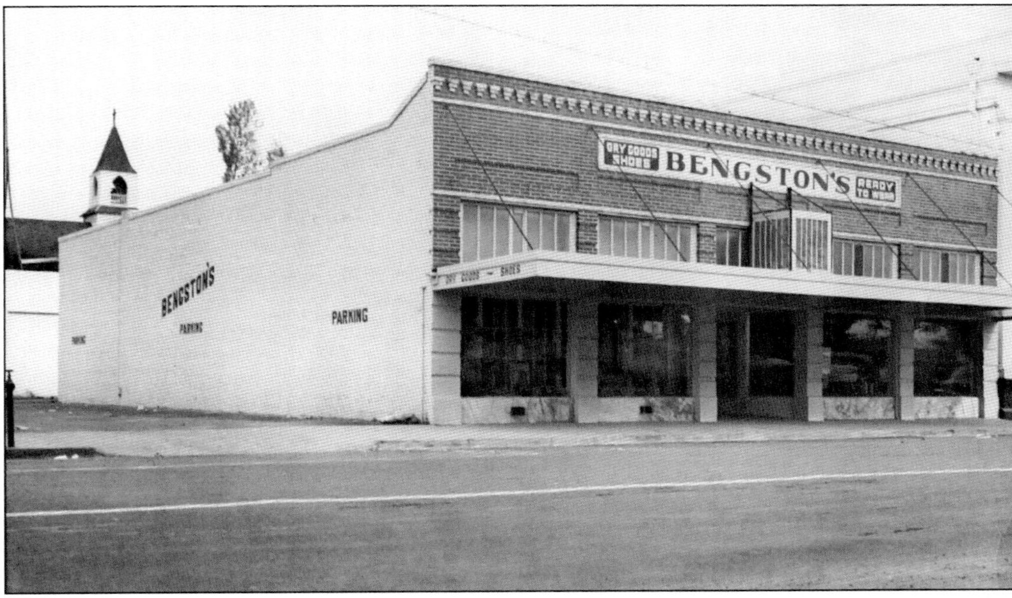


In 1937, Bengston's Dry Goods (offering ready-to-wear shoes and notions) occupied both what had been the dry-goods half and the grocery half of the Fisk Building. In 1997, the Escalon Historical Society purchased the property from the Bengston heirs in order to house the Escalon Historical Museum. Artifacts from the Bengston's store, including signs, merchandise, and photographs, are on display in the museum. This is the third oldest building in the business district of Escalon and retains the original ceiling tiles.

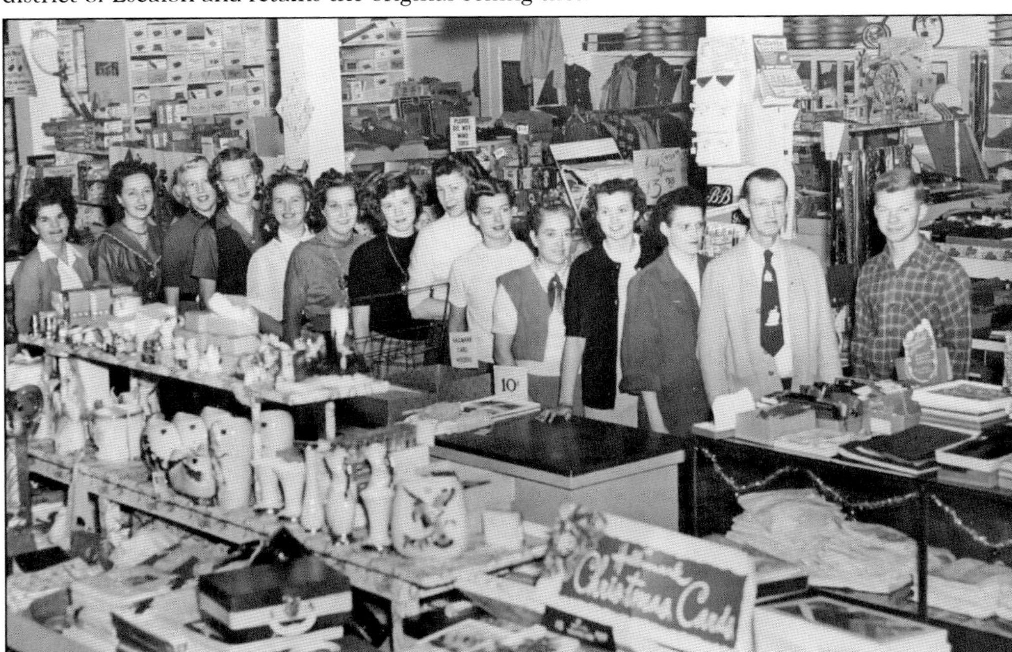


This is Bengston's staff at Christmastime in 1952. From left to right are Catherine Cimpanelli Black, Bernice Short, Carol Strand, Yvonne Hoiymer, Helen Thompson Polhemus, Gladys Johnson, Marion Johnson, Ann Peterson, Frances Hammerquist, Marie Gomes Marston, Vangie Presnell, Bonnie Taylor Macsenti, owner Arvid Bengston, and Don Eliason.

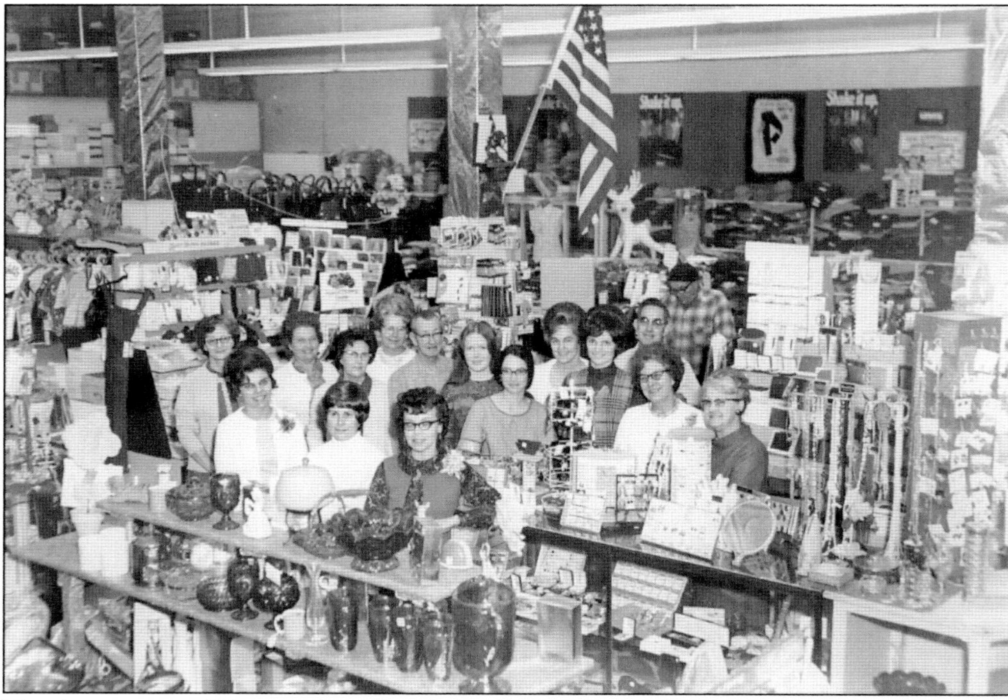

This later group of Bengston's staff includes (from left to right) Lucille Parker, Sandy Crews, Helen Thompson Polhemus, Elsie Fotheringham, Ethyl Marino, Frances Hammerquist, owner Arvid Bengston, Erma Jeanne Barton, Patty Polhemus Santini, Clyta Alders Polhemus, Shirley Vesia, Kathy Prater, Richard Polhemus, Gladys Johnson, and Mary Bookwalter. The customer's identify is unknown.

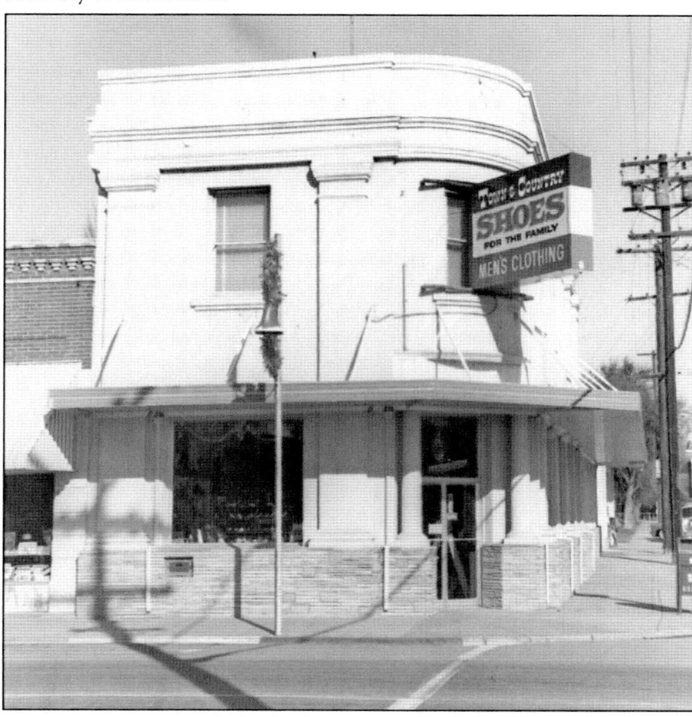


At the time this photograph was taken, Town and Country Men's Clothing, which offered shoes for the whole family, occupied this portion of the Fisk Building at the corner of First and Main Streets. A fire in 1916 had destroyed the addition to the building on the left. When it was rebuilt in 1919, the second floor of the addition where the hotel had been was eliminated. This corner part of the Fisk Building is now occupied by the accounting office of Hogan Manufacturing, Inc.

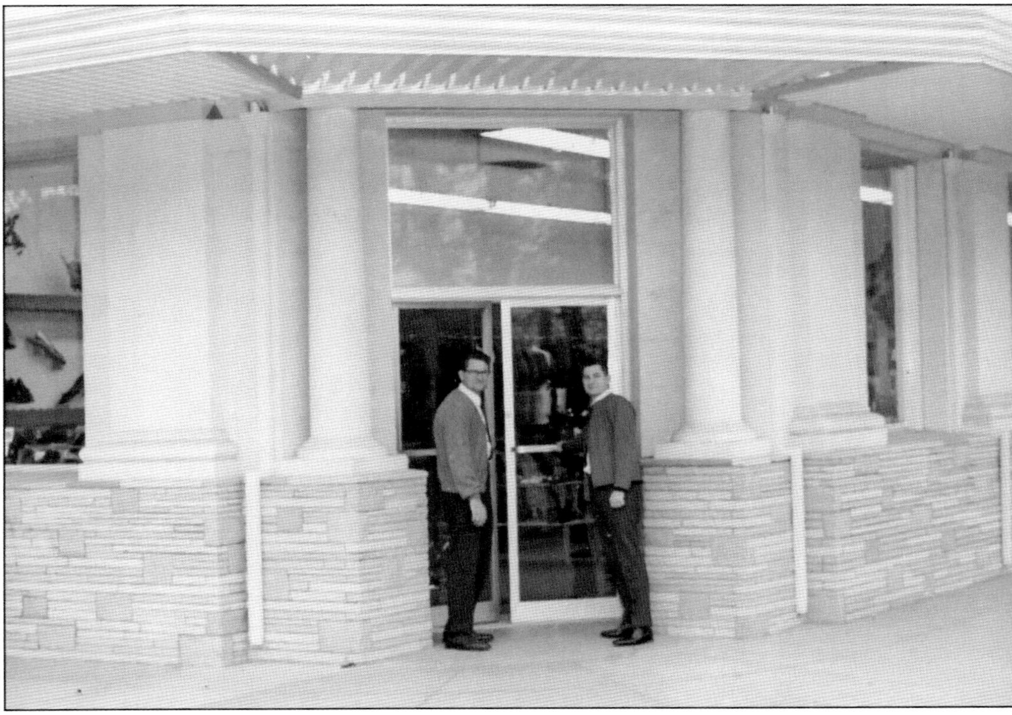

Jim (left) and Orville Johnston stand outside their Town and Country Men's Clothing store at the corner of First and Main Streets. The Johnstons also owned a variety store in the next block of Main Street.

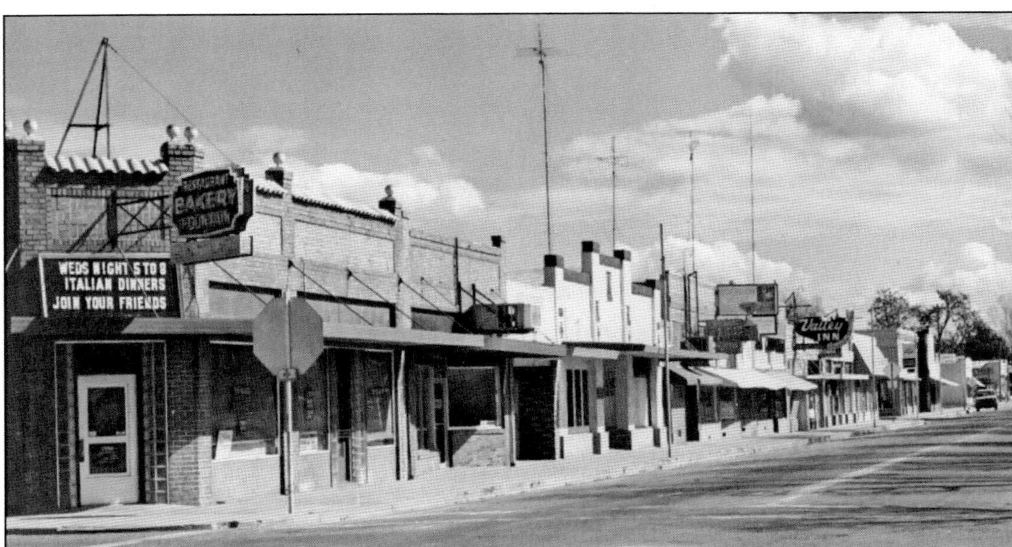


This view of Main Street around 1989 looks southeast from First Street. At this time, the Bakery Restaurant on the corner was well known for its Italian dinners every Wednesday evening. The facades of these downtown buildings look today much like they did historically, the structures having been rebuilt after the fires in the early 1900s that destroyed many of the buildings.

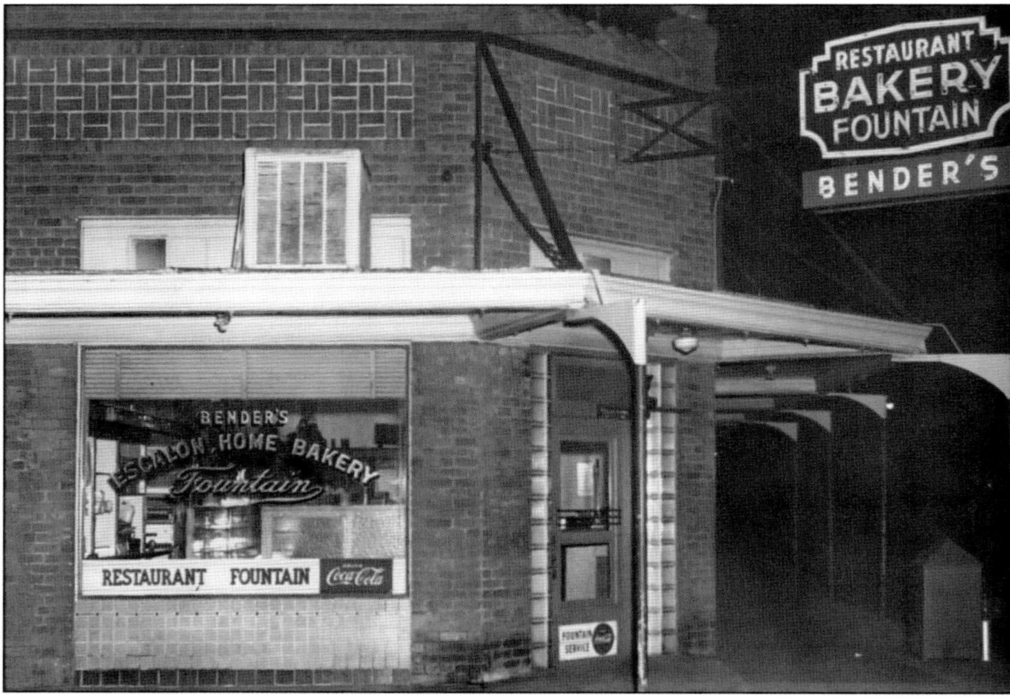


Bender's Escalon Home Bakery Fountain was located at the corner of Main and First Streets for many years, having been built by Arno Bender in 1931. The fountain was added at the time of the move to this location, and the restaurant was added 10 years later. Bender's bakery enjoyed a far-reaching reputation for the selection and quality of its food and baked goods. Bender purchased some of his ingredients, such as black and English walnuts, from local growers.

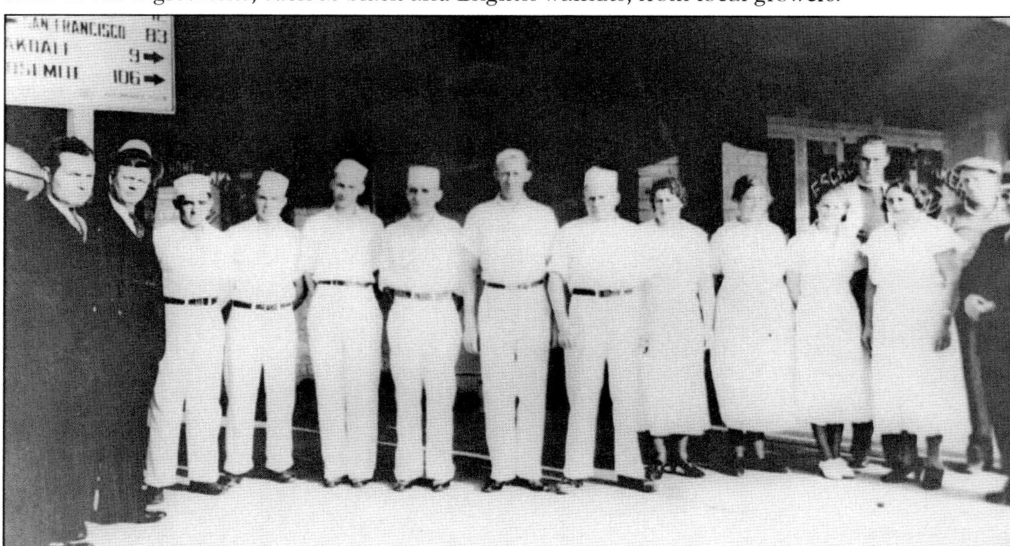

These are employees of the bakery around 1935. Arno Bender is pictured eighth from the left and Vern Lundquist is pictured fourth from the left. This picture was taken in front of the bakery at the corner of Main and First Streets. The mileage sign on the left points out that to the left (west), Stockton is 22 miles, Manteca is 12 miles, and San Francisco is 83 miles away. To the right (east), Oakdale is 9 miles, and Yosemite is 106 miles away.

Frances Bender, Arno's wife, is giving change to a customer at the bakery. The caged bird is one of many that she owned and raised. Many referred to Frances Bender as "Red" because of her red hair. Every year on the final day of swim lessons, Bender's bought each child an ice cream cone. In order to place the time of this picture, one need only remember when Butterfinger candy bars, a "new delight," were available for 5¢ each in the late 1950s and early 1960s.

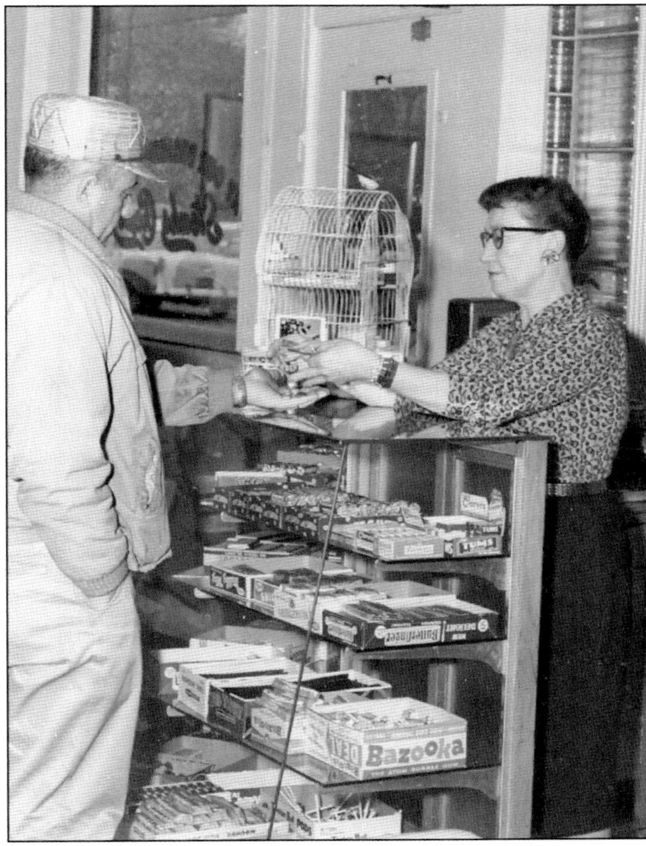


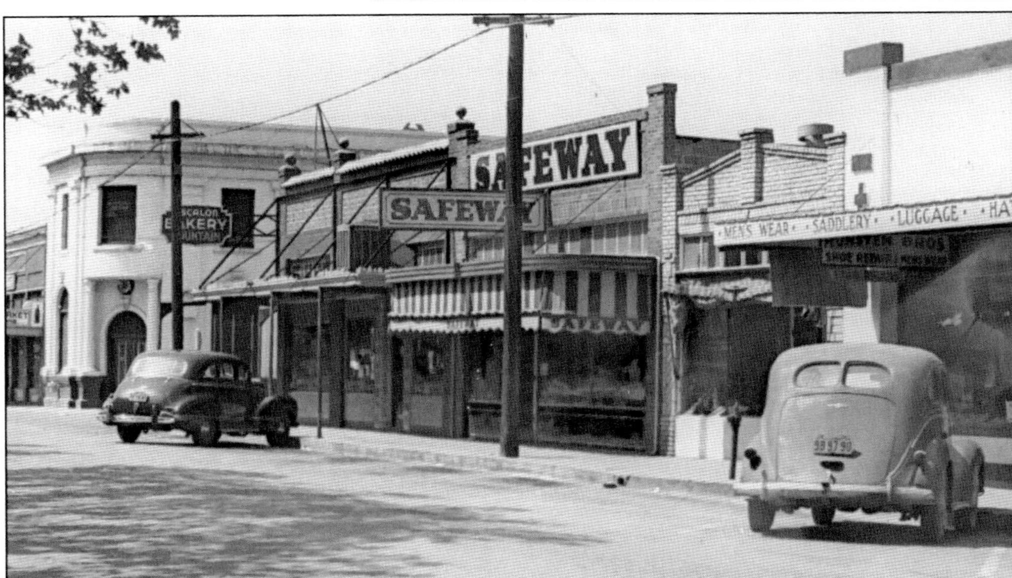


This Safeway store was located on Main Street two doors down from First Street, right next to the Escalon Bakery Fountain on the corner. Two doors from the Safeway was Runsten Brothers, offering men's wear, saddlery, luggage, hats, and rubber footwear. The Safeway store ceased to exist in 1952, becoming Carl's Market Cash and Carry.

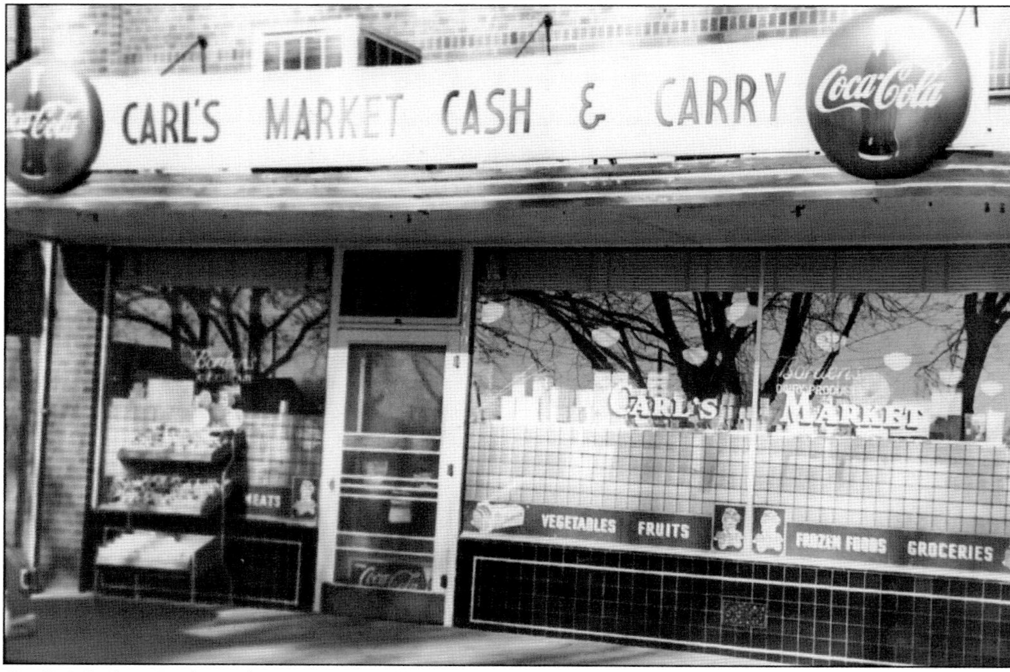


Carl's Market Cash and Carry, owned by Carl and Virginia Cova, occupied the same building on Main Street that the Safeway store had previously, also under their ownership. After just a few years, the Covas would move their market to First Street where Kerner's Home Furnishings had been and where Hogan Manufacturing, Inc., now has engineering offices.

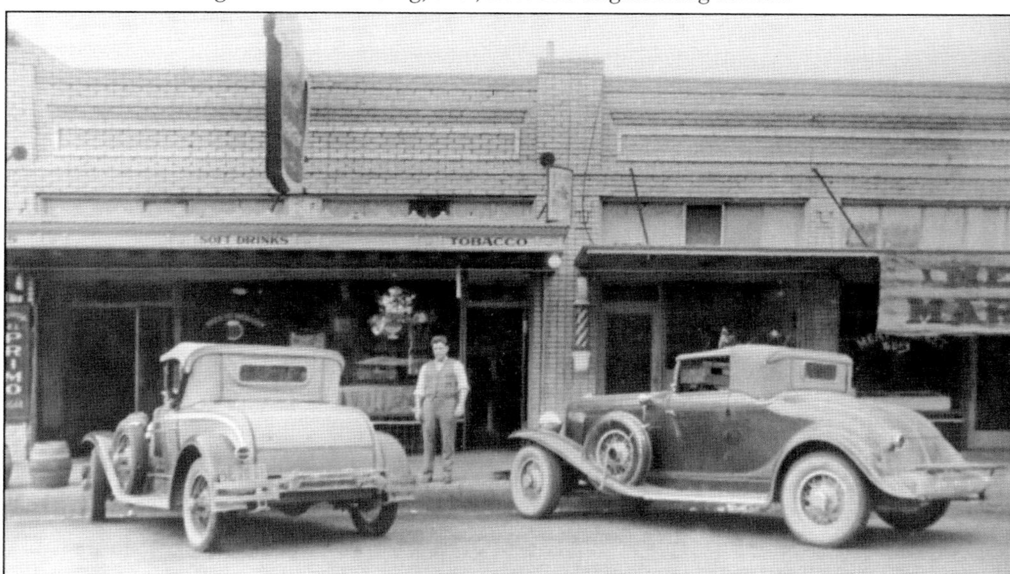


Charles Cadlolo was the owner of the Valley Inn in 1931, when this picture was taken. He had purchased the business from its builder, John Coley. The establishment once had two entrances: one for young people for the sale of ice cream and sodas and the other for adults for the purchase of alcoholic beverages and dancing. During Prohibition, near-beer and other nonalcoholic drinks were sold. In 1937, Cadlolo purchased the winery built by his uncle Louis Sciaroni in 1913, naming it the Cadlolo Winery. Today this winery is known as Stepping Stone Vineyards.

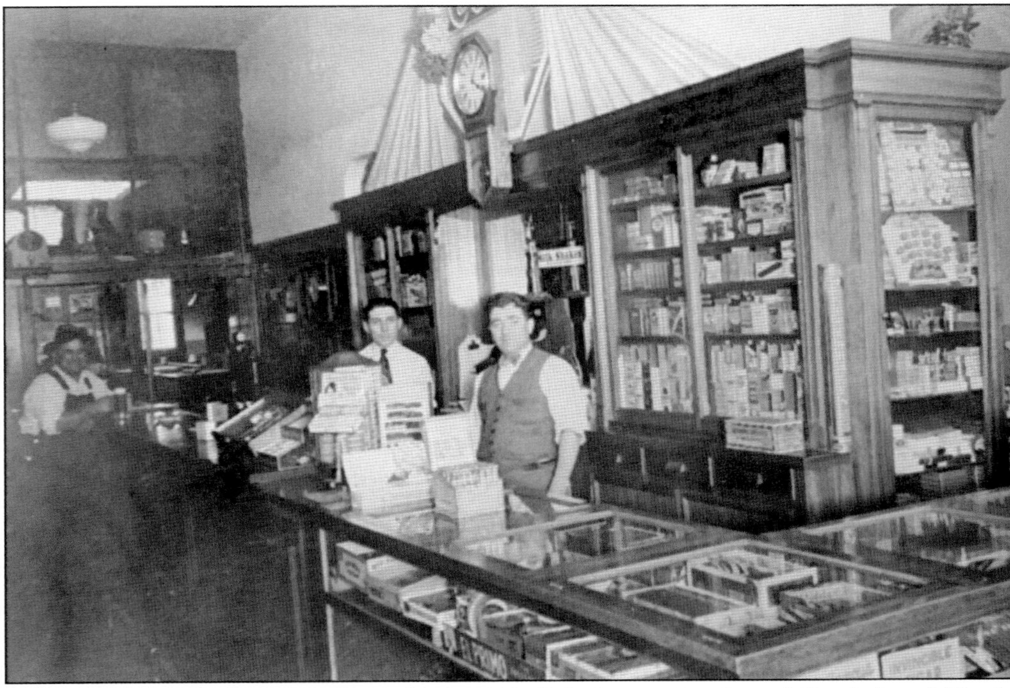

Here Jake Monk (left) is sitting with Michael Cadlolo (center, brother of Charles) and Charles Cadlolo (owner) in the Valley Inn, around 1929 or 1930. The Valley Inn, still in business today, is the oldest business on Main Street.

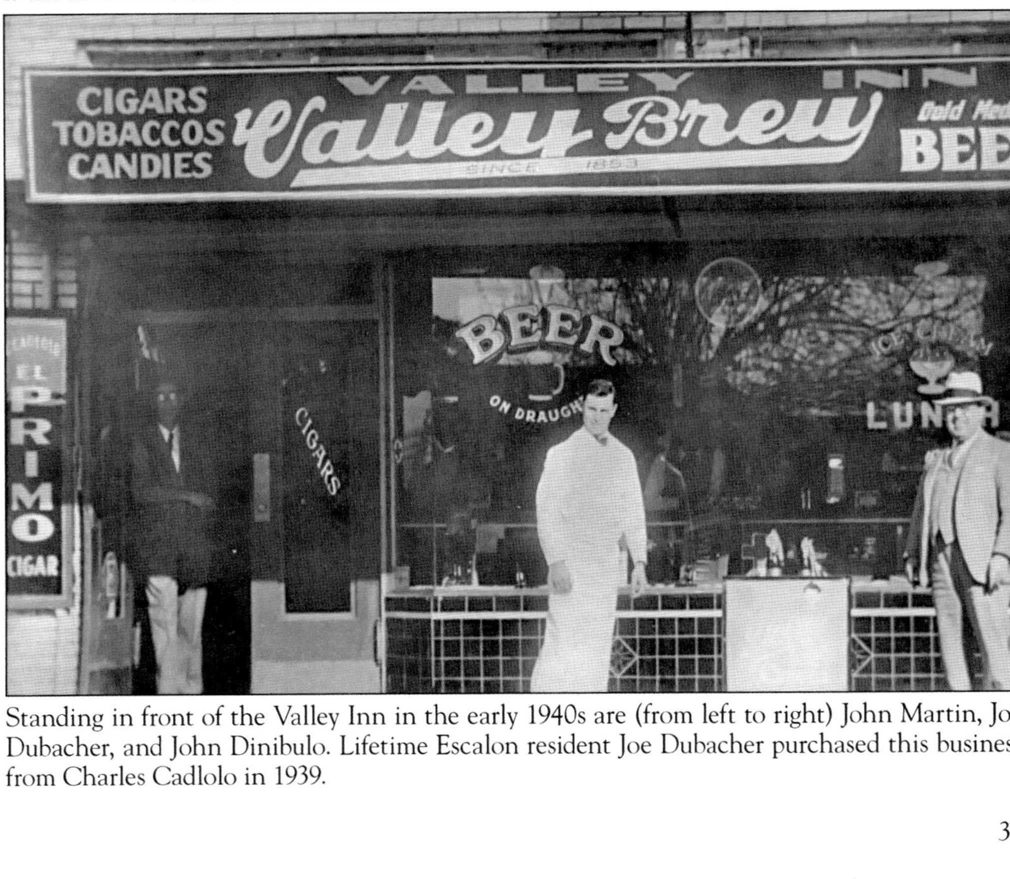


Standing in front of the Valley Inn in the early 1940s are (from left to right) John Martin, Joe Dubacher, and John Dinibulo. Lifetime Escalon resident Joe Dubacher purchased this business from Charles Cadlolo in 1939.

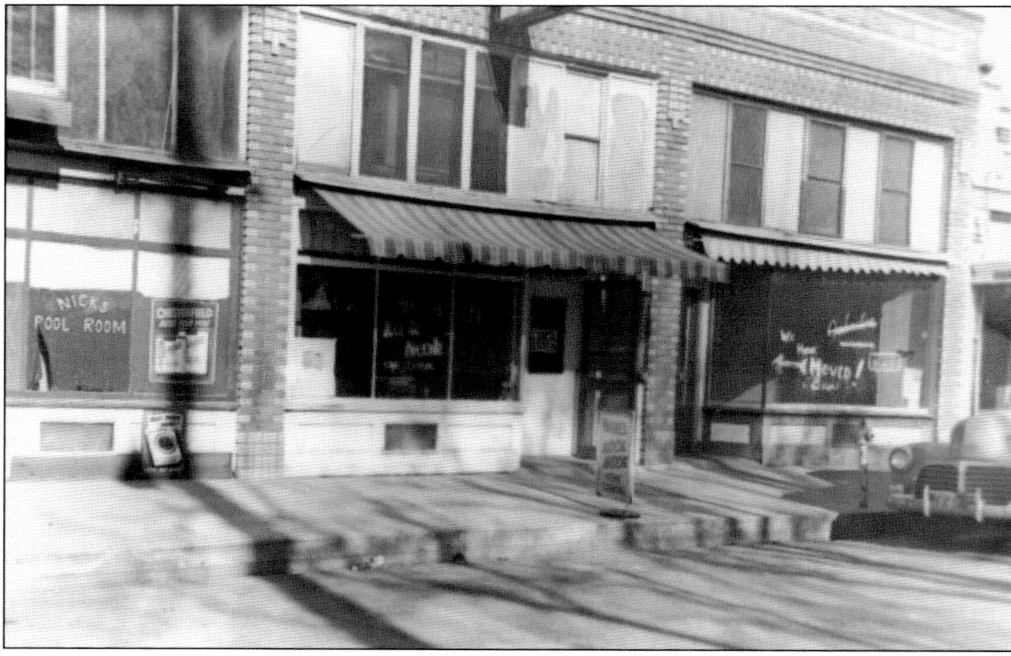


Nick's Pool Room was located on Main Street next to Mabel's Kook Nook, which offered home cooking. Owner Nick Jacono later located his pool hall in the adjacent block, in the building now housing Odette's Fresh Hair Salon.

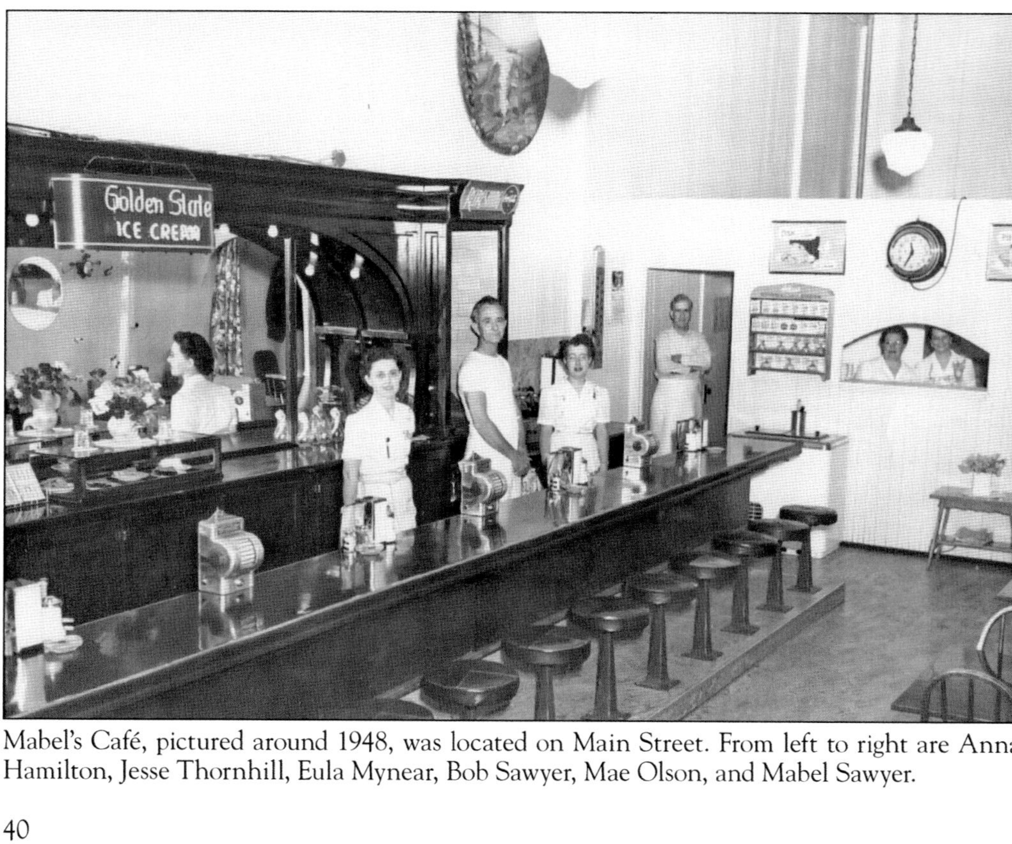


Mabel's Café, pictured around 1948, was located on Main Street. From left to right are Anna Hamilton, Jesse Thornhill, Eula Mynear, Bob Sawyer, Mae Olson, and Mabel Sawyer.

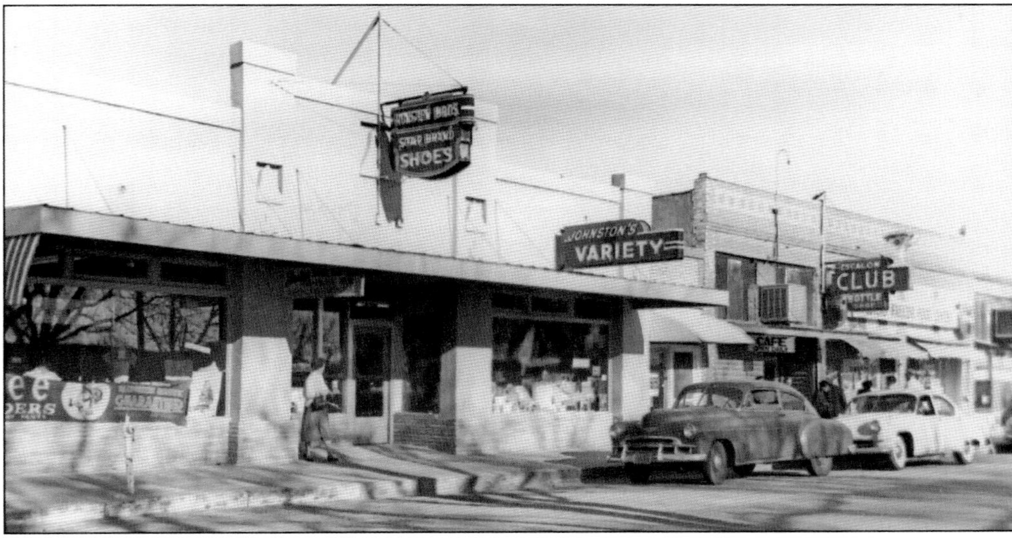


In the early 1950s, Main Street was home to such businesses as Runsten Brothers shoe repair and men's wear. This business made the transition from harness and saddle repair to shoe repair and selling men's clothing. Johnston's Variety, a five-and-dime store next door, offered stationery, notions, toys, and general variety merchandise. Beyond were the Escalon Club Bottle Shop and Fosters Freezer Food Center. These are some of the buildings constructed after the fires in the early 1900s. They remain in use today and house such businesses as the Cromwell and Associates Insurance Agency, Byrd's Main Street Music, Escalon Pet Grooming, and the interior design store Memories.

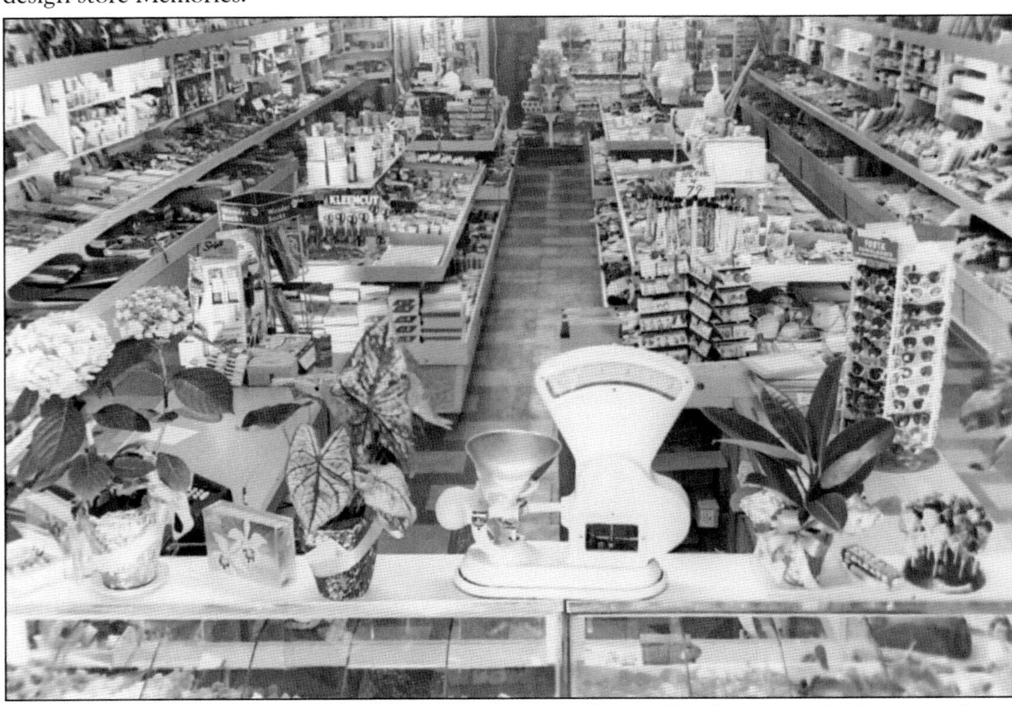

This is the interior of one of the variety stores on Main Street. Candy was weighed and purchased by the pound. Other merchandise for sale included Wonder Books for children, Fosta sunglasses, Kleencut scissors, and much more.

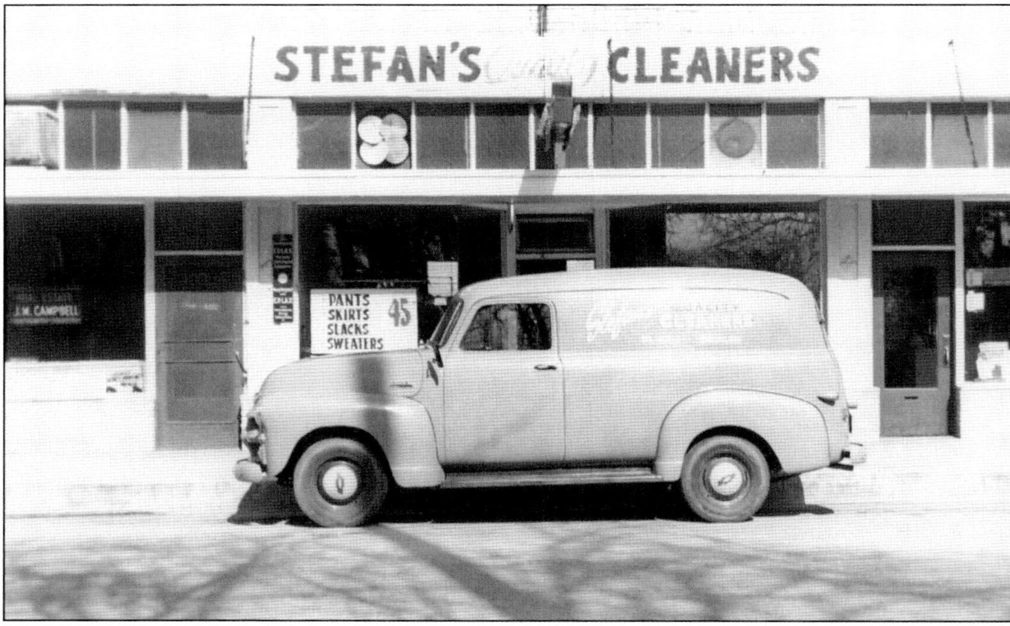


Stefan's Quality Cleaners was located on Main Street between First and Second Streets. According to the sign, pants, skirts, slacks, and sweaters could all be dry cleaned for the same rate of 45¢ each. Four-hour service was offered, and S&H Green Stamps were given out. To the right was Ard's Barber Shop, which was owned and operated by Ard Boyd.

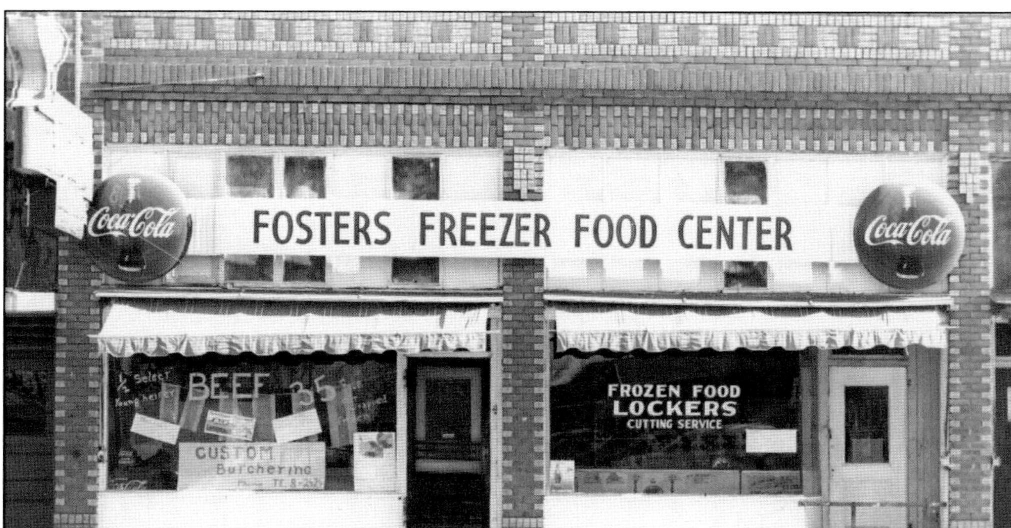


Fosters Freezer Food Center, offering frozen food lockers and a cutting service, was located on Main Street next to the Escalon Club Bottle Shop. For custom butchering, customers called TE8-2424. According to the writing on the window, one half of a select young heifer was cut and wrapped for 35¢ per pound. This business later belonged to Vern and Mabel Plemmons under the name Vern's Frozen Food Lockers.

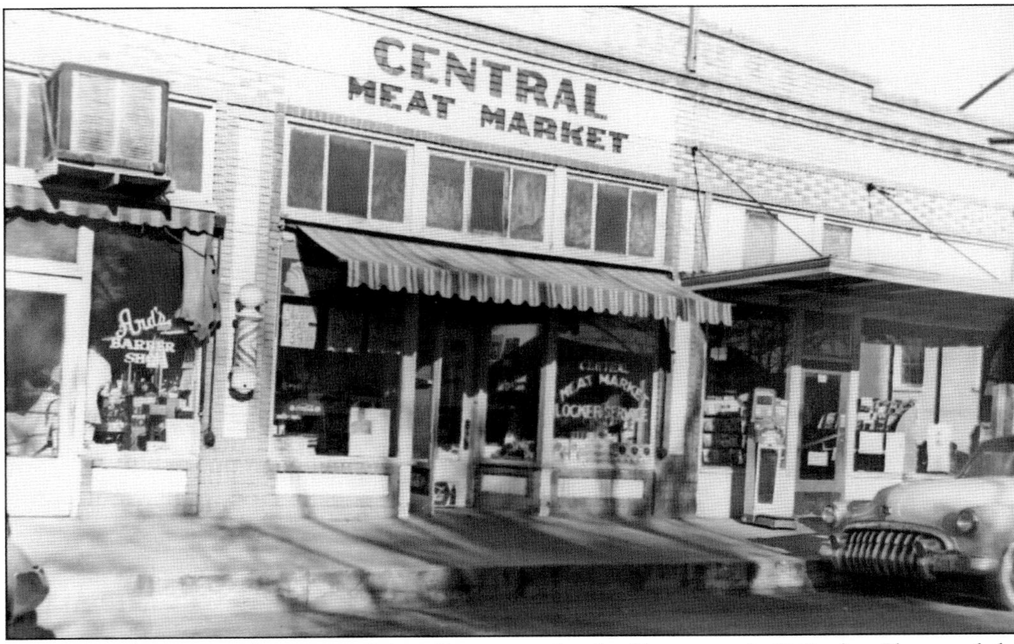


The Central Meat Market was on Main Street, sandwiched between Ard's Barber Shop and the Rexall Drug Store, which was on the corner with Second Street. Today this spot is occupied by Realty World.

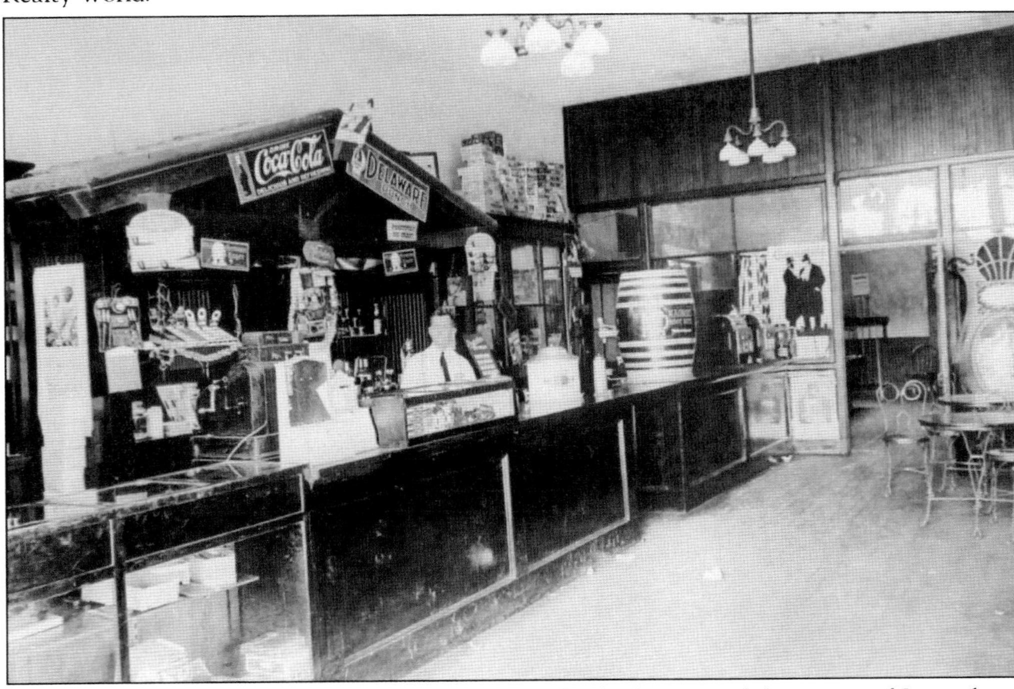


This is the interior of James Coley's bar and pool hall, which occupied the corner of Second and Main Streets. Among the surviving memorabilia from this establishment are tokens good for 5¢ in trade, which are currently on loan to the Escalon Historical Museum. Additional businesses owned by Coley included a hotel, an ice cream parlor, a card room, a feed store, a soda fountain, a telephone office, and a second bar.

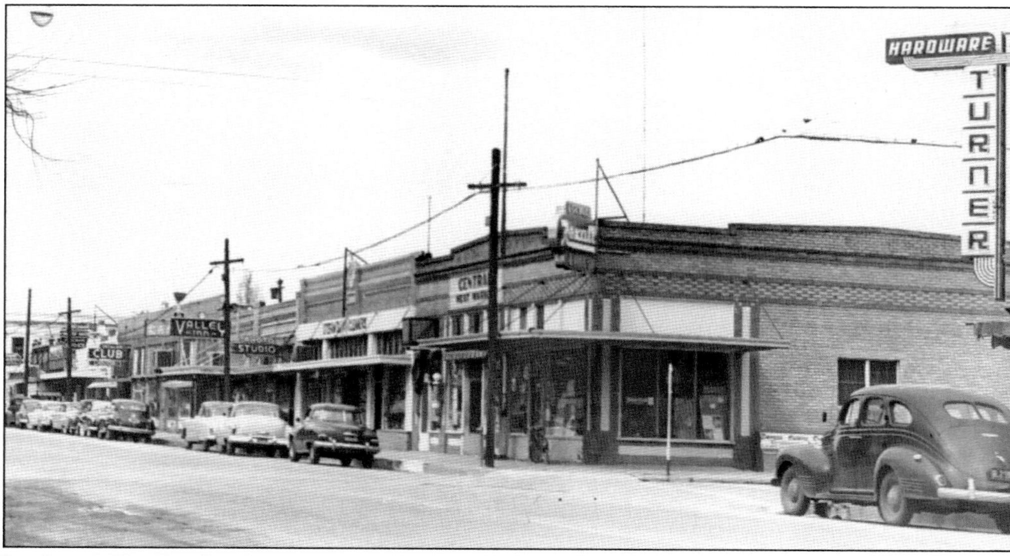


In the 1950s, Escalon Drug was a part of the Rexall chain of drugstores, and it occupied the corner of Main and Second Streets across from Turner Hardware. Other Main Street businesses visible here proceeding north from right to left include the Central Meat Market, Ard's Barber Shop, a café, Marshall Studio, the Valley Inn (still there today), another café, the Escalon Club Bottle Shop, Runsten Brothers, and the Escalon Bakery Fountain. The back of the bench beside the Second Street wall of the drugstore is an advertisement for the Deegan Funeral Chapel. The Turner Hardware building was later home to Strand's Ace Hardware for many years and is now being remodeled to showcase antiques for sale. It is the oldest building in the downtown business district.

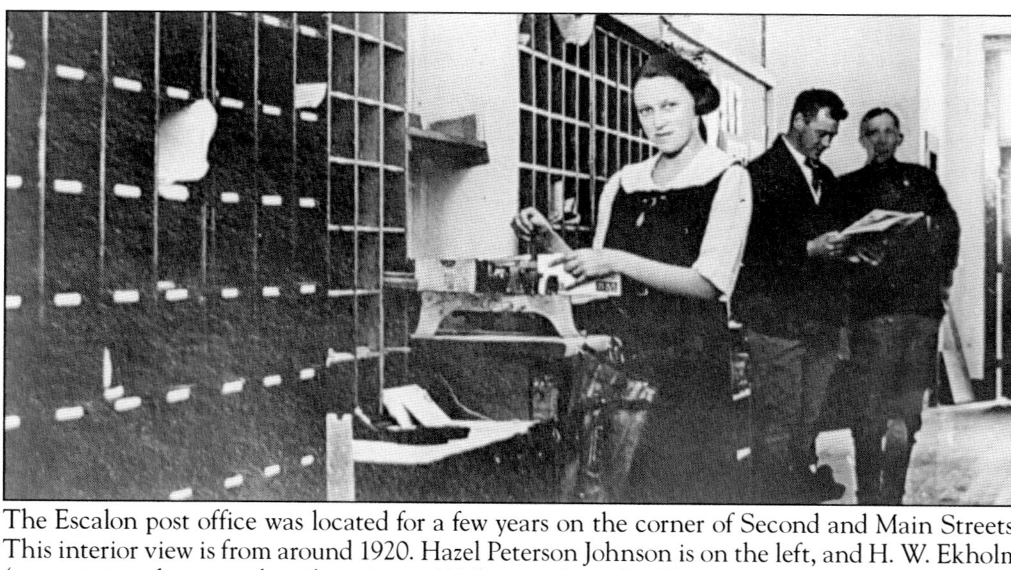

The Escalon post office was located for a few years on the corner of Second and Main Streets. This interior view is from around 1920. Hazel Peterson Johnson is on the left, and H. W. Ekholm (commissioned as a rural mail carrier in 1916) is on the right. The other man is unidentified. At this time, only rural routes received mail delivery. City delivery would begin in 1961, ten years after the post office moved across Second Street to the building that now houses the American Legion Gustafson-Thompson Post. In 1963, the post office moved to its current location at the corner of Coley Avenue and Third Street. The corner of Main and Second is now home to Leonardo's Café.

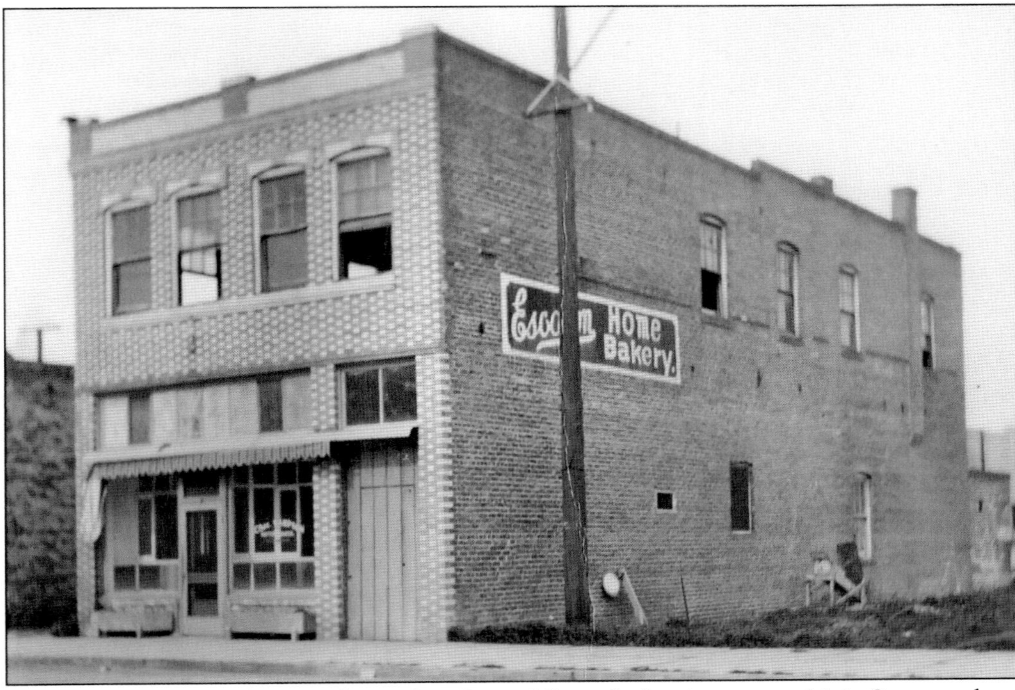


The Escalon Home Bakery was located on Second Street before its move to Main Street and was owned by Arno Bender. The bakery had its own vehicle and offered free delivery. The business was the home of Blue Bird Bread and proclaimed that its baked goods were "made from the purest ingredients obtainable." The original building was destroyed in the fire of 1917 and was rebuilt as this two-story brick building. This building then sustained a fire and was replaced by the building that would later house the city hall.

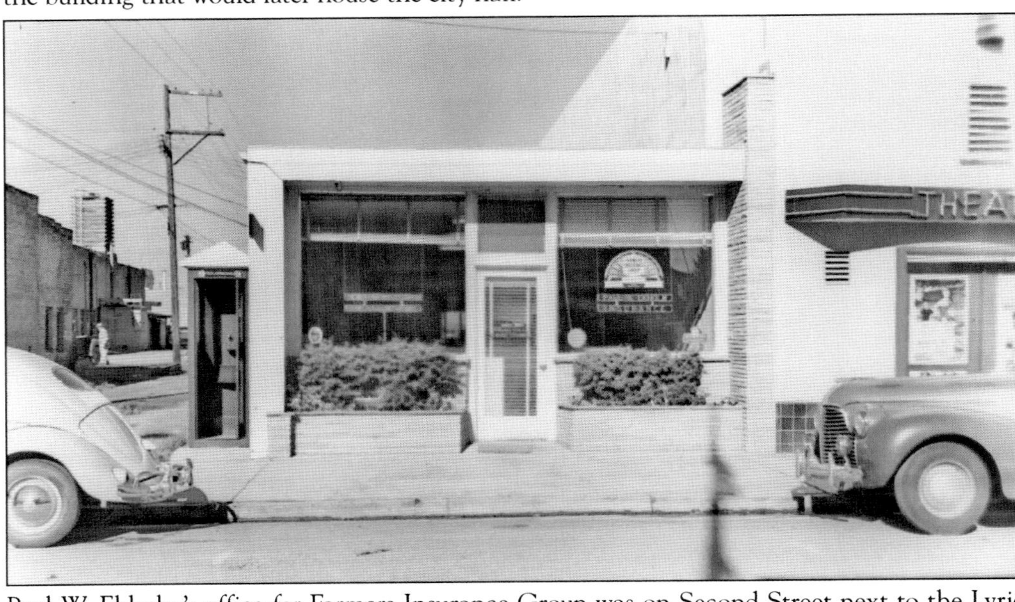

Paul W. Ekholm's office for Farmers Insurance Group was on Second Street next to the Lyric Theatre. Ekholm was a certified public accountant, provided bookkeeping services, and owned several properties in Escalon. The meeting room in the Escalon Branch Library was named after him.

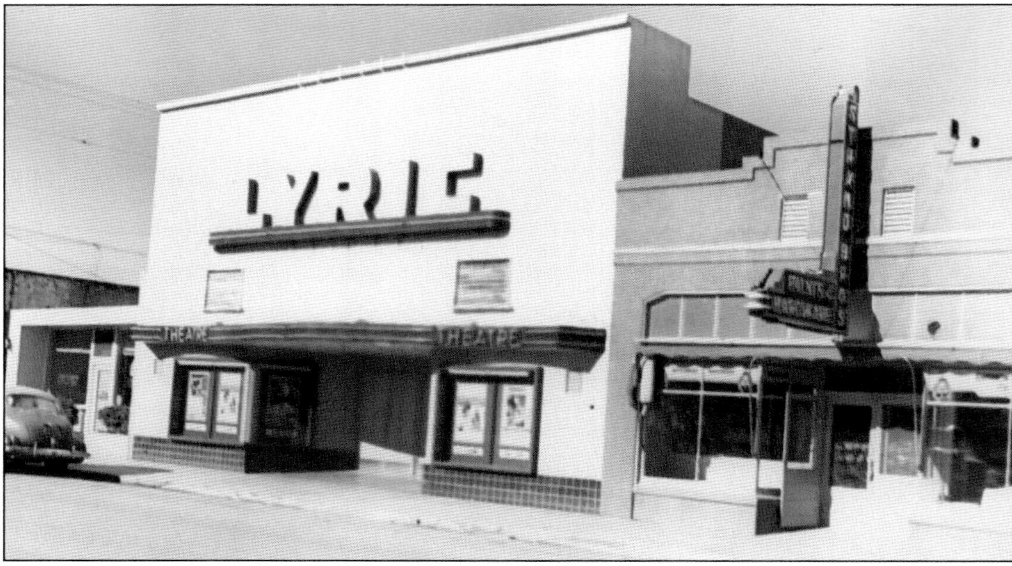


The Lyric Theatre enjoyed a brief run on Second Street between Main Street and Coley Avenue in the 1940s and 1950s. There was one screen, admission was less than $1, and the venue was a popular gathering place for teenagers. Business was best on Saturday and Sunday, when families would come into town from their farms or ranches. On the left (to the west of the theater) was Paul W. Ekholm's insurance office. On the right (to the east) at the corner with Coley Avenue was Strand Brothers Paint and Hardware, which opened in 1946. Strand's moved to Main Street in the 1970s to occupy the old Turner Hardware building and then became Strand's Ace Hardware under the ownership of Larry Swanson. Ace Hardware is now located on McHenry Avenue.

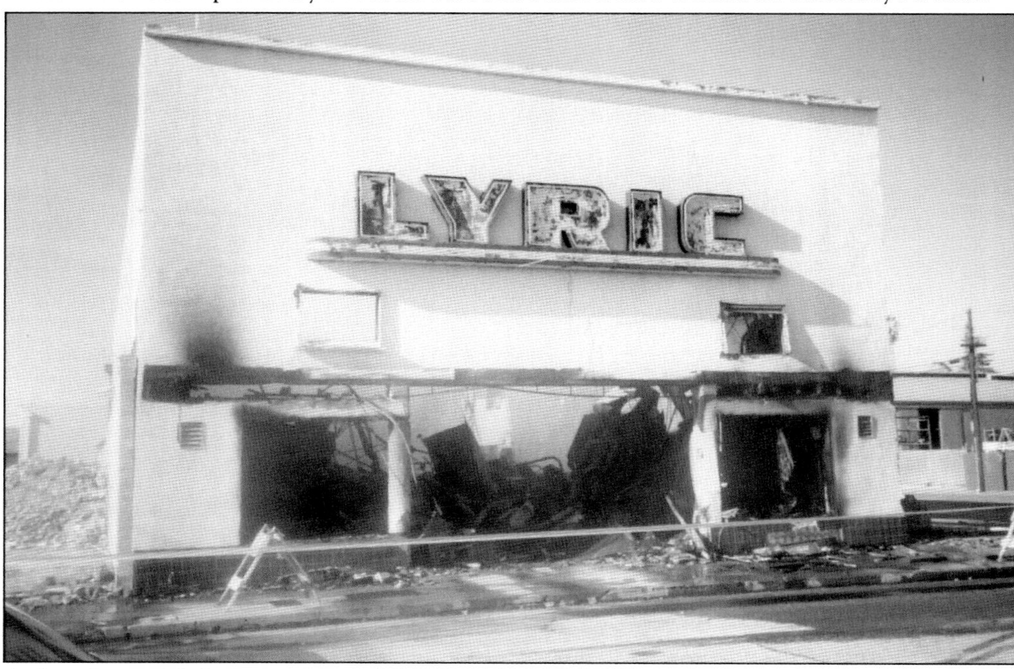


A fire destroyed the interior of the Lyric Theatre building. The city considered using the remaining structure for a new library building, but the property was deemed unsafe and was eventually torn down.

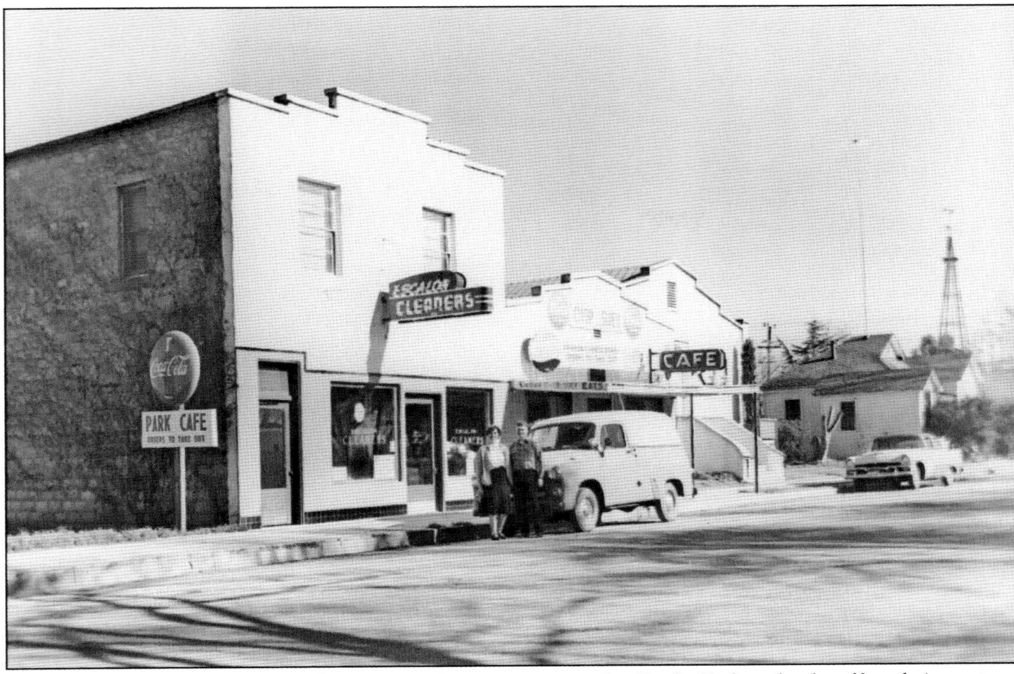


Escalon Cleaners was located on Main Street next to the Park Café, which offered American and Chinese dishes to take out. Today the leftmost building is vacant, while the other is home to Odette's Fresh Hair Salon. Beyond the café is the Escalon Grange Hall.

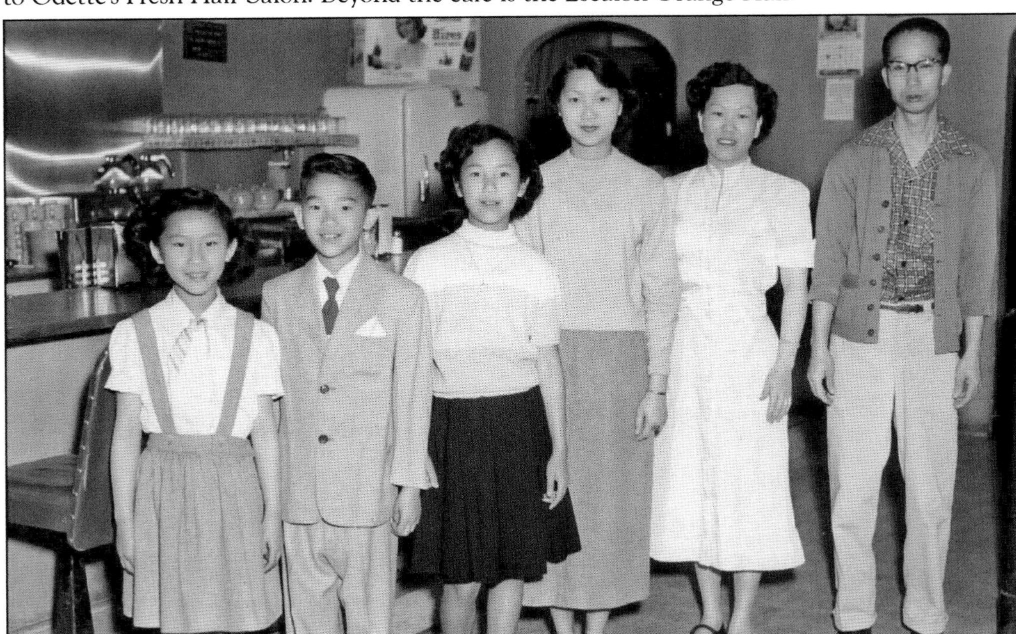

The Wong family owned the Park Café on Main Street in the 1950s. Afterward the Sargenti family, namely Walt and Julie, operated an Italian restaurant in that spot. Pictured from left to right are Bonnie, Bryant, Bev, Connie, Sue, and Yuen Wong.

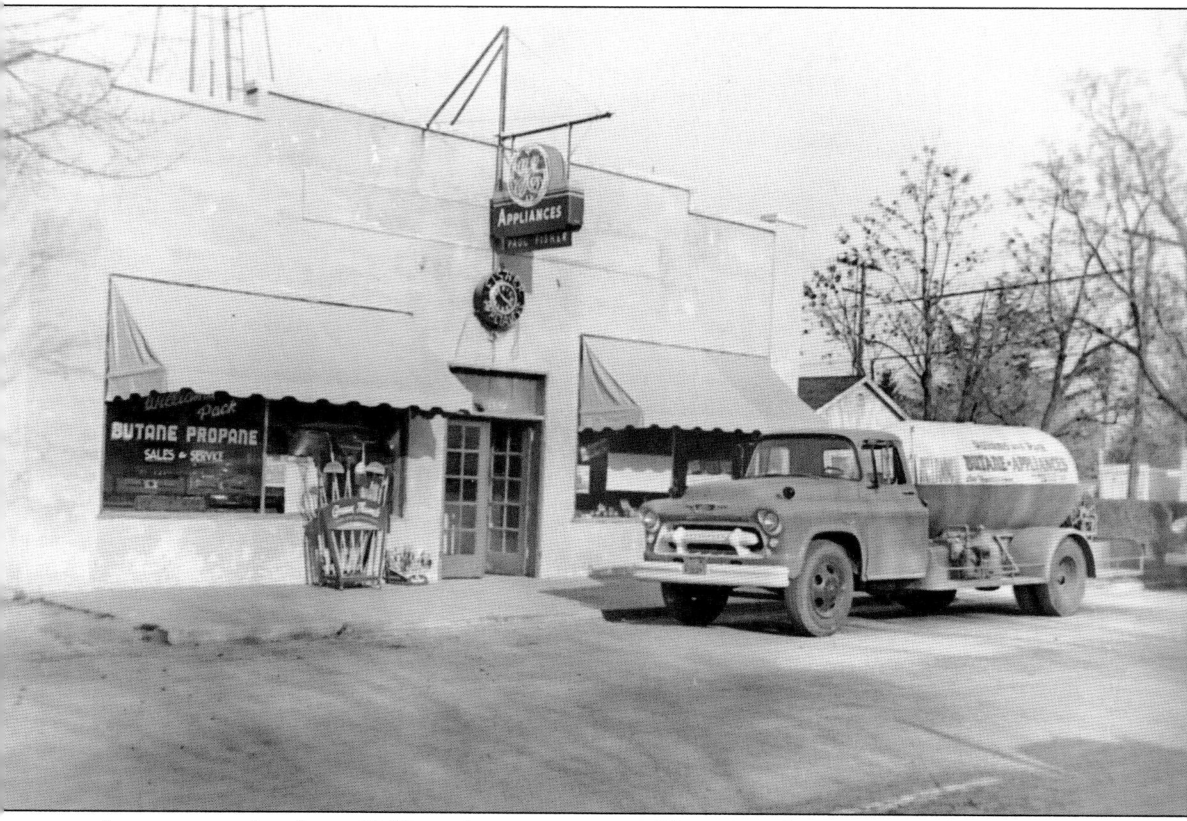


It appears to be about 10:20 in the morning or 3:50 in the afternoon at Williams and Pack on Main Street. This store had butane, propane, Green Thumb gardening implements, and General Electric appliance sales and service. The building now contains city hall offices. The house behind and to the right still stands.

# *Five*

# HISTORIC HOMES

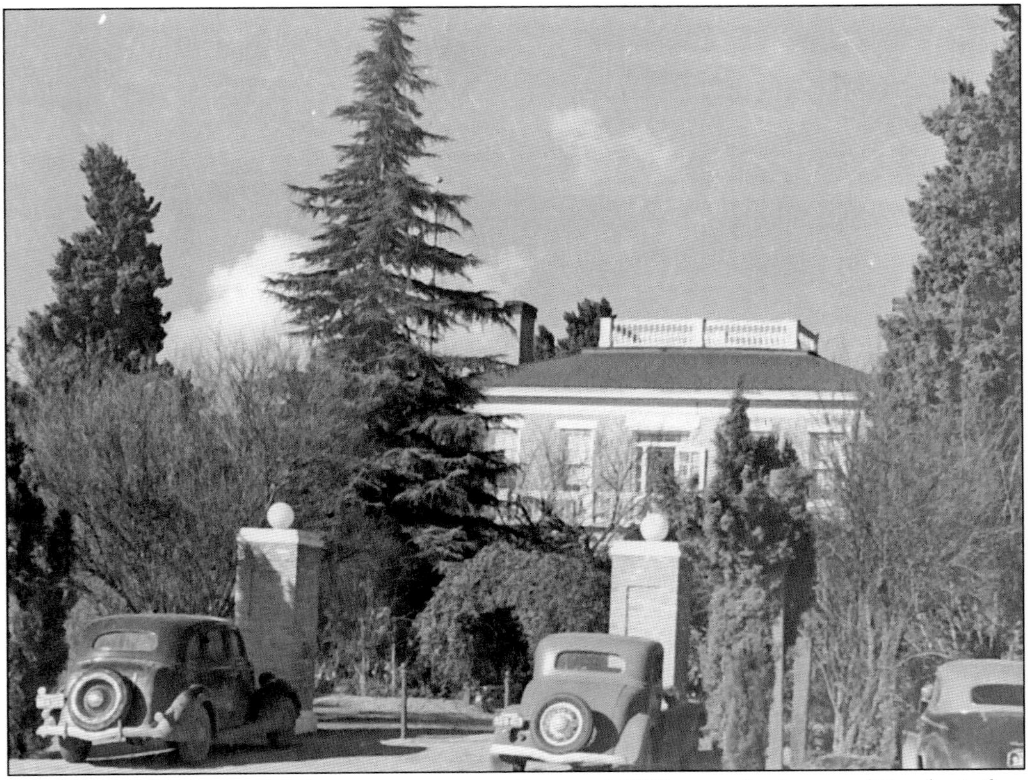

This square, two-story, brick mansion, pictured around 1950, was the home of Escalon's first settler and founder, John Wheeler Jones. It was built in the 1860s and still stands today at the intersection of Pioneer and Park Avenues. After being a residence, the building belonged to a women's club, served as a high school while a permanent high school was being built, operated as the first Pioneer Memorial Hospital (so named because of John Wheeler Jones's pioneer status), and then returned to being a residence. When used as a women's club, the grounds were known as Jones Park. While it was the high school, the student body increased from 35 to 79 students. When serving as a hospital, the delivery room was located on the second floor, requiring expectant mothers to walk up the flight of stairs to the maternity area. The bricks used in the original construction were made by Richard Jones, John's brother, from clay found in a field west of town.

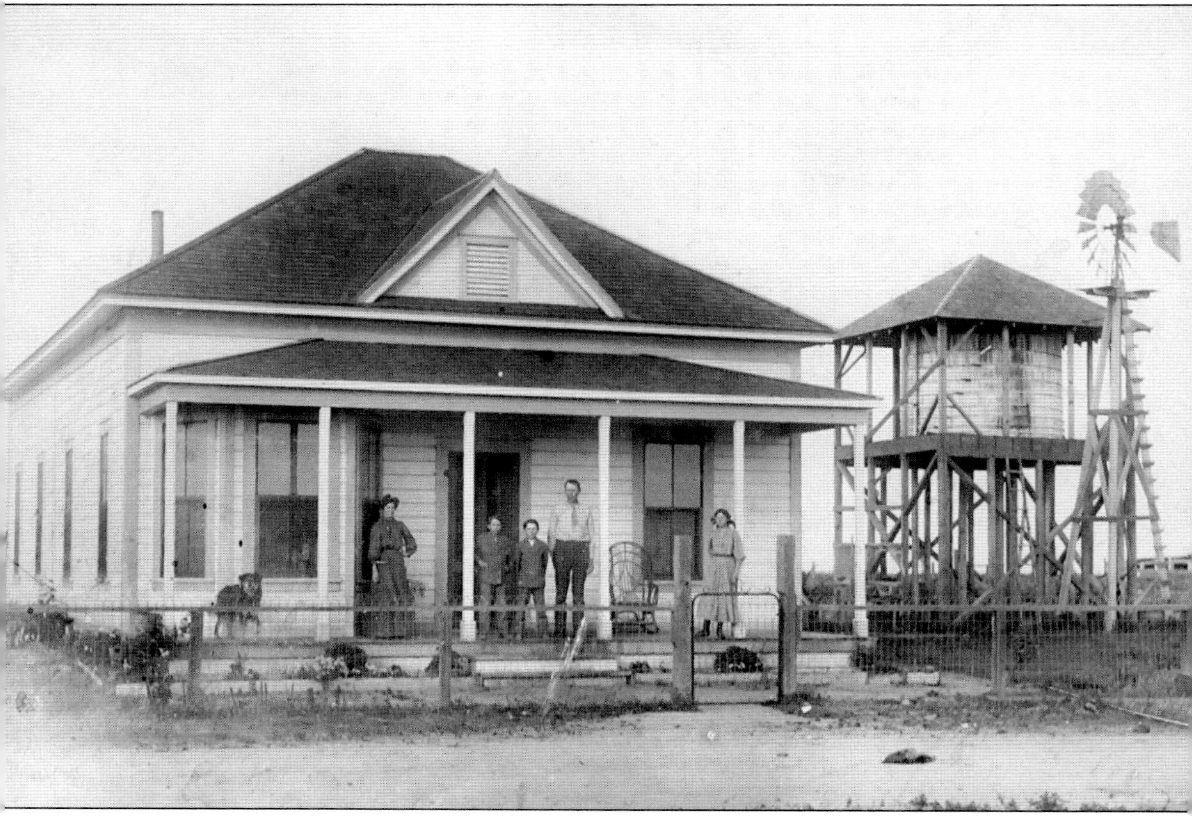

The home of James H. and Olive Jackson and their children is pictured here in 1906. It was built in the late 1800s and stood at the corner of Jackson Avenue and Second Street. Pictured from left to right are Olive Jackson, Clayton Jackson, Carl Jackson, James H. Jackson, and Myrtle Jackson. The Jacksons owned a hotel and the first saloon in Escalon. Olive Jackson served as the postmistress in 1900 when the post office was located for a brief time in the Jackson home. Clayton, born in Escalon in 1896, served as one of the grand marshals in the Spring Festival parade in 1974. He was honored at that time as one of the oldest native-born citizens in Escalon. As a young boy, Clayton attended the elementary school on First Street.

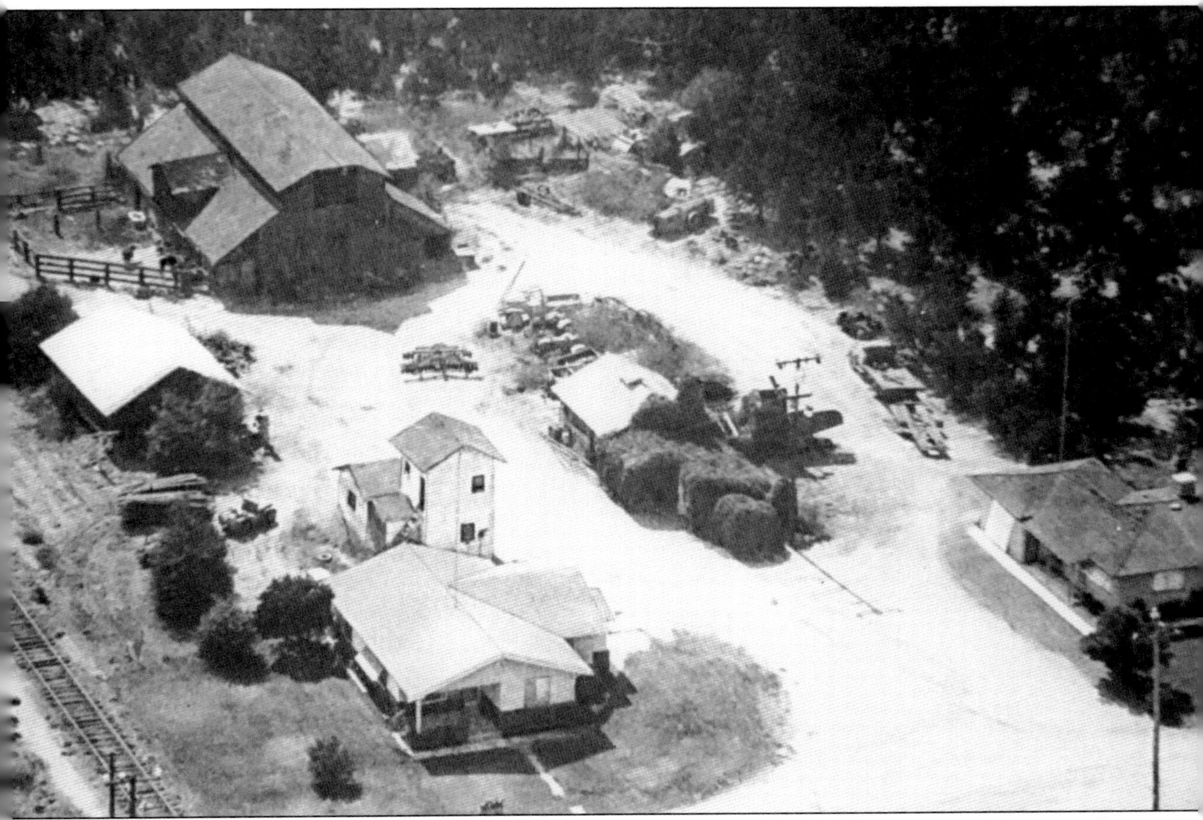

The Ullery Ranch was owned by Florence Ullery and was located on the southwest corner of McHenry and Ullery Avenues. The barn had a unique side door that enabled it to be used by stagecoaches on their way to Farmington and Collegeville. Inside was a wooden track for the hayfork. The farm at one time produced melons and sweet potatoes, and one of the outbuildings close to the railroad tracks served as the packing shed for those crops. Eventually, peach trees, and then almond trees, would be planted. Today the two homes and a few of the outbuildings remain. Orchard trees now grow on the barn's previous location.

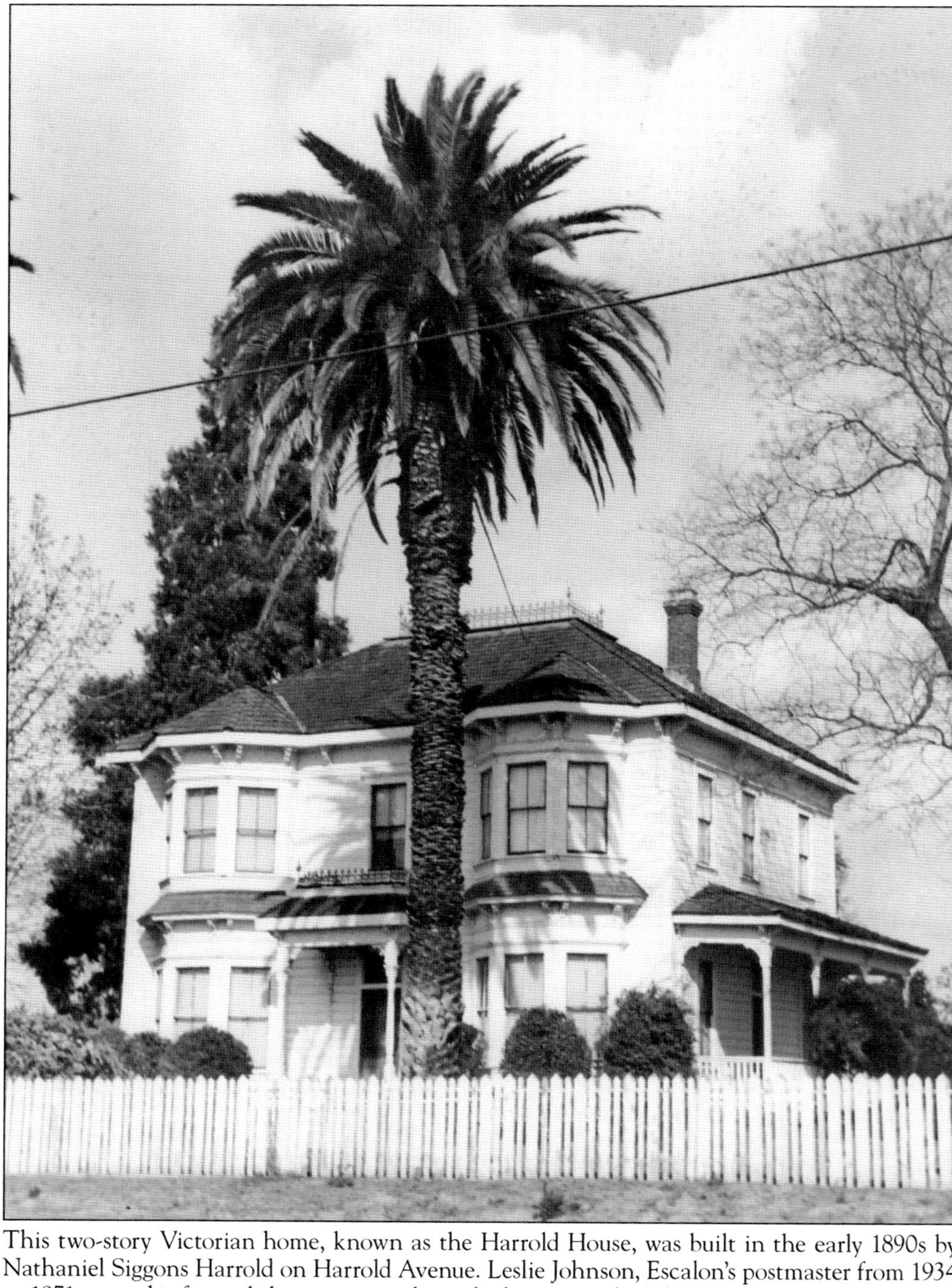

This two-story Victorian home, known as the Harrold House, was built in the early 1890s by Nathaniel Siggons Harrold on Harrold Avenue. Leslie Johnson, Escalon's postmaster from 1934 to 1971, owned it for a while, causing it also to be known as the Johnson House.

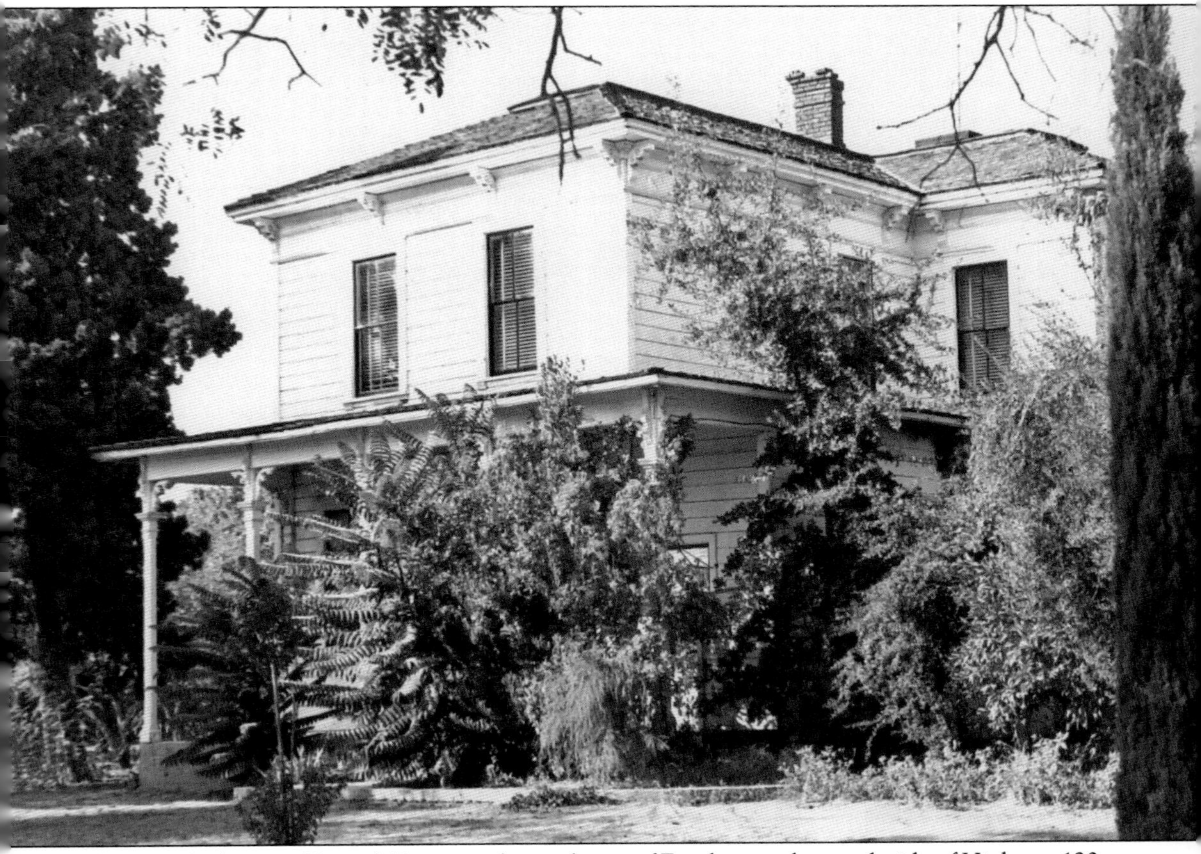

This was the home of Patrick Brennan, located west of Escalon on the north side of Highway 120 between Van Allen and Carrolton Roads. He built the house in the late 1800s. Brennan helped in the planning and laying out of French Camp Road, which would later become this highway. He also donated land for the first Van Allen Elementary School property. Prior to farming his many acres of wheat, he had been in the business of supplying mining camps.

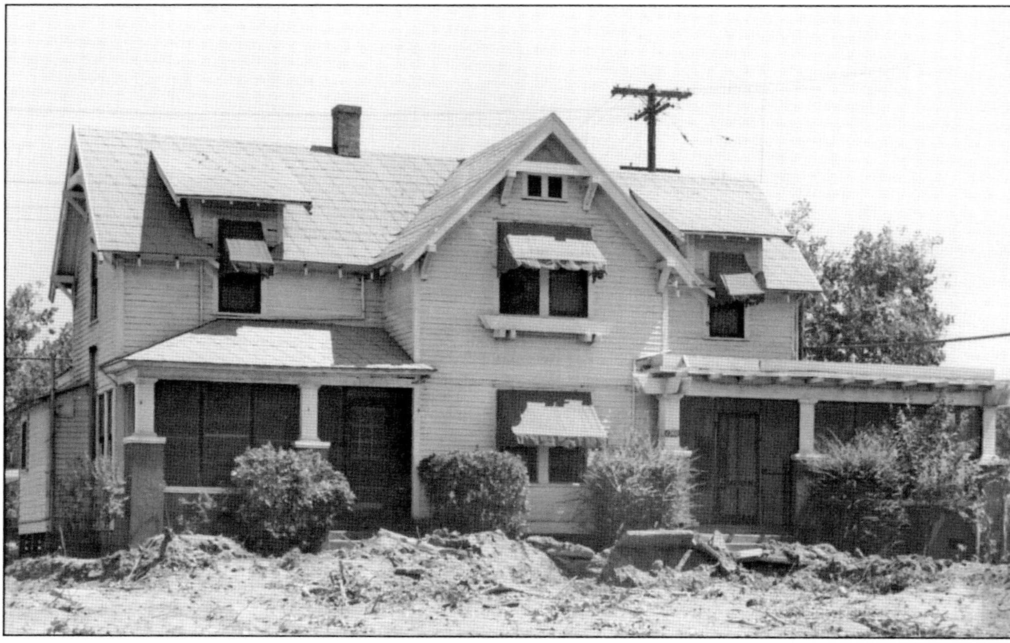

The Blackmore House was built by Andy Kern at the beginning of the 20th century and was located for many years at the intersection of St. Clair Street and Highway 120. The house was built for $2,000 in the midst of what was then a flourishing vineyard. The Shell Oil Company purchased the property in the 1960s for the operation of a Shell gas station. Currently occupying this spot is McDowell and Davis Towing and Auto Repair. Pat and Dexter Moore bought the house when it was moved in its entirety to the property of Stan and Eula Sherwood on Stewart Road in Del Rio.

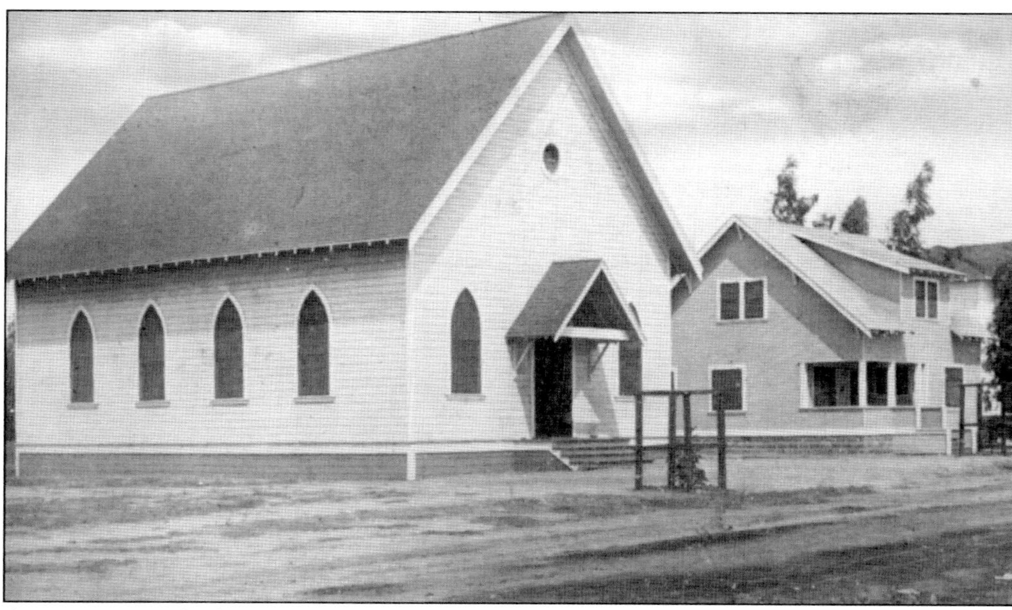

A parsonage was built in 1915 between the Swedish Lutheran Church (center) and the elementary school on First Street. It remains today next to the Escalon Presbyterian Church as a private residence.

# Six

# NOTEWORTHY EVENTS

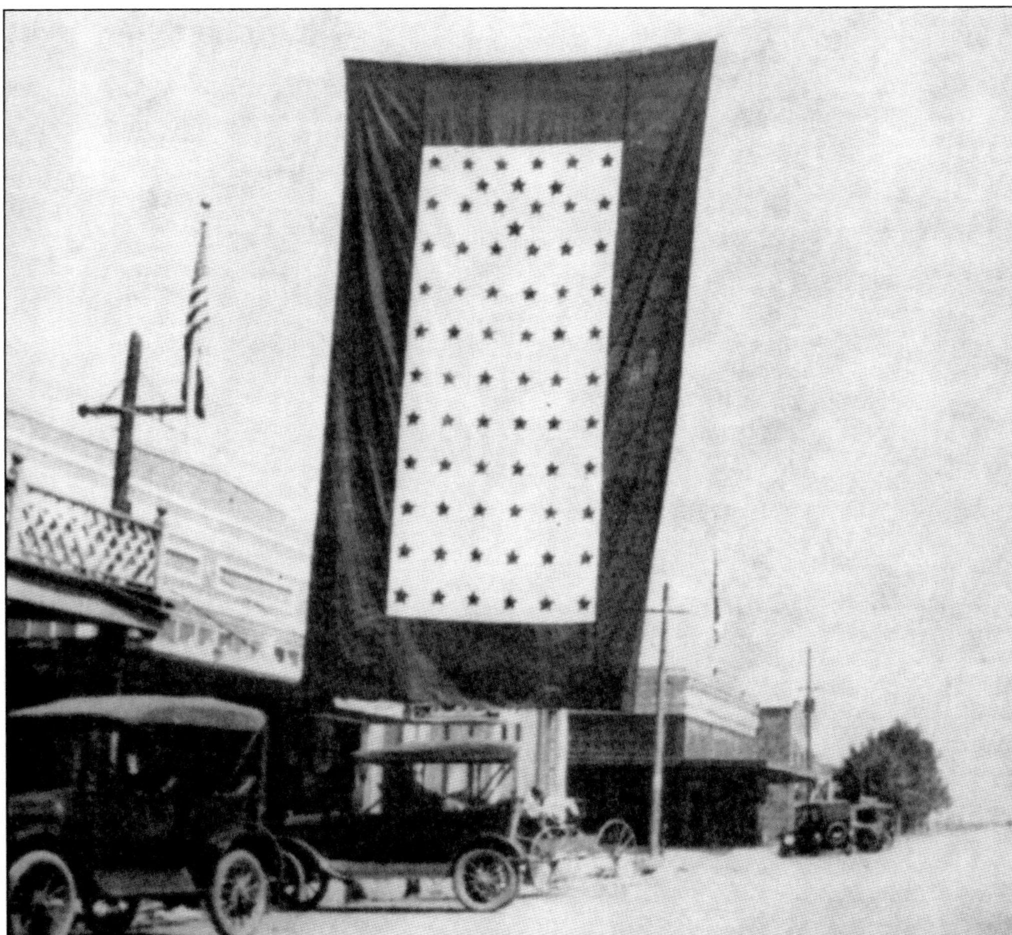

This service flag was suspended above Main Street at Second Street to represent local soldiers who had gone to fight in World War I. There are 70 stars shown here, but eventually, 92 individuals from Escalon served. Two died in service (Bert Gustafson and Cecil Thompson, for whom the American Legion Post was named). This was a rate of two percent, tied with one other city (in South Carolina) for the highest rate of loss for a community in the nation. The flag was rimmed in blue and had blue stars on a white background. This southeast view was taken in 1918.

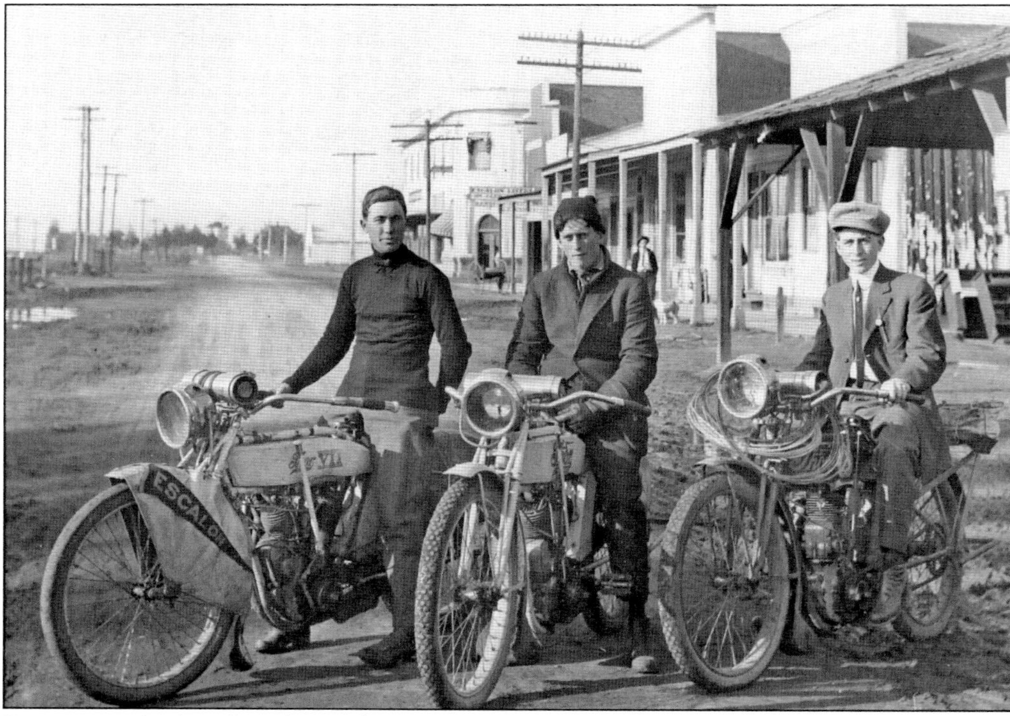


Sitting astride their bicycles in downtown Escalon around 1913 are (from left to right) Bob Harder, Woodson L. Drew, and Clifford Huelsick, installers of Escalon's first telephone lines. In the background is the Fisk Building, which housed the first bank in Escalon and now houses the accounting office of Hogan Manufacturing, Inc. The wooden structures pictured were destroyed by the fires that occurred in the decade after this picture was taken. Notice the carbide, gas-fueled headlamps on the bicycles.

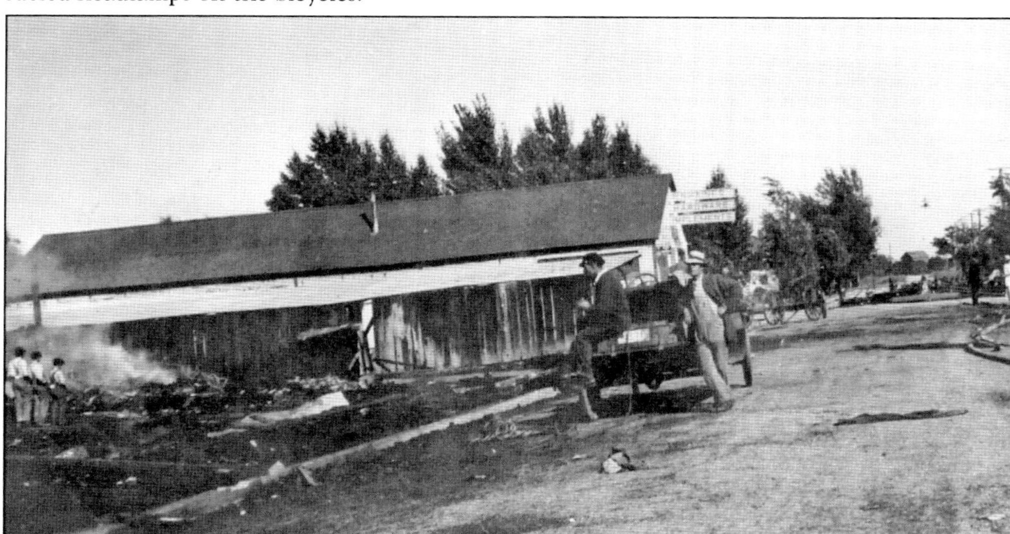

This is a view of the fire damage on Second Street in 1917. The building still standing was home to Haines Hardware and Implements at the corner with Coley Avenue, coincidentally where concerned citizens had met in 1912 to propose the formation of a fire district for the growing Escalon community.

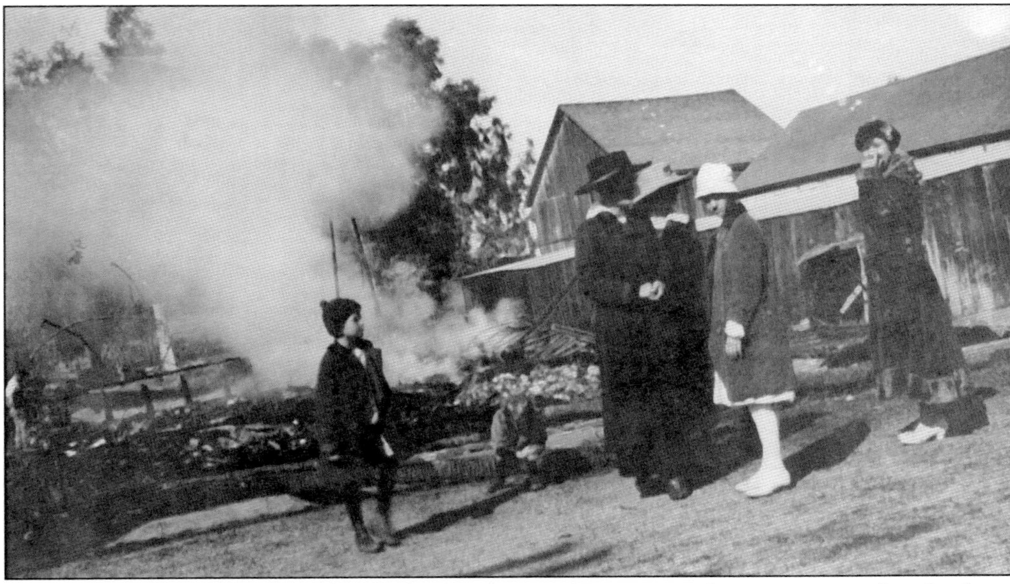

Some concerned citizens stand near the fire-damaged businesses downtown just after the fire of 1917 or 1920.

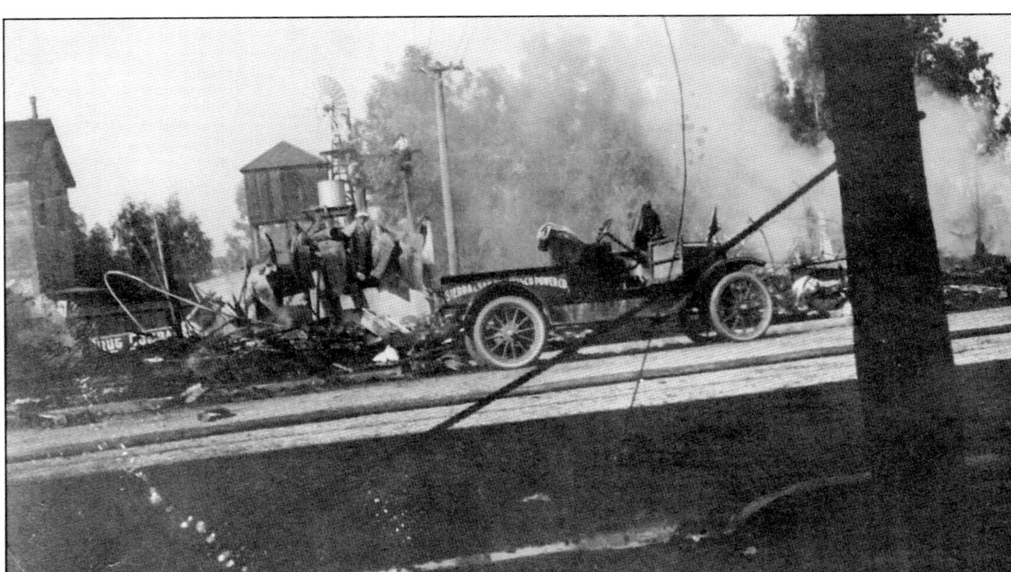

Barely visible through the rubble on the left is a sign from the Escalon Drug Company, the occupant of one of the buildings destroyed by fire in the early 1900s.

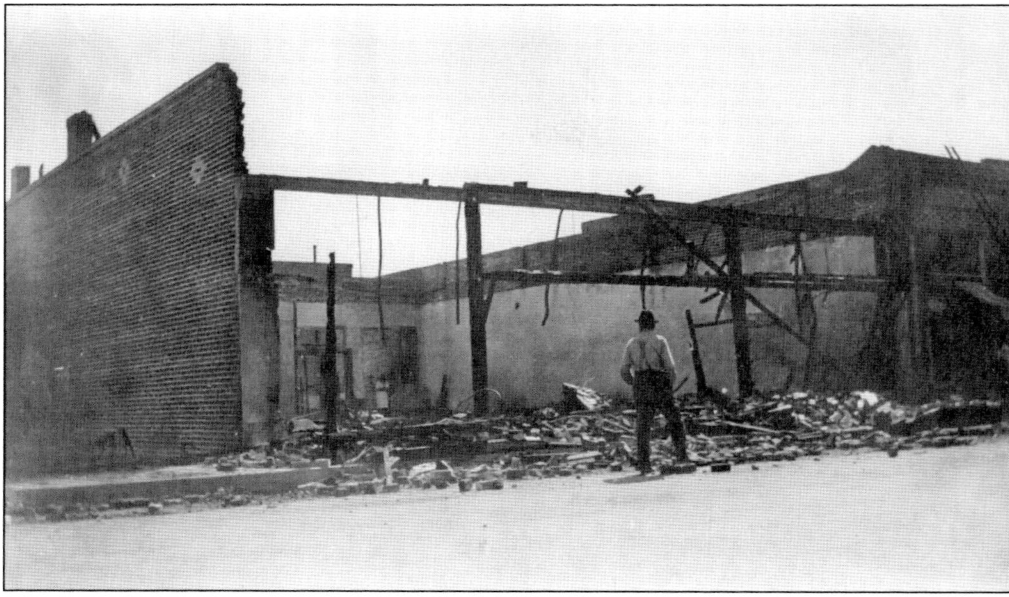

These are pictures of some of the damage on Main Street done by the fire of 1920. The photographs were donated to the Escalon Historical Museum by Don Anderson.

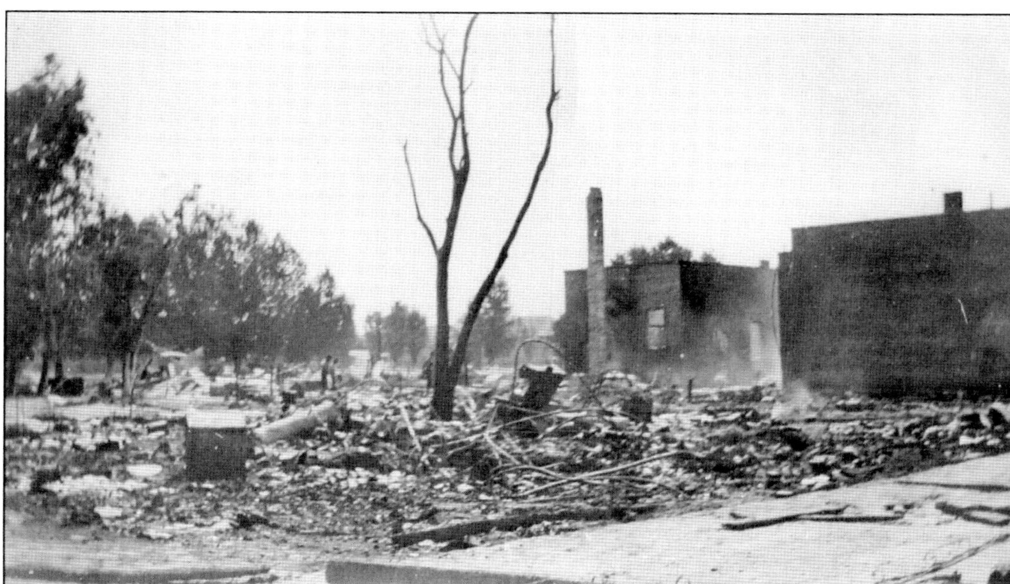

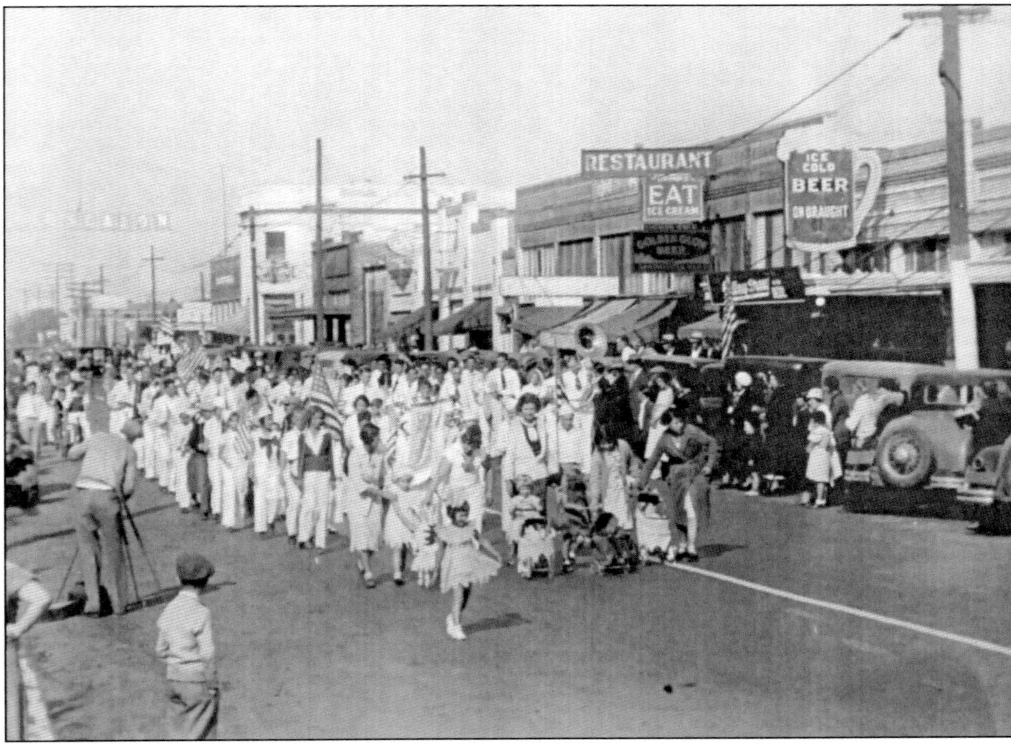


Participants in the Armistice Day parade of 1934 or 1935, as seen on the cover, proceed southeast on Main Street. In those days, Escalon High School had a rivalry with Ripon, a nearby community. The football games matching these two teams were played every year on this holiday. Game time was 2:30 p.m., as the field did not yet have lights for evening games. While the games were being played, this downtown street was deserted.

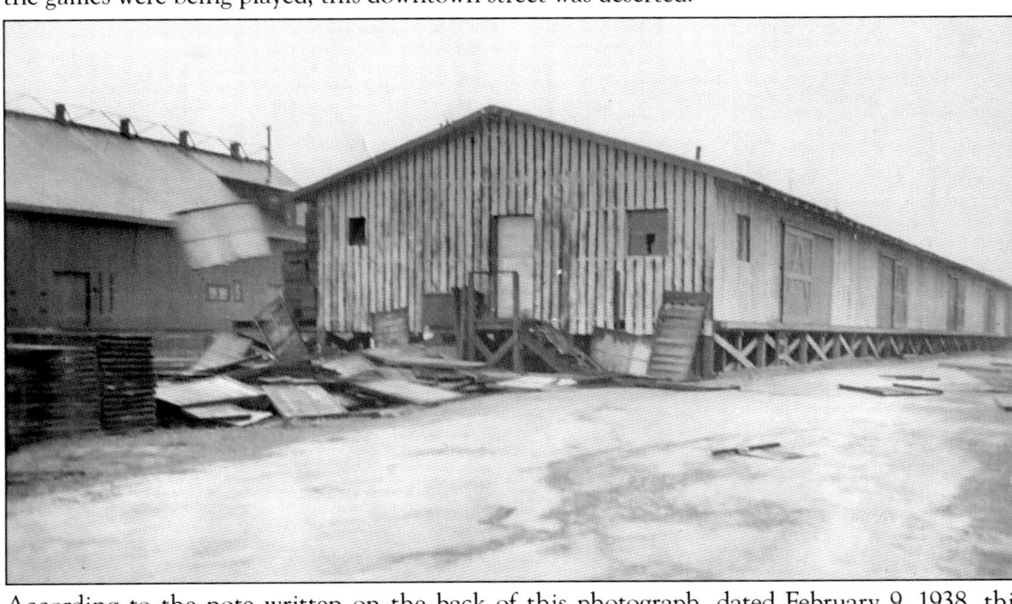

According to the note written on the back of this photograph, dated February 9, 1938, this picture was taken during a storm with high winds. On the left is a drying tray in midair. After the storm, according to the note, there were drying trays scattered all over town.

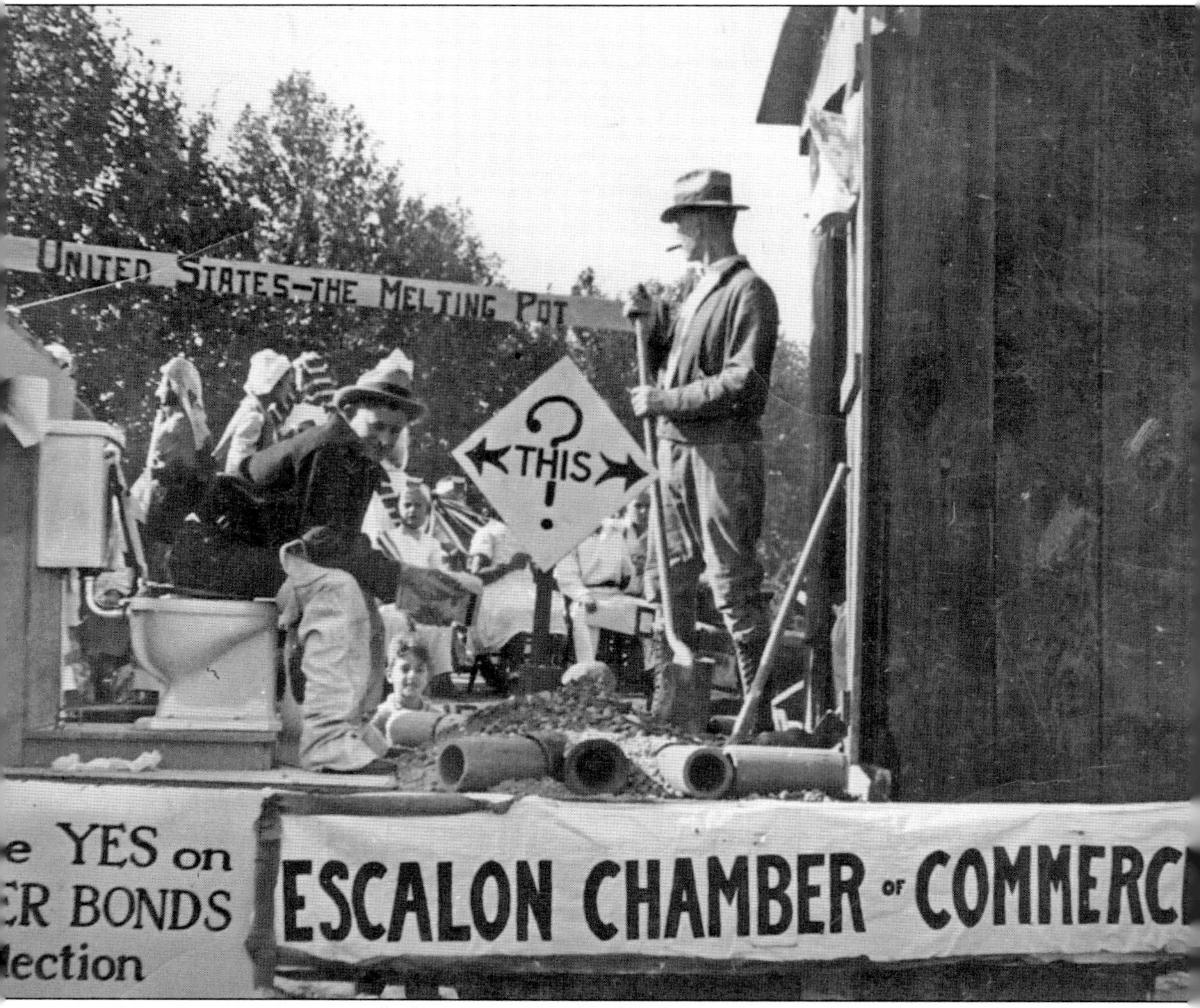


This appears to be a parade float sponsored by the Escalon Chamber of Commerce advocating a "yes" vote on sewer bonds in the November 23rd election of that year. Pictured are Jack Riesenbeck (seated) and C. T. Brayton, two local businessmen.

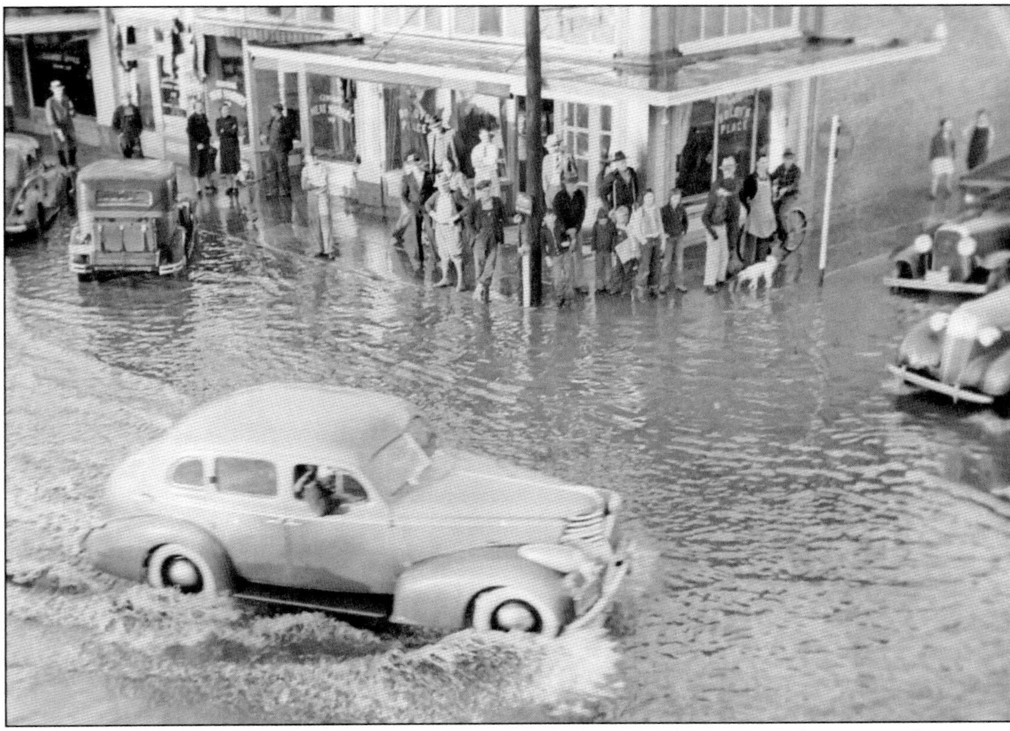

Manuel Silveira drives down Main Street in this 1940 rainstorm. At this time, the corner structure at Second and Main Streets was the home of Boldt's Place, an ice cream parlor owned by Todd Boldt.

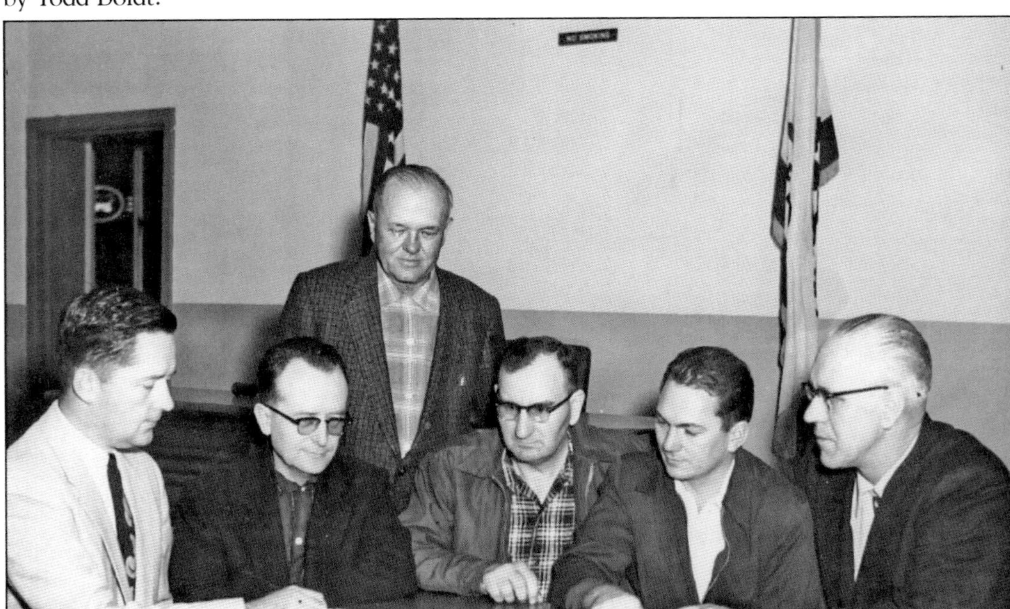

The city of Escalon was incorporated on March 12, 1957. From left to right are Escalon's city attorney, Leo Milich, and the first city council: Monroe Kerner (owner of Kerner's Home Furnishings), Carl Peterson (businessman, farmer, and insurance agent), Adolf Reichert (vice mayor), Ralph Verschoor (owner of Ralph's Garage), and Francis Blixt, Escalon's first mayor.

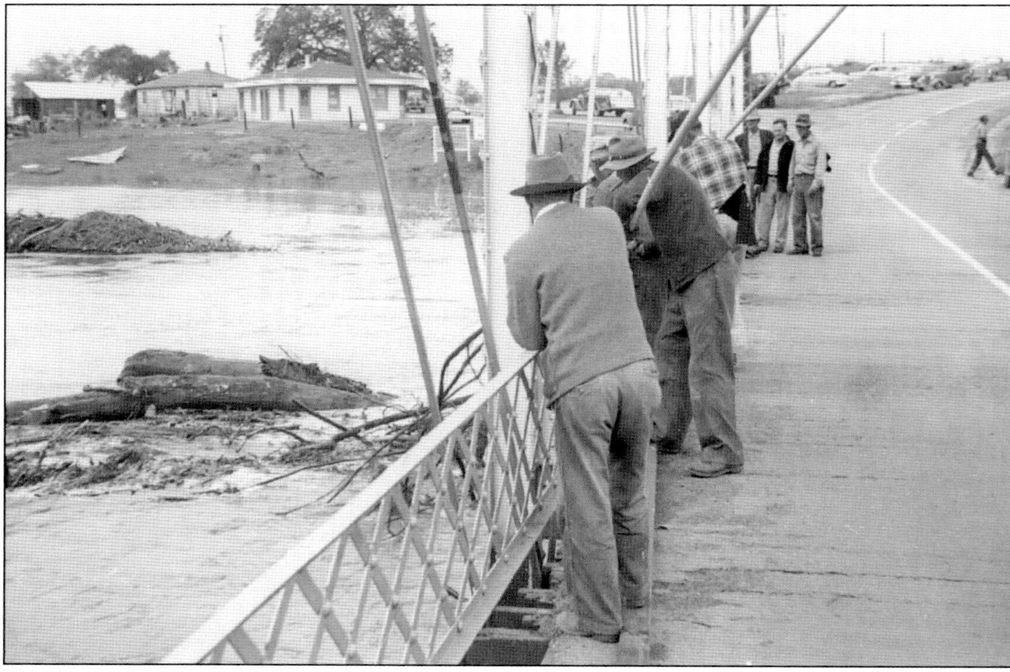

Watching the Stanislaus River rise to near flood stage and the debris get hung up on the underpinnings of the bridge was more interesting than watching paint dry in the winter of 1950–1951. This bridge met its demise in the flood of 1956. The original of this photograph was donated to the Escalon Historical Museum by Case van Zwalenburg.

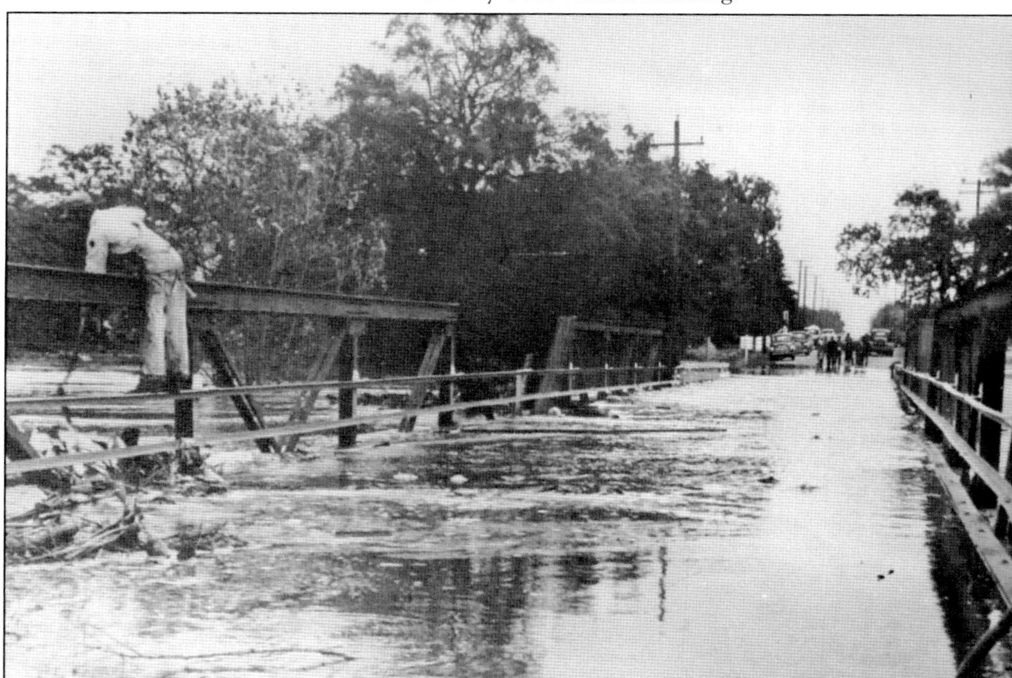

During the flood of 1950–1951, the Stanislaus River rose to a threatening height, but this bridge south of Escalon remained intact.

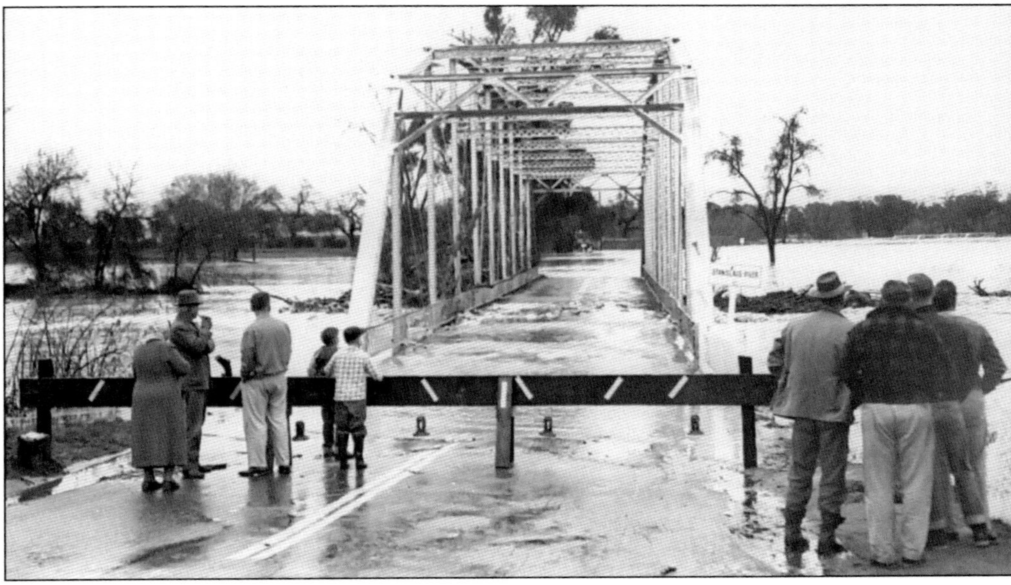

In the flood of 1956, the bridge beyond the metal supports was washed away. The bridge had spanned the Stanislaus River south of Escalon. A new bridge was built where the ground was higher and less susceptible to flooding.

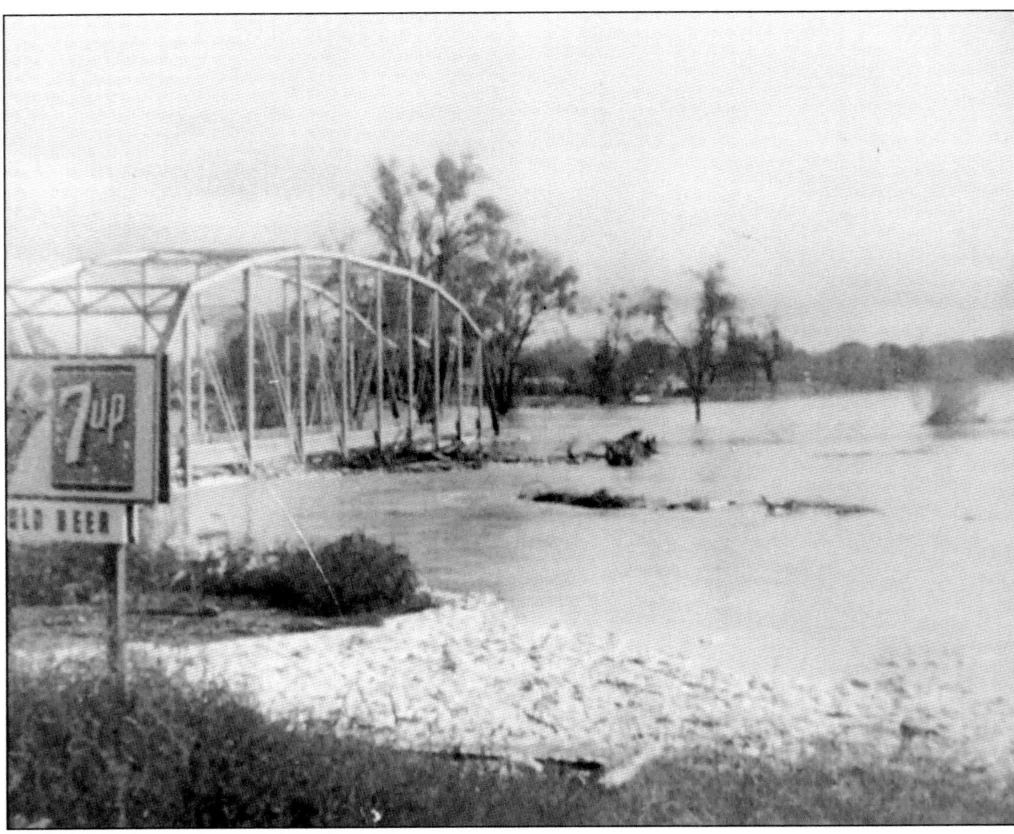

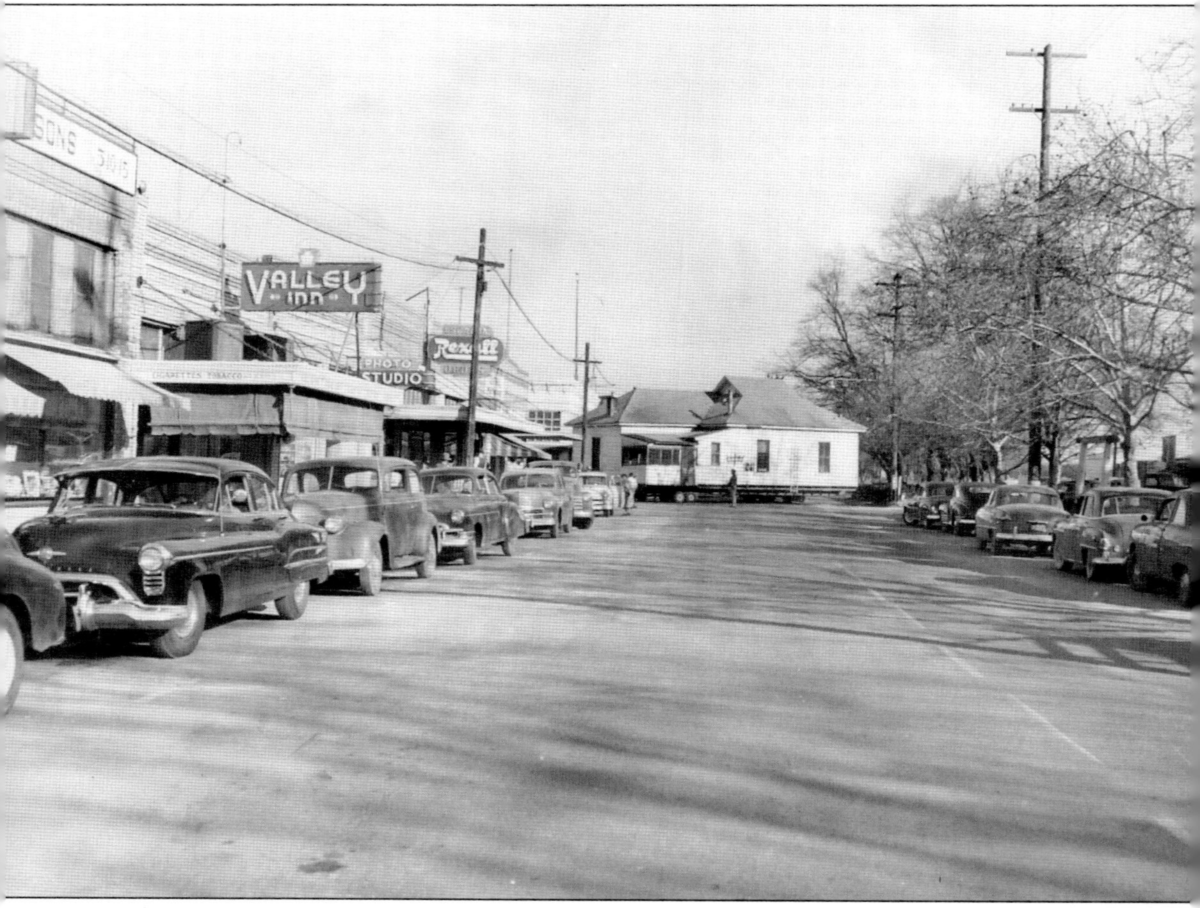


In the 1950s, the term "moving day" apparently had a different connotation than it does today. Here a house is being transported down Main Street to its new location.

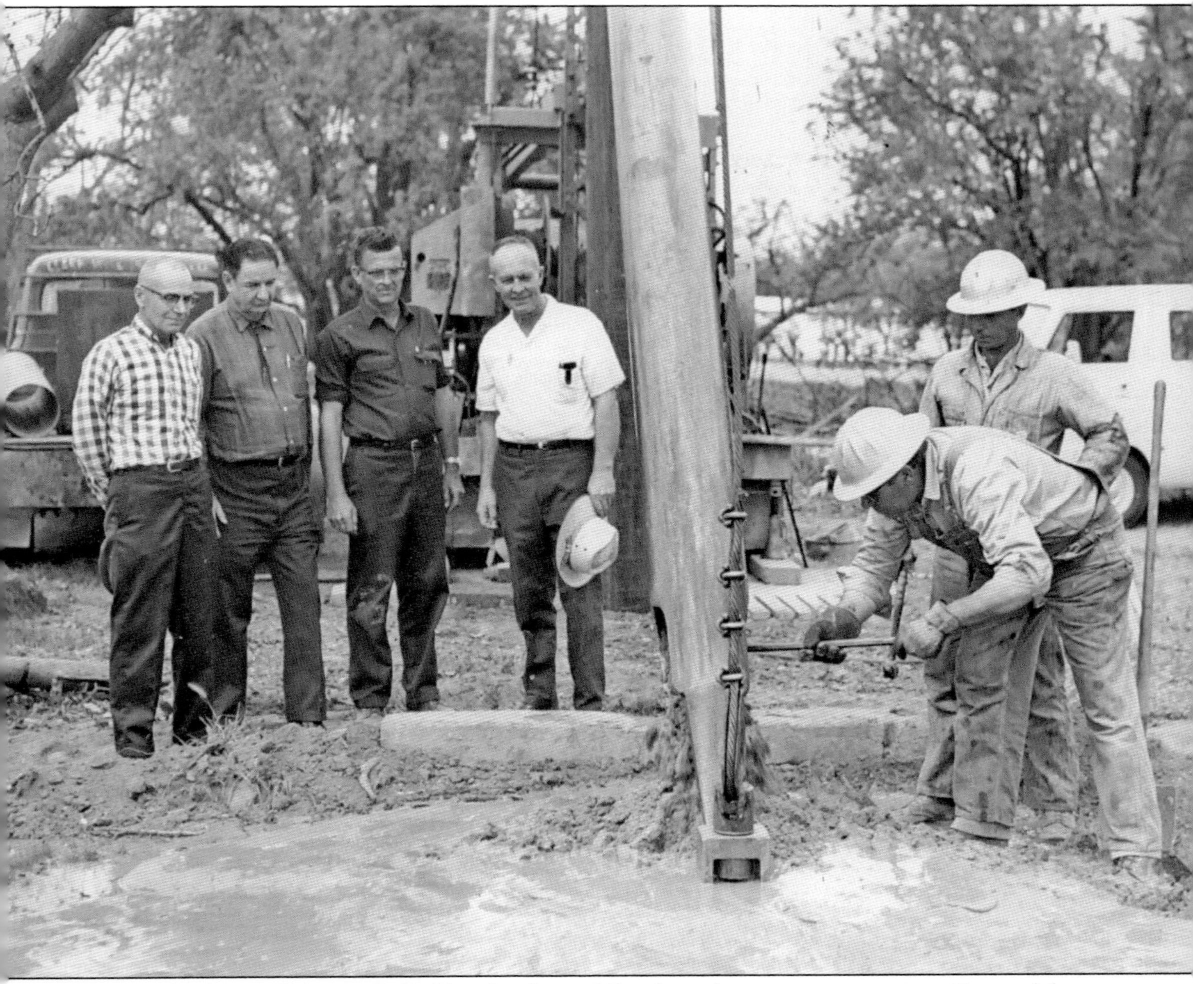

This is the first well being drilled by the City of Escalon after its incorporation. Pictured from left to right in 1958 are Case Rietveld (city employee), John McCloud (first city clerk and first city administrator), Vern Paddack (prominent almond farmer), and Tom Hagan (veterinarian and future city council member and mayor). John McCloud began in city administration in 1957 with a $500 loan from a local bank.

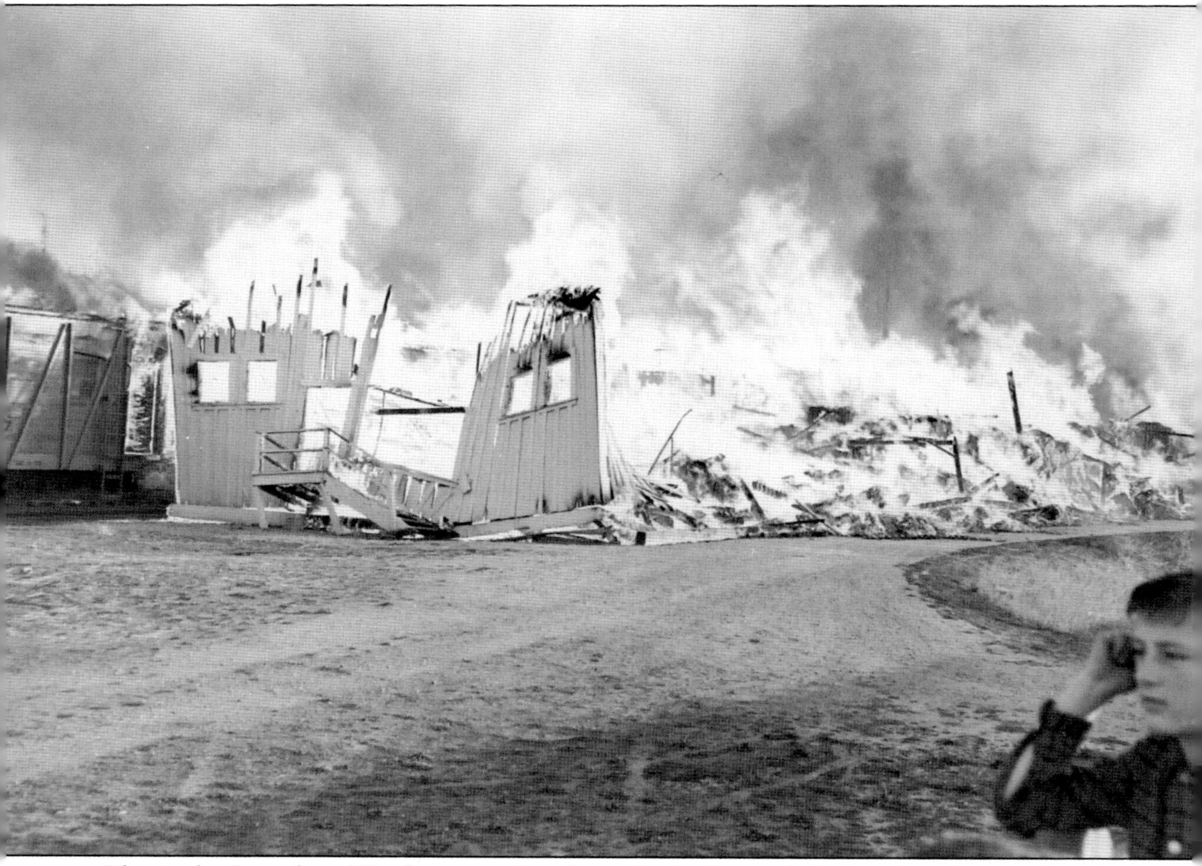

This is the Rosenberg Warehouse on fire alongside the Santa Fe Railroad tracks in 1959. The building was located between what are now the Bank of the West and Boat Country.

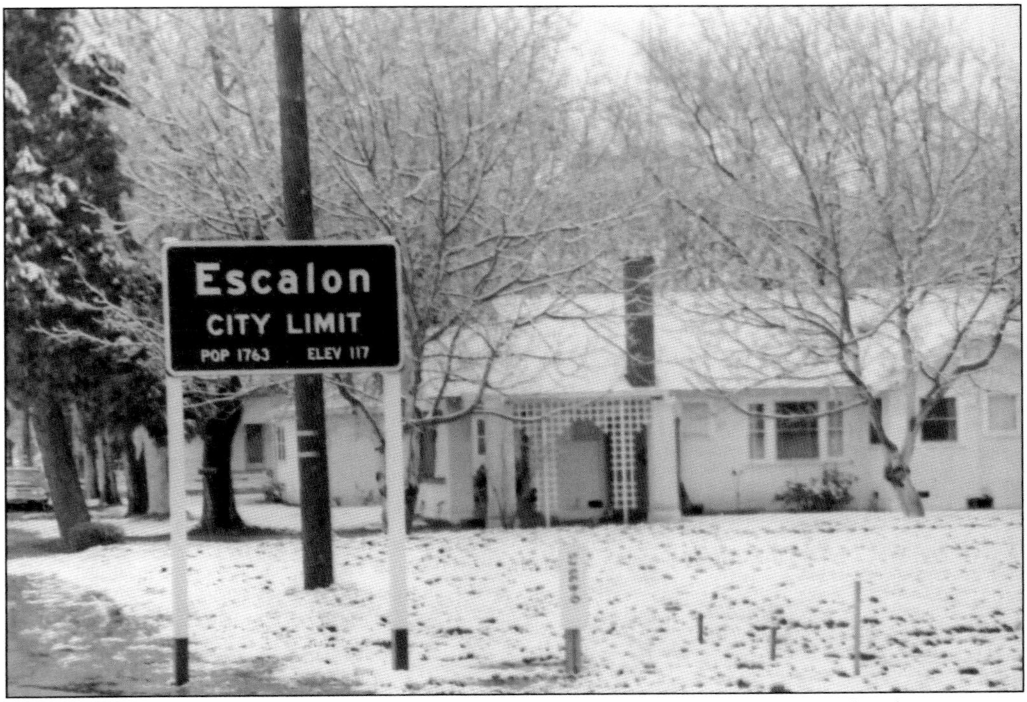


Snow fell in Escalon when the population was 1,763. Snow was recorded in Escalon from a storm in 1918, on the ground in 1932, as flurries in 1950 (when this photograph was believed to have been taken), and again on the ground in 1962. The home pictured above was built in 1918.

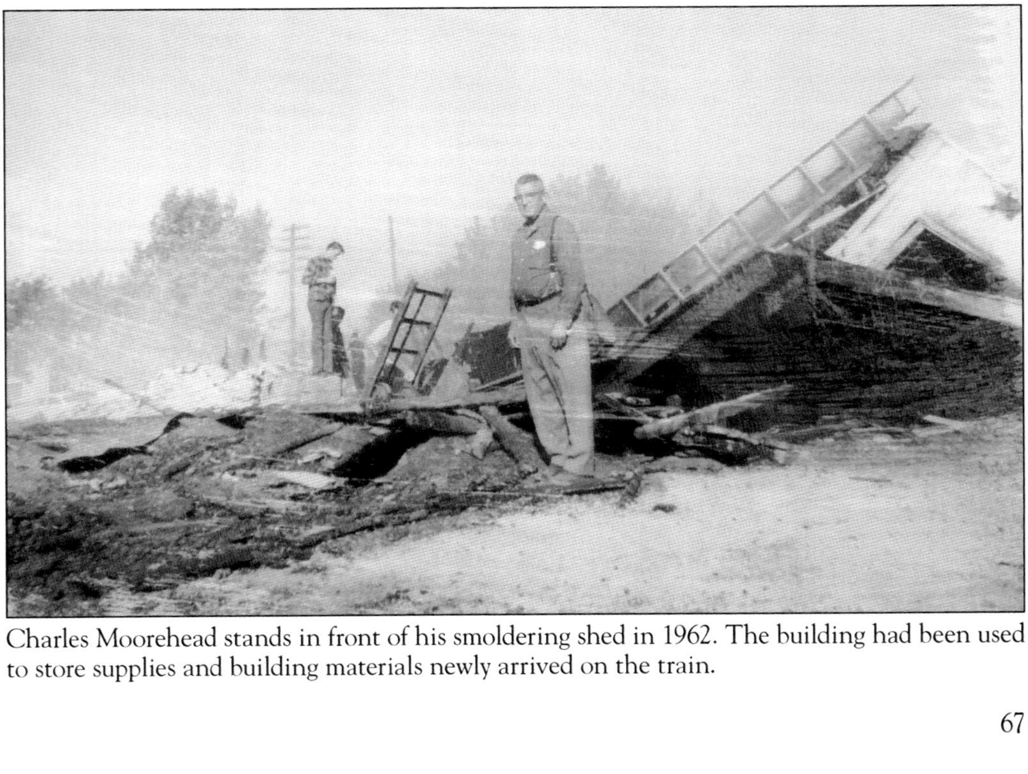

Charles Moorehead stands in front of his smoldering shed in 1962. The building had been used to store supplies and building materials newly arrived on the train.

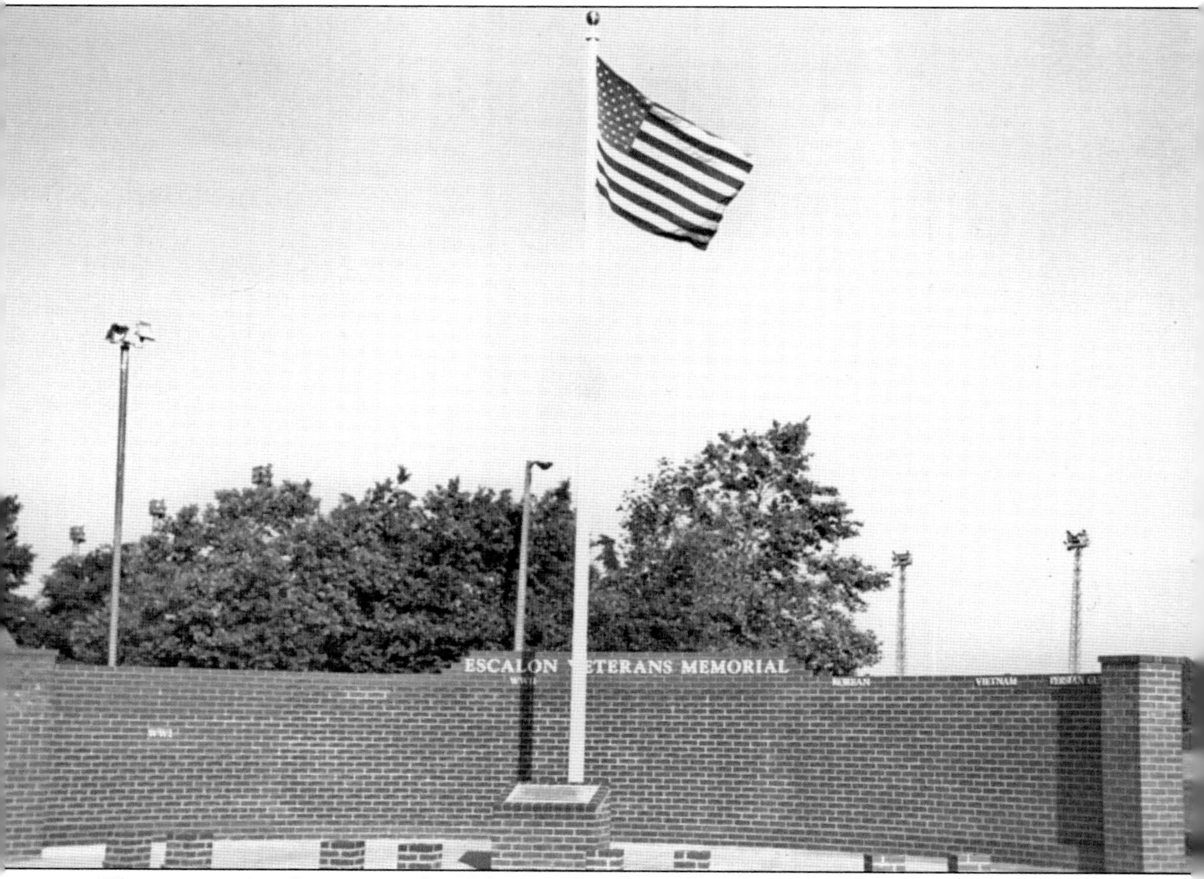


This veterans' wall was erected and dedicated in the mid-1990s in front of the community center. Bricks were available for $25 each. A veteran's name was inscribed on each brick, and they were placed in the wall alphabetically within each war's or era's section. A star on a brick denoted a life given in wartime. This memorial tribute was provided by the Veterans of Foreign Wars and the American Legion.

On January 30, 1989, the Escalon Historical Society was founded. It consisted of a group of citizens concerned with the preservation of Escalon's history, and the society was charged with acquiring and maintaining a historical museum. The city council of the City of Escalon issued this resolution of commendation in appreciation of the society's continuing efforts.

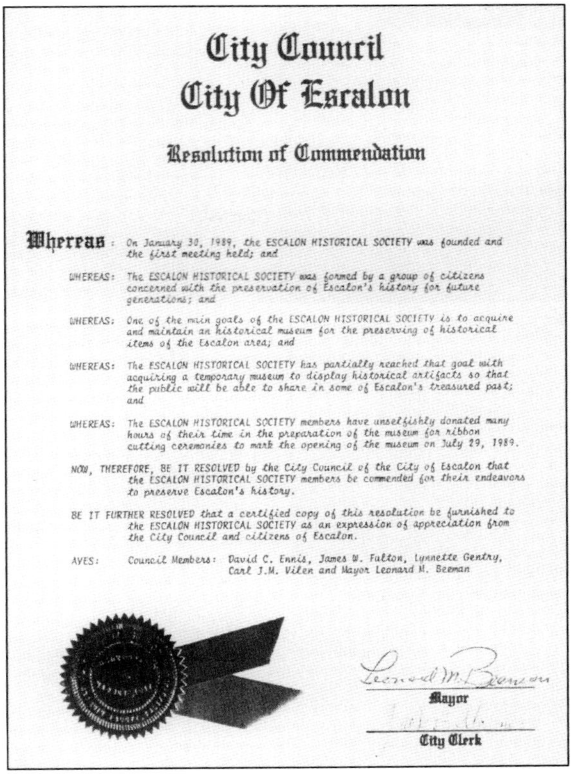

City Council
City Of Escalon

Resolution of Commendation

Whereas: On January 30, 1989, the ESCALON HISTORICAL SOCIETY was founded and the first meeting held; and

WHEREAS: The ESCALON HISTORICAL SOCIETY was formed by a group of citizens concerned with the preservation of Escalon's history for future generations; and

WHEREAS: One of the main goals of the ESCALON HISTORICAL SOCIETY is to acquire and maintain an historical museum for the preserving of historical items of the Escalon area; and

WHEREAS: The ESCALON HISTORICAL SOCIETY has partially reached that goal with acquiring a temporary museum to display historical artifacts so that the public will be able to share in some of Escalon's treasured past; and

WHEREAS: The ESCALON HISTORICAL SOCIETY members have unselfishly donated many hours of their time in the preparation of the museum for ribbon cutting ceremonies to mark the opening of the museum on July 29, 1989.

NOW, THEREFORE, BE IT RESOLVED by the City Council of the City of Escalon that the ESCALON HISTORICAL SOCIETY members be commended for their endeavors to preserve Escalon's history.

BE IT FURTHER RESOLVED that a certified copy of this resolution be furnished to the ESCALON HISTORICAL SOCIETY as an expression of appreciation from the City Council and citizens of Escalon.

AYES: Council Members: David C. Ennis, James W. Fulton, Lynnette Gentry, Carl J.M. Vilen and Mayor Leonard M. Beeman

Mayor

City Clerk

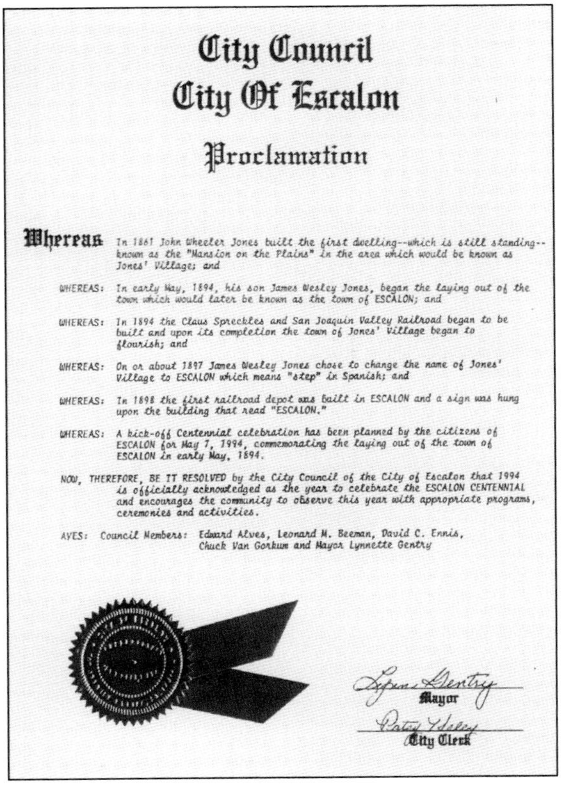

City Council
City Of Escalon

Proclamation

Whereas In 1861 John Wheeler Jones built the first dwelling--which is still standing--known as the "Mansion on the Plains" in the area which would be known as Jones' Village; and

WHEREAS: In early May, 1894, his son James Wesley Jones, began the laying out of the town which would later be known as the town of ESCALON; and

WHEREAS: In 1894 the Claus Spreckles and San Joaquin Valley Railroad began to be built and upon its completion the town of Jones' Village began to flourish; and

WHEREAS: On or about 1897 James Wesley Jones chose to change the name of Jones' Village to ESCALON which means "step" in Spanish; and

WHEREAS: In 1898 the first railroad depot was built in ESCALON and a sign was hung upon the building that read "ESCALON."

WHEREAS: A kick-off Centennial celebration has been planned by the citizens of ESCALON for May 7, 1994, commemorating the laying out of the town of ESCALON in early May, 1894.

NOW, THEREFORE, BE IT RESOLVED by the City Council of the City of Escalon that 1994 is officially acknowledged as the year to celebrate the ESCALON CENTENNIAL and encourages the community to observe this year with appropriate programs, ceremonies and activities.

AYES: Council Members: Edward Alves, Leonard M. Beeman, David C. Ennis, Chuck Van Gorkum and Mayor Lynnette Gentry

Mayor

City Clerk

Since the town of Escalon was laid out by James Wesley Jones beginning in 1894, and since the construction of the railroad began in 1894, the year 1994 was officially acknowledged as the year to celebrate the Escalon centennial. This proclamation by the city council of the City of Escalon officially acknowledged the year of the celebration and encouraged an appropriate observance of the commemoration.

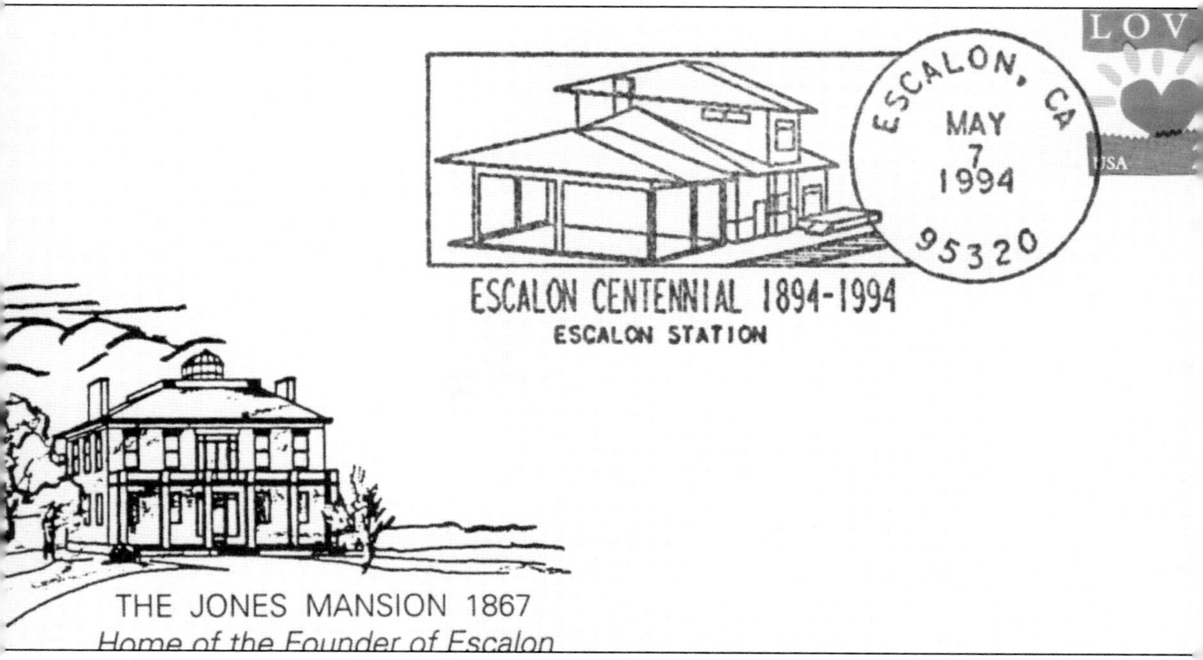


In honor of the city's centennial in 1994, special postal envelopes were printed, stamped, and canceled that depicted the Jones Mansion, home of the founder of Escalon, and bore the stamp of the Escalon Station. A few of these remain for sale in the museum for interested collectors.

# *Seven*

# PEOPLE

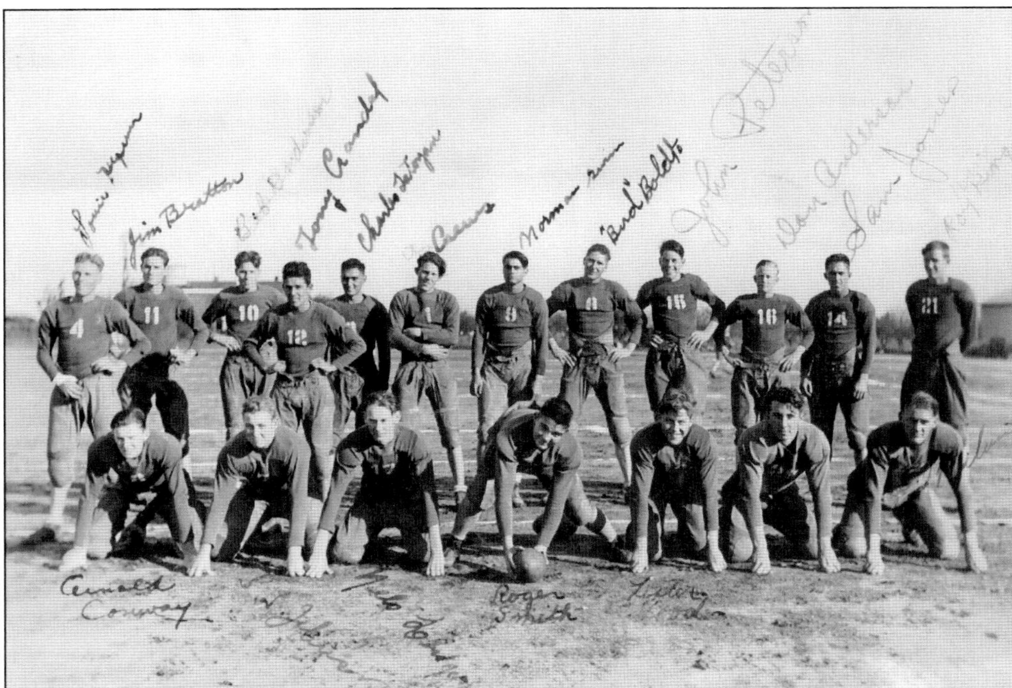

*Leatherheads*, a movie about football in the 1920s, took its title from the leather headgear worn in the early days of the sport. Escalon's own leatherheads of 1935, coached by Harold J. Whitlock, are, from left to right (first row) Arnold Conway, S. T. Johnson, Nels Lindgren, Roger Smith, Lester Good, Warren Moorehead, and Melvin Berg; (second row) Louis Hegwer, Jim Bratton, Bob Anderson, Tony Crandal, Charles Tatoyan, Arden Crews, Norman Gwin, Foster "Bud" Boldt, John Peterson, Don Anderson, Sam Jones, and Roy King. In 1935, the field consisted of dirt, not grass or turf. On a rainy day, the lines indicating the playing field would be worn away by halftime. The spectators on the sidelines would gradually edge onto the field during play, unable to determine where the playing field started or stopped. Turf or grass on the field came into use about 1938.

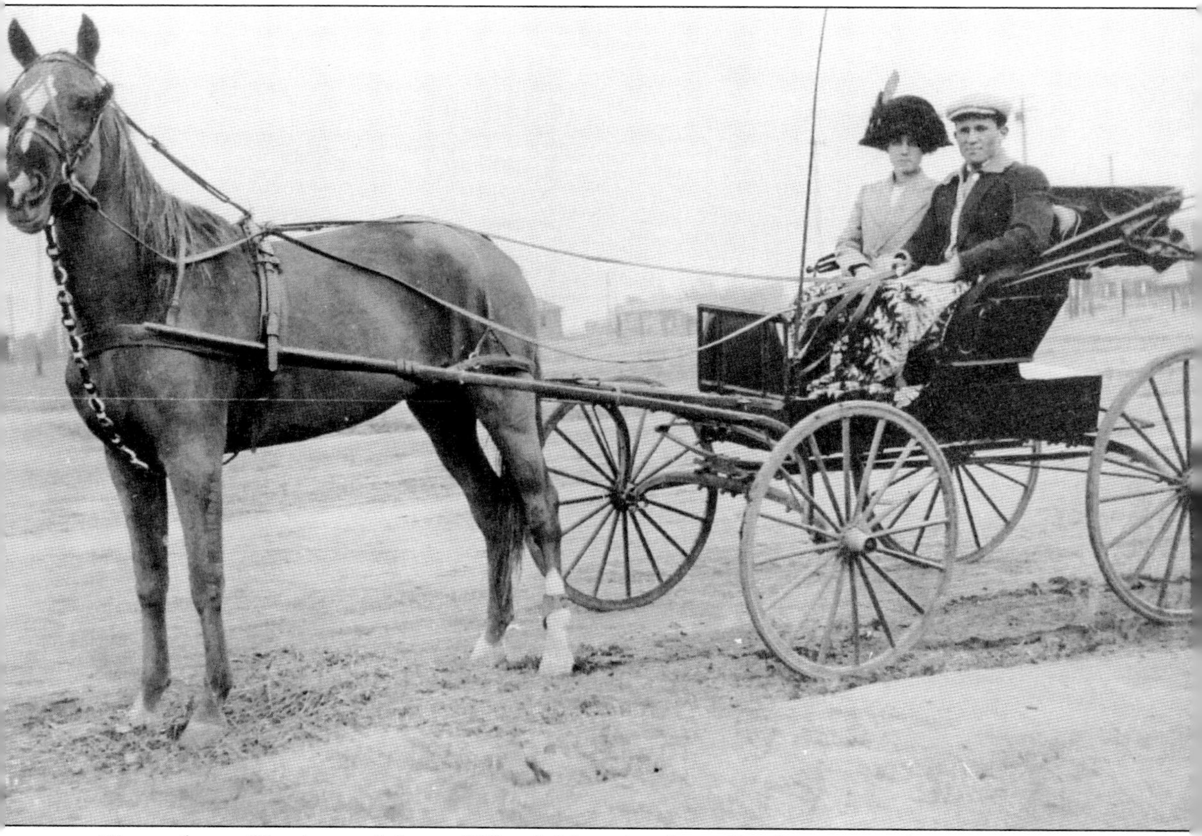

Pictured are Charles and Irma (Ullery) Moorehead in October 1914. This one-horsepower vehicle made it from Modesto to Escalon in 55 minutes and served as Moorehead's mode of transportation to and from work for a period of time. Irma had been a bookkeeper at Irwin Lumber before marrying Charles and before Charles purchased the lumber company. In 1919, Charles was instrumental in starting the San Joaquin County Fair, having aided in 1917 with the Escalon Community Fair. He served on the county fair board for several years. A table from Irma Moorehead's home is on display in the Escalon Historical Museum.

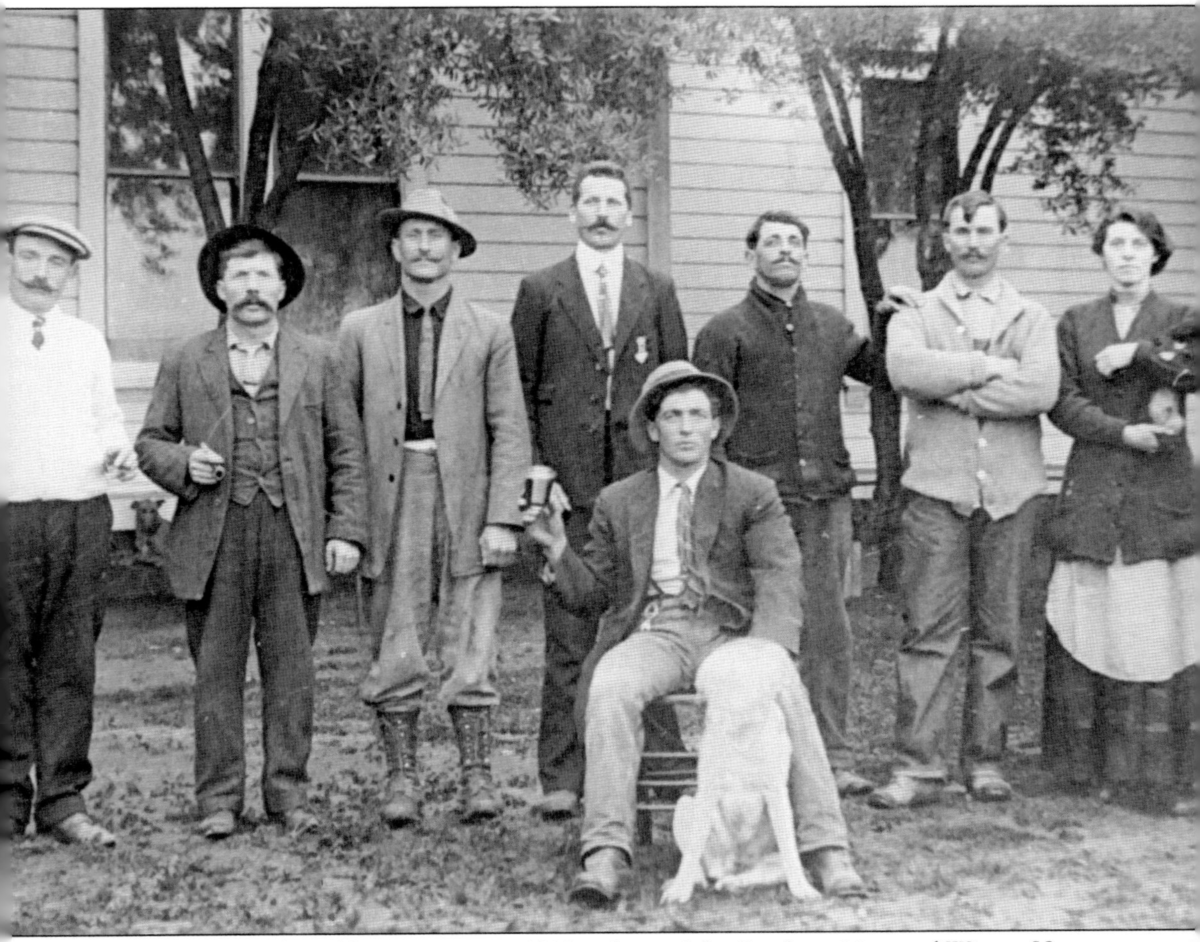

This group of Escalon old-timers poses c. 1915 in front of the Stockton Vineyard Winery House on property that over the years belonged to Petri Winery, Heublein Winery, and Canandaigua, among others. Charles Cadlolo is in front with his dog. Charles worked for the Stockton Vineyard from 1913 to 1917 before working for his uncle Louis Sciaroni at his winery, the first in Escalon. This picture was donated to the Escalon Historical Museum by John Pereira.

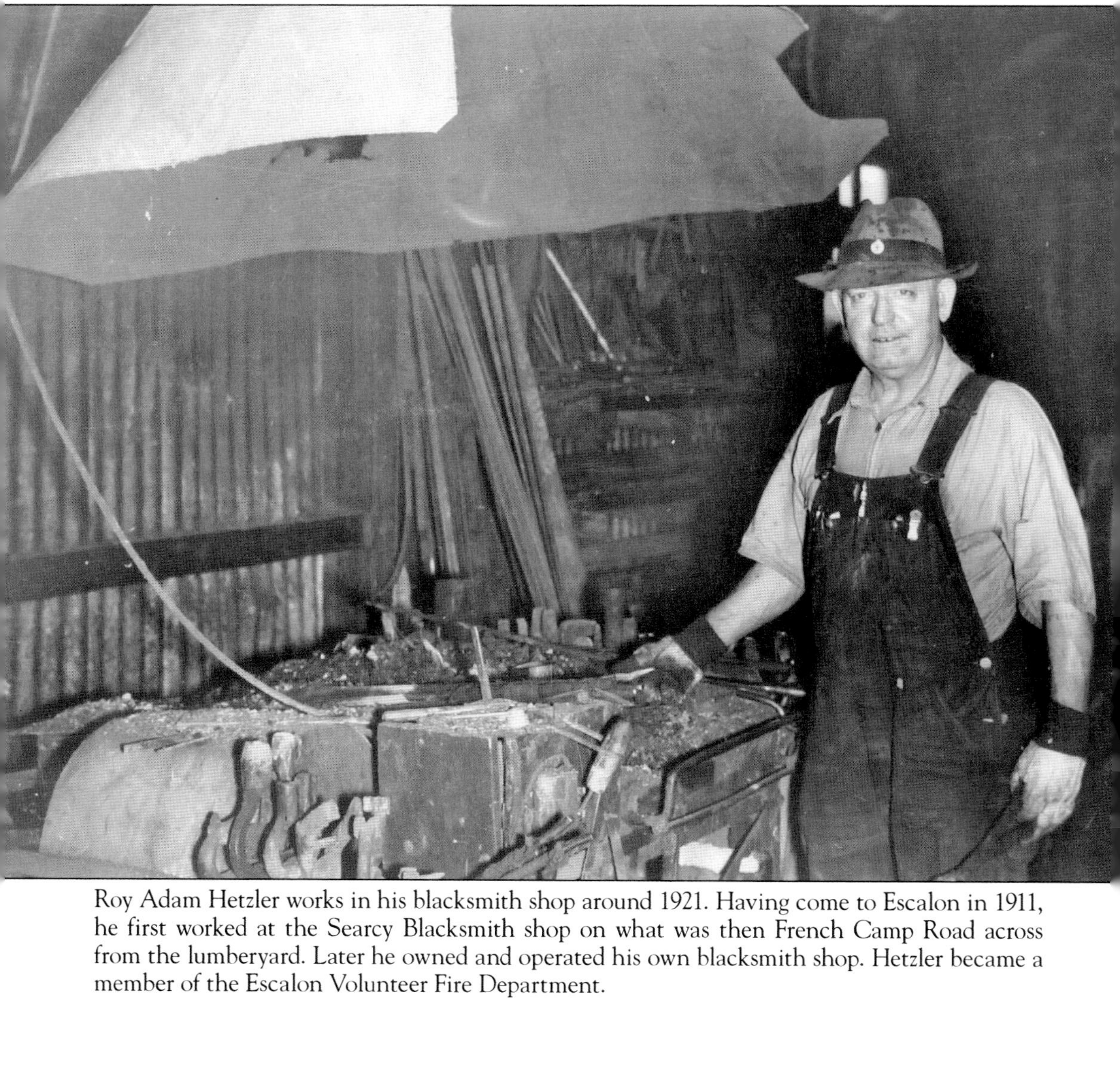

Roy Adam Hetzler works in his blacksmith shop around 1921. Having come to Escalon in 1911, he first worked at the Searcy Blacksmith shop on what was then French Camp Road across from the lumberyard. Later he owned and operated his own blacksmith shop. Hetzler became a member of the Escalon Volunteer Fire Department.

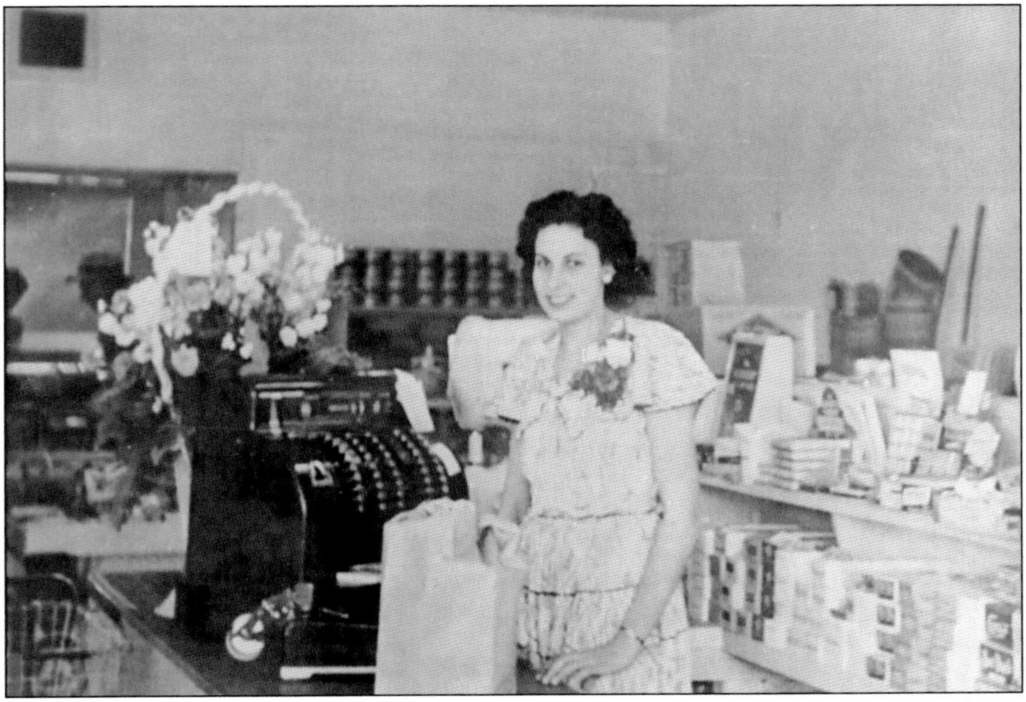

Lena Silveira Doyle is ready at the cash register at the opening of the B&L Market in 1945.

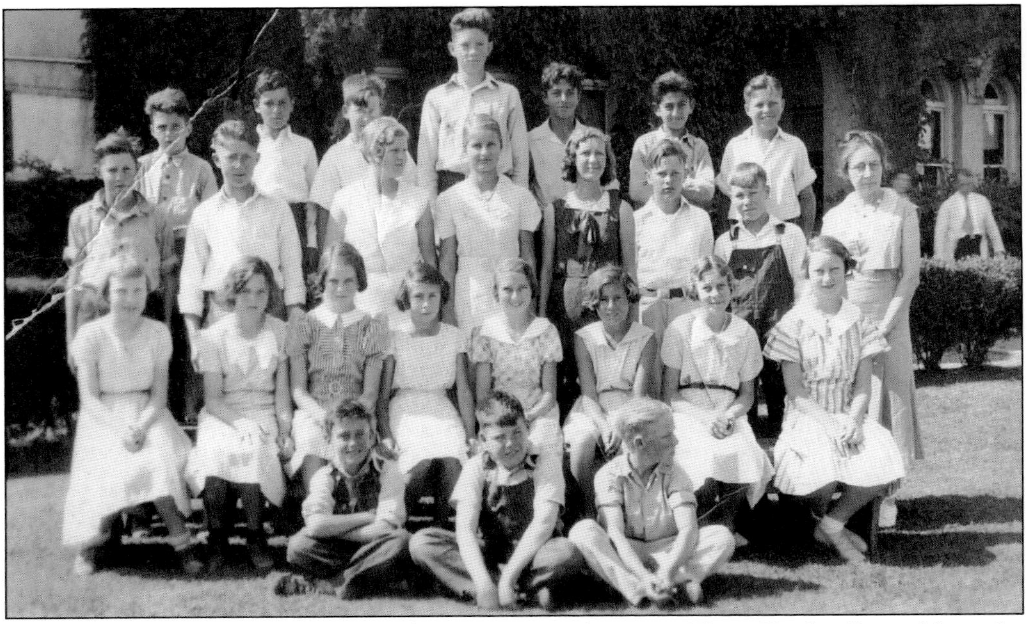

This is the seventh-grade class in April 1934. Front and center is Elmer Hetzler. Second from the left in the third row on the bleachers is Bruce Moorehead. Second from the right in the fourth row is Carl Dugo. All three of these surnames figure in the history of Escalon.

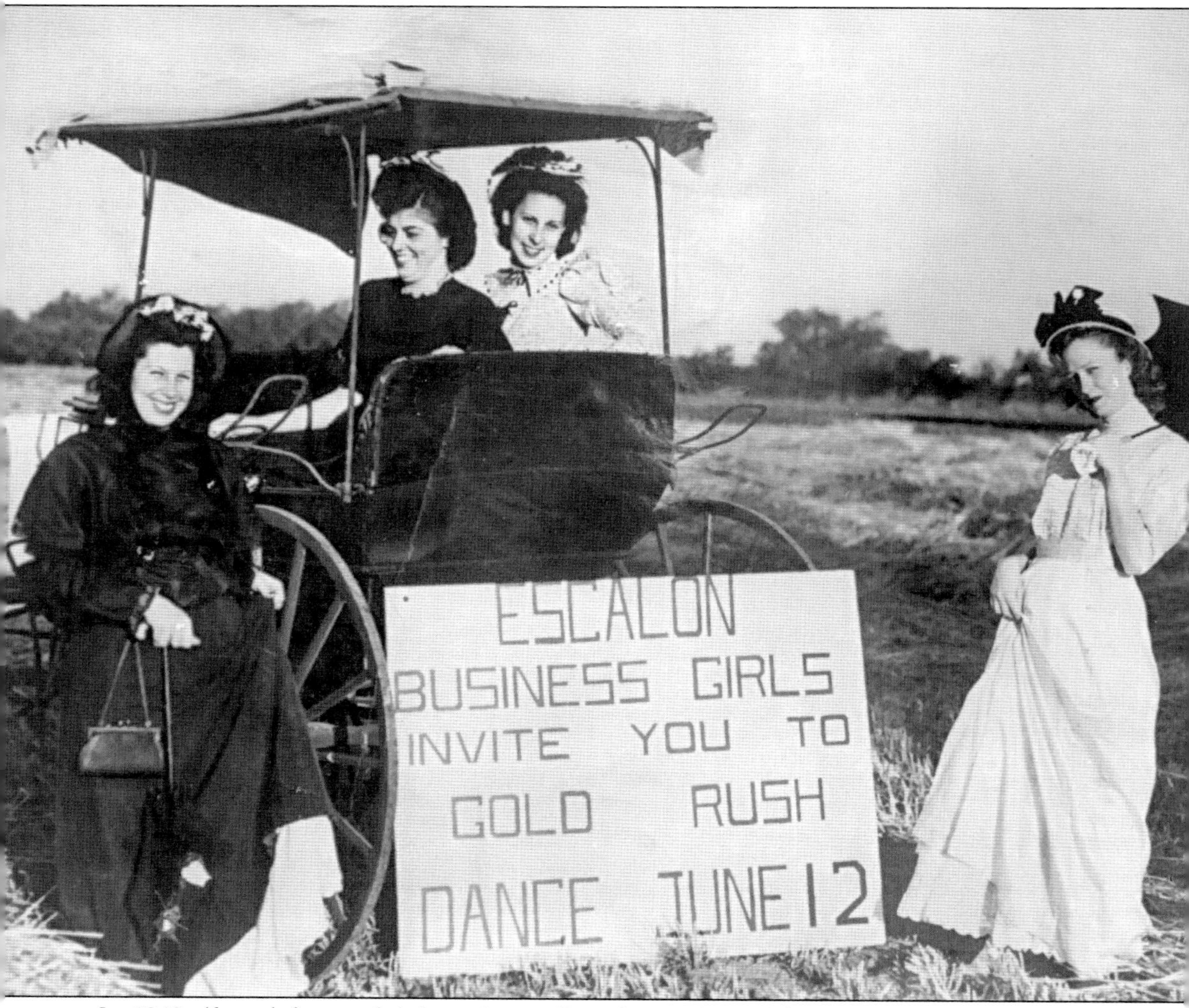


In 1948, (from left to right) Lena Lema, Rose Lopes, Lena Silveira, and Frances Washburn George of the Escalon Business Girls invited one and all to the Gold Rush Dance to be held on June 12. This women's group was formed in Escalon 60 years ago to provide a social outlet for working women. As members of the state group, they held meetings, attended conventions, sponsored dances at the American Legion, and held fund-raisers. This lively group consisted of 15 members and lasted for 30 years, until being disbanded.

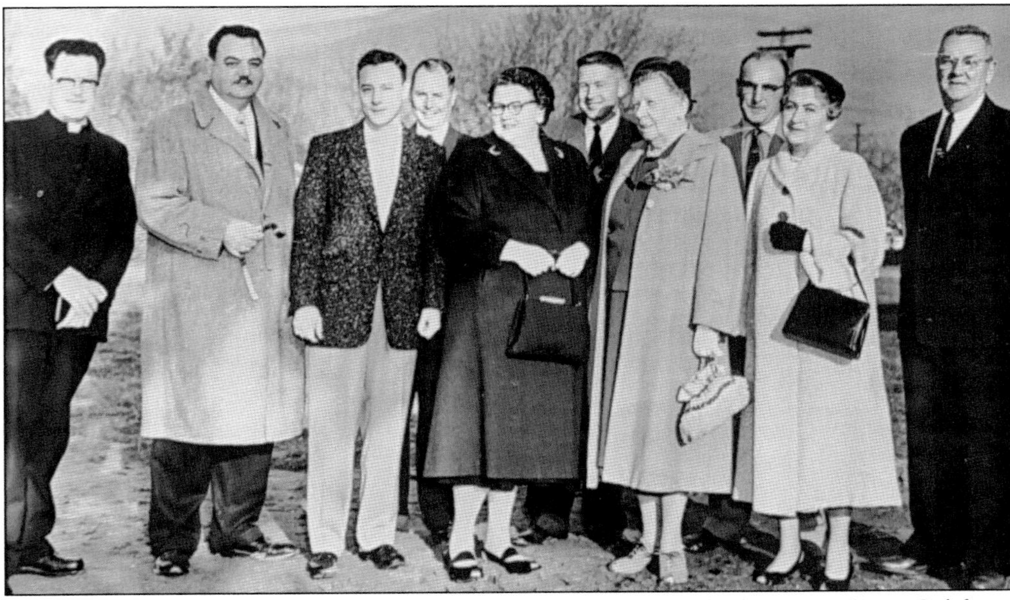

The ground-breaking for the new Pioneer Memorial Hospital took place in 1959 on California Street. From left to right are Fr. Richard Prendeville, Dr. Phillip von Hungen, Dr. Clifford Haskin, Joe Dubacher, Evelyn Bishop, Clark Swanson, Martha Clough, Jim Bonelli, Barbara Malspina, and Cecil Oliver, members of the Escalon Community Hospital Association.

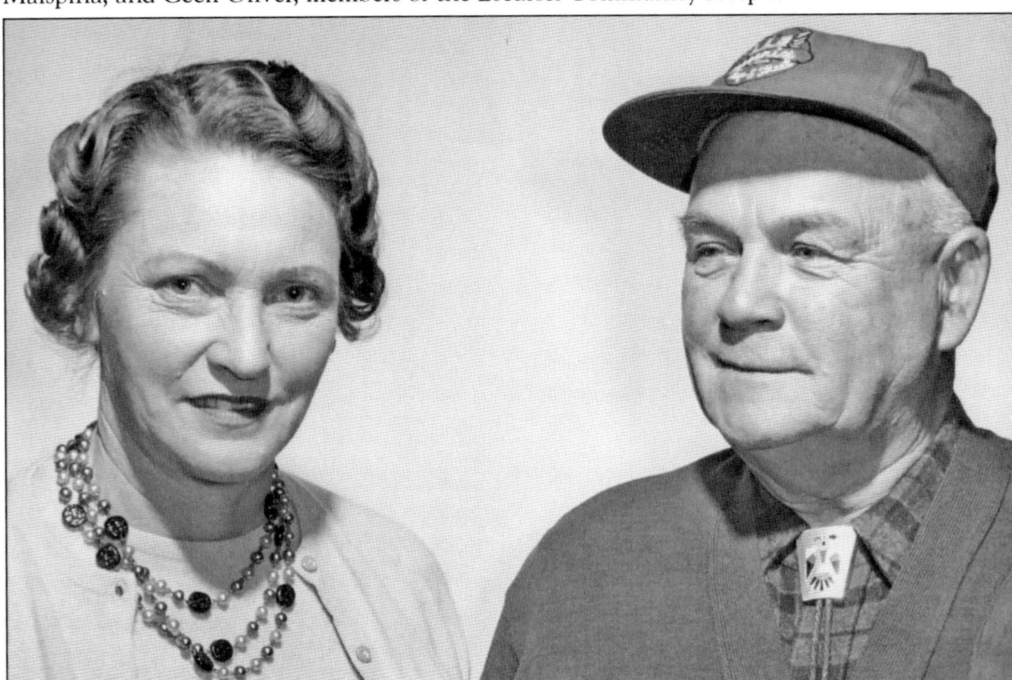

Pictured here are Sam and Effie Latta. Sam farmed peaches, was active in the Escalon Sportsmen's Club, and was an accomplished trap shooter with his 20-gauge shotgun. Effie was a planning commissioner for the City of Escalon and an excellent farmer in her own right after the death of her husband. Latta Children's Park, located at the corner of Oklahoma Avenue and California Street, was named for these involved and committed citizens of Escalon.

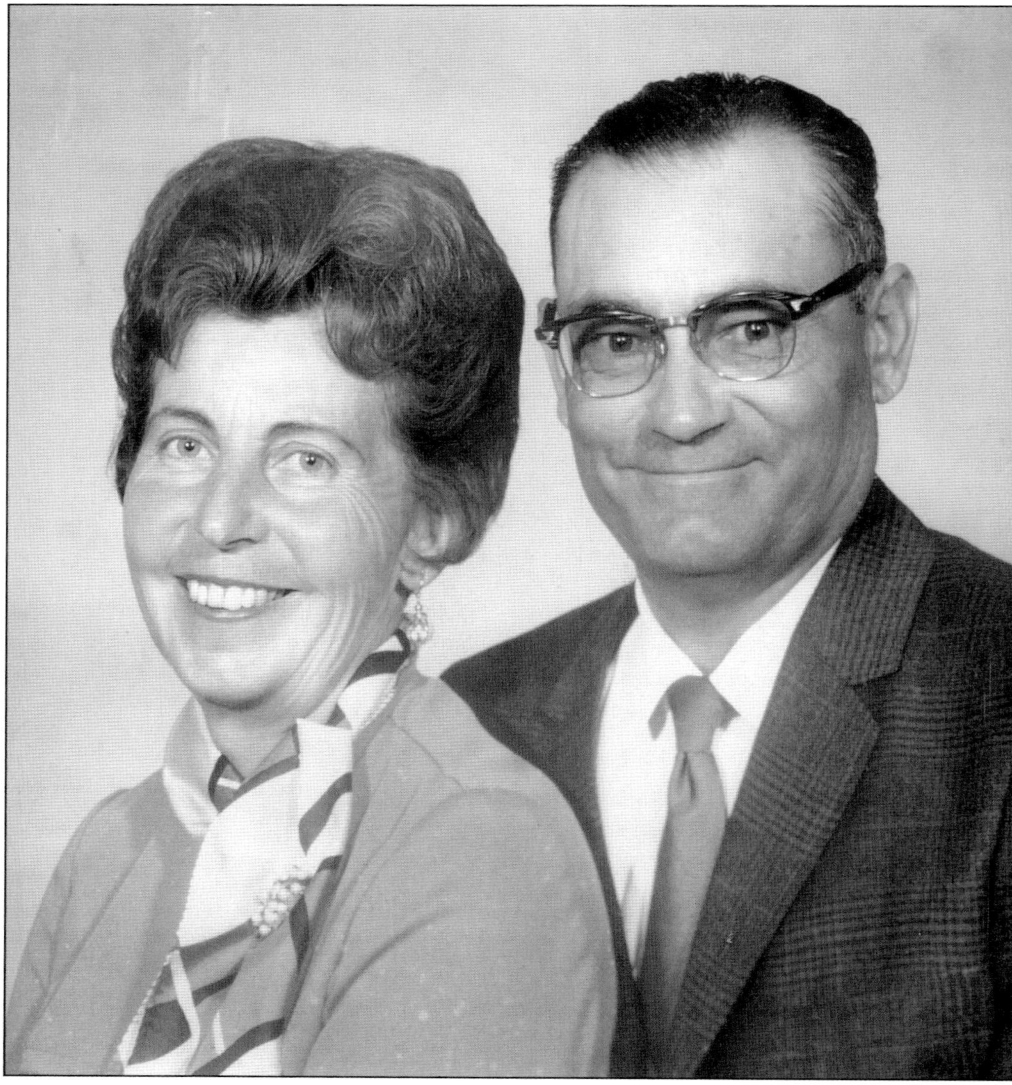

Mary and Charles Sanchez grew grapes, melons, and almonds on their ranch in Escalon. They sold some of their acreage to the Escalon Unified School District in order for El Portal Middle School to be built. On the remaining land, they developed Vintage Estates, the largest subdivision to be built in Escalon. This subdivision contains Sanchez Park and Sanchez Way, named after this couple. Mary, now Mary Loumena, is active with the Escalon Historical Society, the Escalon Historical Museum, and her church.

# *Eight*

# SCHOOLS AND CHURCHES

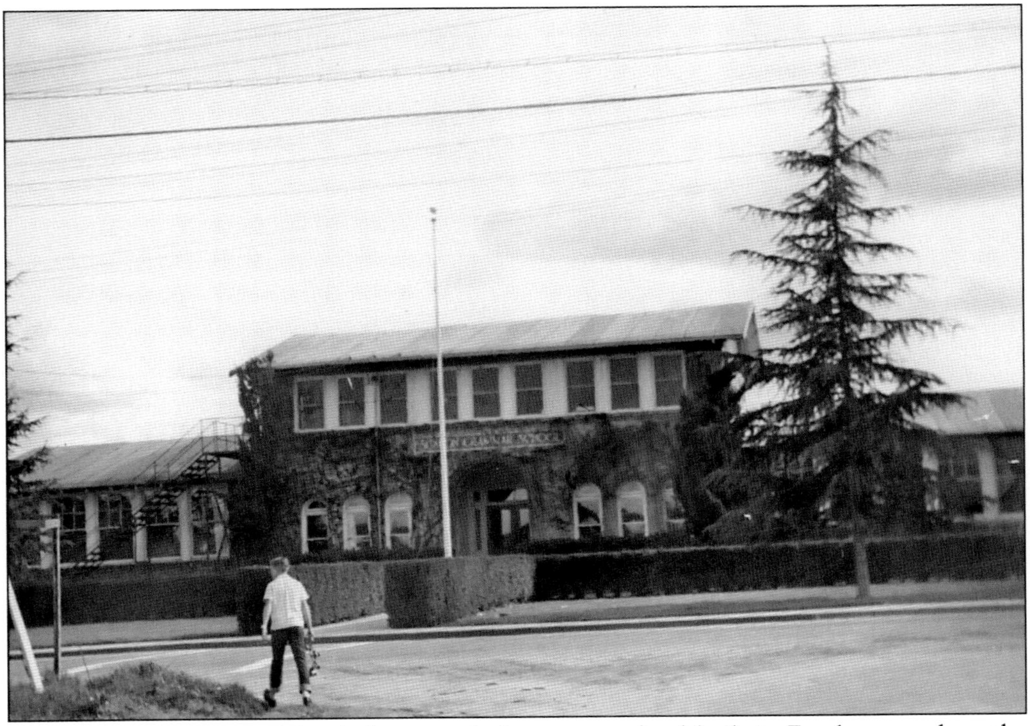

The Escalon Grammar School, the second elementary school built in Escalon, stood on the south side of Jackson Avenue/Highway 120 across from the intersection with Brayton Avenue. A laundromat, Escalon Chiropractic, and Fourth Street now occupy this spot. This grammar school operated until 1948 when a newer, larger elementary school was needed for the growing community. The Escalon Historical Museum has on display two wooden supports (believed to be the only surviving items from this school) that had been used for the flagpole in front of the school.

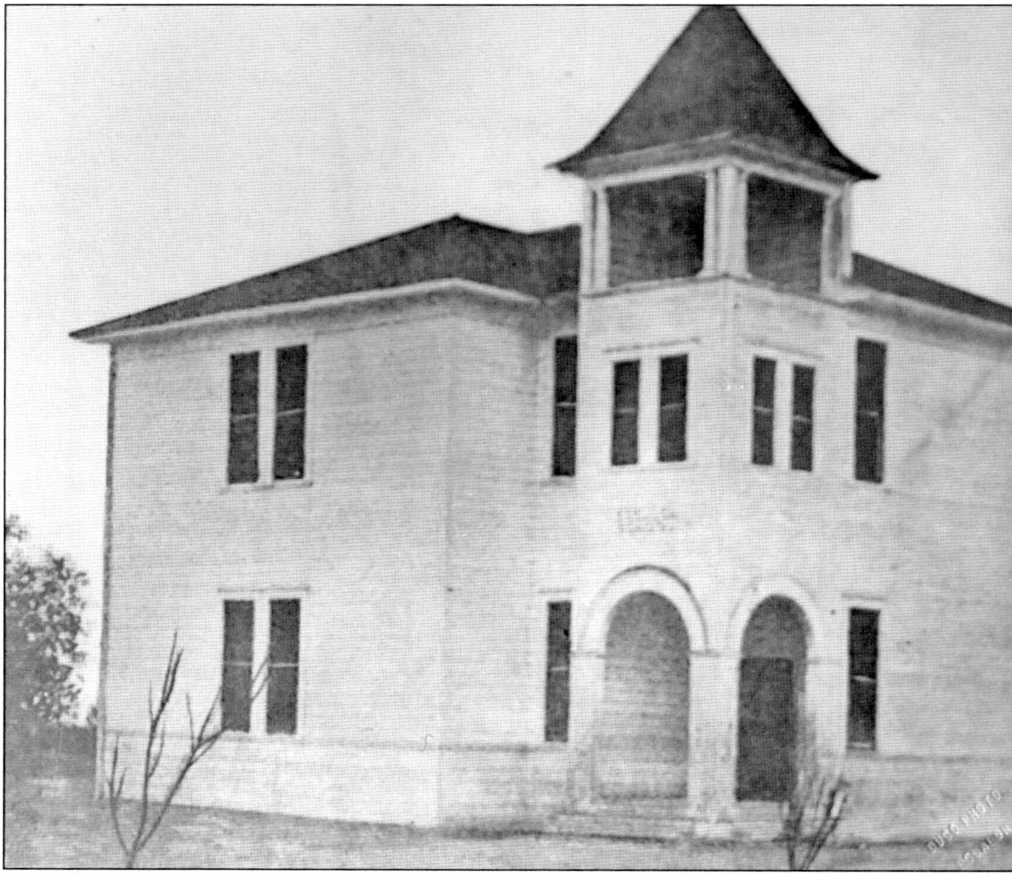

This was the first elementary school in Escalon, built in 1904 on First Street at the corner with what is now Highway 120. Prior to the building of this structure, the Jones children and others were tutored in their homes. The Escalon Presbyterian Church purchased this school building in 1915, used it for a number of years, and now has newer structures occupying this spot.

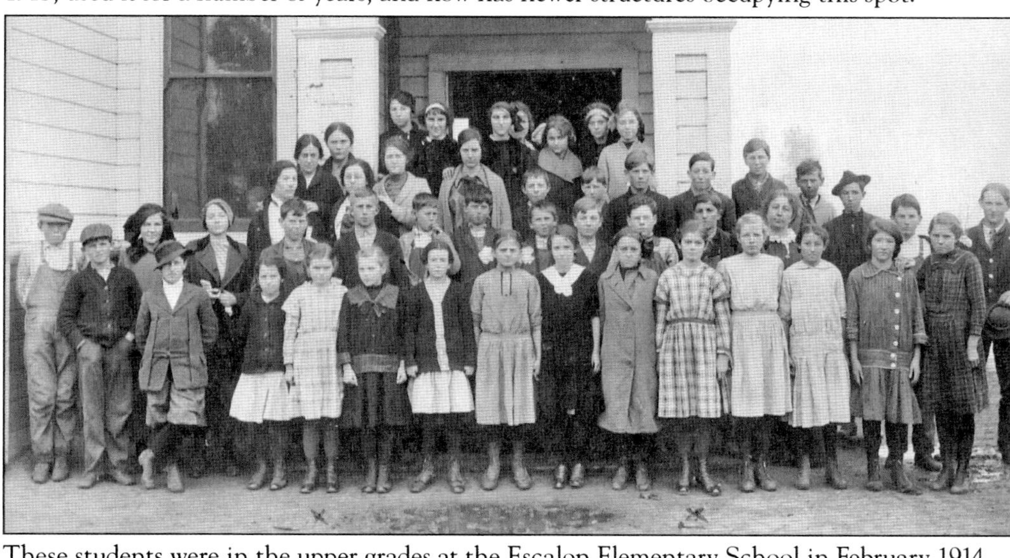

These students were in the upper grades at the Escalon Elementary School in February 1914.

## CLASS OFFICERS

**FIRST PERIOD**

Pres. Marvin Johnson
Vice-P. Patsy Skiles
Secty. Bonnie Thompson
Treas. J. C. Parker

**SECOND PERIOD**

Pres. Joseph Dugo
Vice-Pres. Raymond Mynear
Secty. Patsy Skiles
Treas. Marvin Johnson

**THIRD PERIOD**

Pres. Philamina Bianchet
Vice-P. George Reid
Secty. Bettyann Good
Treas. Joseph Dugo

**FOURTH PERIOD**

Pres. Marvin Johnson
Vice-P. Otto Peterson
Secty. David Derickson
Treas. Myron Johnson

**FIFTH PERIOD**

Pres. Otto Peterson
Vice-P. Patsy Skiles
Secty. Eugene Kizarr
Treas. June Jorgenson

**SIXTH PERIOD**

Pres. George Reid
Vic-P. Raymond Byrd
Secty. Tommy Rampoldi
Treas. Philamina Bianchet

* * * *

## FACULTY

C. Leonard Blomquist, Principal
Veryl Galt, Instrumental Music Instructor
Thomas Olaeta
Bessa Butler
Anna M. White
Ethelia Prater
Muriel Hale
Edith Henson
Lorena Colson
Mary B. Bracy

* * * *

## BOARD of TRUSTEES

James H. Vincent, President
Carl H. Peterson
L. Stanley Blixt, Clerk

# Escalon Elementary School Commencement

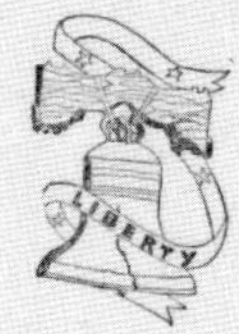


Monday June 3, 1946

Escalon Union High School Auditorium

Eight O'clock P. M.

Escalon California

This program is for the Escalon Elementary School commencement on June 3, 1946. This year, 45 students were graduating. Their class flower was the sweet pea.

## PROGRAM

Orchestra ........ Directed by MISS VERYL GALT
Flowers of Spring — Skernicka
Processional ........ CLASS
Invocation ........ REV. C. W. JOHNSON
Preamble ........ CLASS
Address of Welcome ........ GEORGE REID
Song ........ CLASS
I Pledge Allegiance to My Flag
Bridges -Riegger
Speech ........ DONALD DECOSTA
Piano Solo ........ JUNE JORGENSON
Waltz in A Flat - Brahms
Speech ........ MYRON JOHNSON
Song ........ GIRL'S CHORUS
In The Garden of Tomorrow
Clarence Lucas
Address ........ JOHN R. WILLIAMS
Co. Supt. of Schools
Instrumental Number ........ MEMBERS of GRADUATING CLASS
Gavotte in F - Martini
Citizenship Award ........ MRS. VICTOR GONZALES
Pres. P. T. A. 1945-46
Introduction of Class ........ C. L. BLOMQUIST
Awarding Diplomas ........ JAMES H. VINCENT
Farewell Speech ........ BONNIE JEAN THOMPSON
Class Song ........ CLASS
Benediction ........ REV. ROBERT E. BUZZA
Recessional ........ CLASS

* * * *

ESCALON UNION HIGH SCHOOL AUDITORIUM

Monday, June 3, 1946 Eight O'clock P. M.

## CLASS ROLL

Gladys Baxter
Philamina Bianchet
Betty Lou Bonney
Raymond Byrd
LaMoyne Caudle
Gordon Dahlin
Donald DeCosta
David Derickson
Lloyd Dickerson
Joseph Dugo
Vernon Dutey
Bruce Eliason
Celivo Farinelli
Ronald Fitch
Richard Ford
Jean Foutch
Willora Foutch
Alma Gillespie
Bettyann Good
Marvin Johnson
Myron Johnson
Iona Jones
June Jorgenson
Eugene Kizarr
Louise Light
Ronald Marshall
Donald Merrill
Louise Mynear
Raymond Mynear
Clarence Nelson
J. C. Parker
Otto Peterson
Tommy Rampoldi
James Reeves
George Reid
Wilber Robertson
Wilma Sharp
Patsy Skiles
Bonnie Jean Thompson
Wanda Thompson
Mary Jean Trager
Nina Twedt
Clarence Uthe
Bobby Williams

Sue Daughtery

* * * *

Class Motto: ALL FOR ONE, ONE FOR ALL
Class Colors: BLUE and WHITE
Class Flower: SWEET PEA

"NOT FINISHED, BUT BEGUN"

# Escalon Grammar School

## Commencement 1919

| | |
|---|---|
| Music | Orchestra |
| Invocation | Rev. W. L. Bone |
| Song, "America, the Beautiful" | School |
| Greeting | Mrs. Pearce |
| Vocal Solo | Dr. Snare |
| Music | Orchestra |
| Address | Dr. J. M. Skinner |
| Song | Seventh and Eighth Grades |
| (a) Cycling Song | |
| (b) Lullaby and Good Night | |
| Presentation of Diplomas | Supt. John Anderson |
| Music | Orchestra |

### CLASS

Ewing Bone
Fred E. Talbot
Clarence W. Dahlin
Ida D. Tacker
Gladys I. Shull
Stella M. Berglund
Mabel E. Popp
Marjorie A. Peterson

### TEACHERS

Mrs. Grace T. Pearce
Miss Jessie E. Flagg
Mrs. Mary N. Saunders
Miss Florence Reed

This program is for the Escalon Grammar School commencement in 1919. Eight students graduated this year.

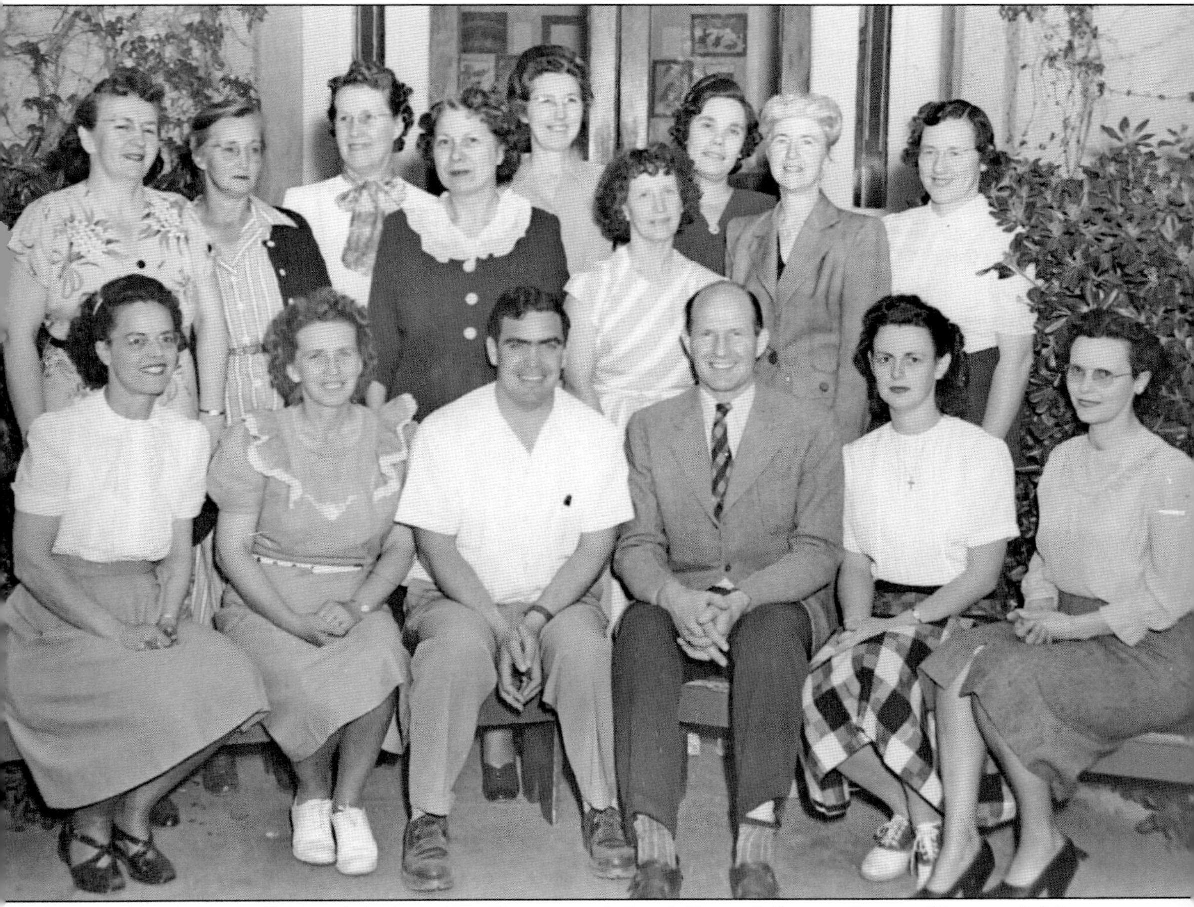

Teachers pose in front of the Escalon Grammar School. From left to right are (first row) Mary Bracy Lee (eighth grade), Esther Applequist Palmer (second and third grades), Thomas Olaeta, principal Leonard Blomquist, Audrey Olaeta (wife of Thomas), and Muriel Hale (fourth grade); (second row) Verna Chrysler, Irene Hatcher, Edith Henson (first grade), Lydia Festerling, Lorena Colson (second grade), Ethel Harriman, Margaret Battee, Ellen Mummey (first grade), and Eleanor Todd (kindergarten).

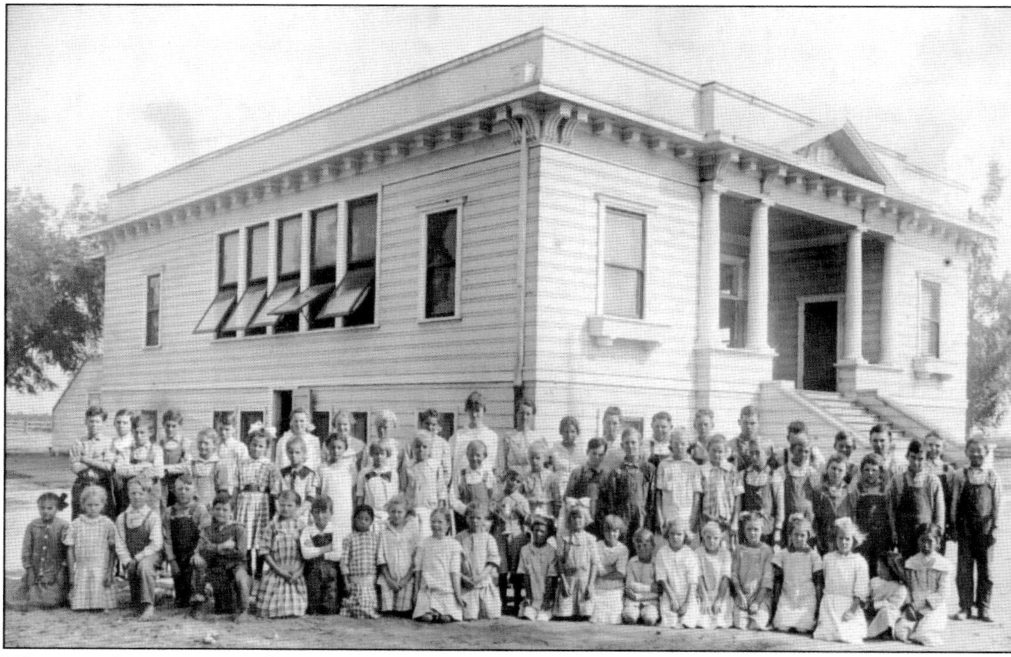

These students are posed in front of Van Allen School House No. 3 in the 1920s. This school building was constructed in 1913 at the northeast corner of Van Allen Road and what was then French Camp Road (now Highway 120). The original Van Allen building and its first successor had been located on the northwest corner of this same intersection on property donated by Patrick Brennan. This school was named after L. C. Van Allen, then the superintendent of schools.

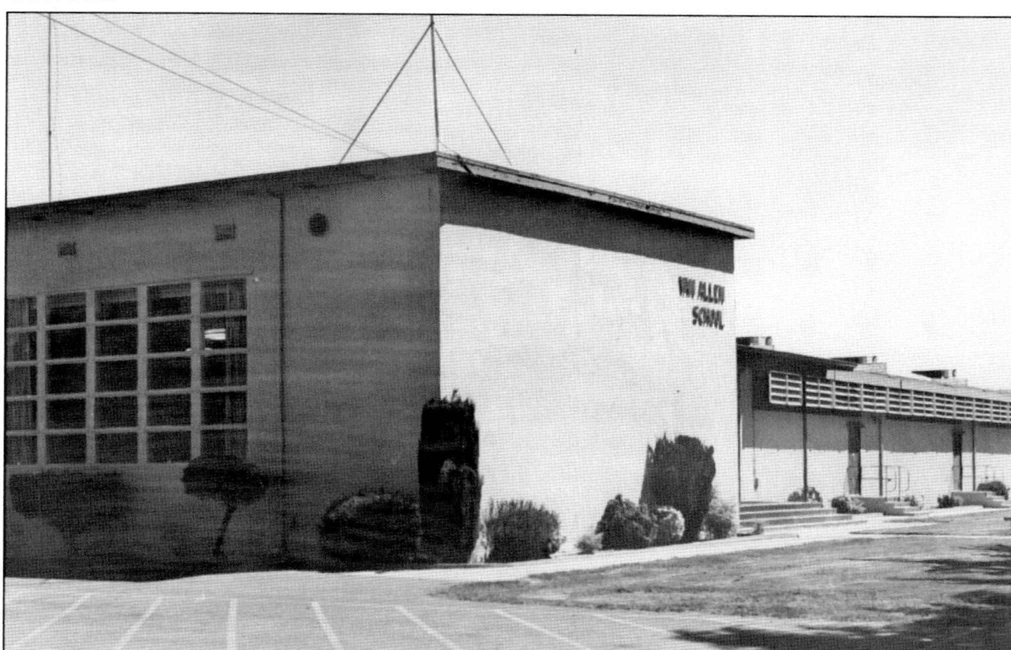


This is the current Van Allen Elementary School, built in 1953. The previous building had been razed earlier in the 1950s. The land for this location was donated by John O'Malley.

TEACHERS

Goldie M. Brennan, Principal

Lucy J. Hunt

Grace Harter

Adele Kenefick

COMMENCEMENT EXERCISES

CLASS OF 1924

# VAN ALLEN GRAMMAR SCHOOL

MAY 15, 1924

This program is from the commencement exercises at Van Allen Grammar School on May 15, 1924. At the time, the school employed a principal and three teachers for 10 students. Richard Blackmore, of the Blackmore Grocery Store, was the valedictorian. The class motto was "Work and Win."

PROGRAM

| | |
|---|---|
| Flag Salute | |
| Choruses | |
| Anvil Chorus | |
| Vacation Time | School |
| Salutatory | John Second |
| Group of Songs | Primary Children |
| Class Prophecy | Fourth Grade |
| Chorus | |
| Amaryllis | Grammar Grades |
| Class History | Class |
| Chorus | |
| Blossom Bells | First Five Grades |
| Class Will | Alpha Blakesley |
| Reading | Mrs. Edna Orr James, General Supervisor of Rural Schools. |
| Chorus | |
| Questions | Grammar Grades |
| Valedictory | Richard Blackmore |
| Chorus | |
| Stars Brightly Shining | Grammar Grades |
| Presentation of Diplomas | H. W. Bessac, County Superintendent. |
| Floral March | |

CLASS ROLL

Thelma Blackmore

Dalena Second

Amy Peterson

Alpha Blakesley

Earl Coggin

Howard Robinson

John Second

Frank Bushka

John Ponte

Richard Blackmore

CLASS COLORS
Rose and Gold

CLASS MOTTO
Work and Win

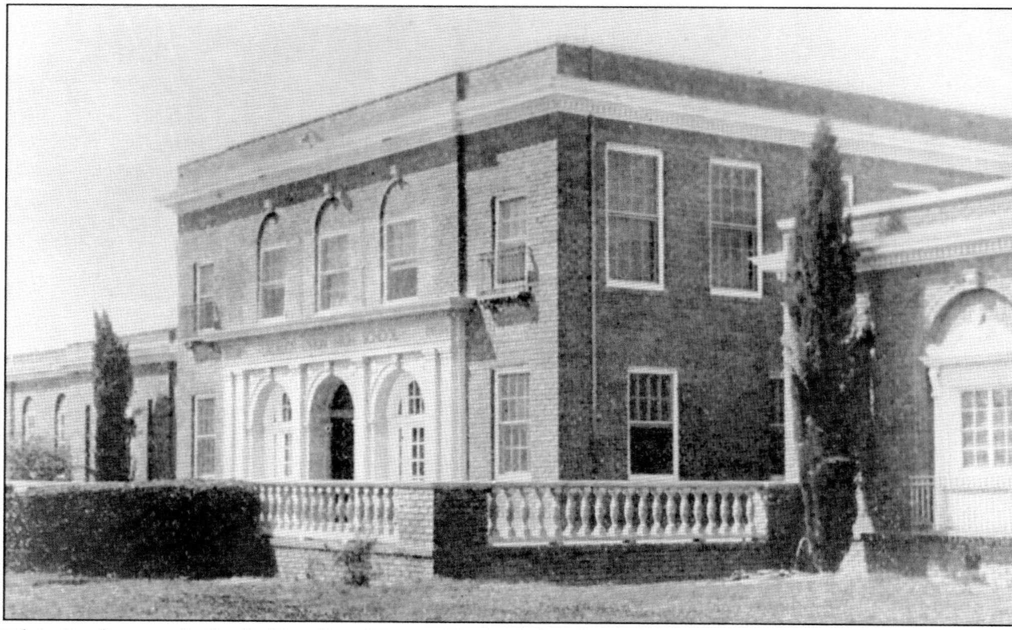

This is the newly built Escalon Union High School. Construction was completed in 1922, and students began attending the new school instead of the Union High School at the brick mansion, as they had since 1919. This building remained in use on the site of the current Escalon High School until 1955, when it was determined that the school did not meet earthquake safety requirements.

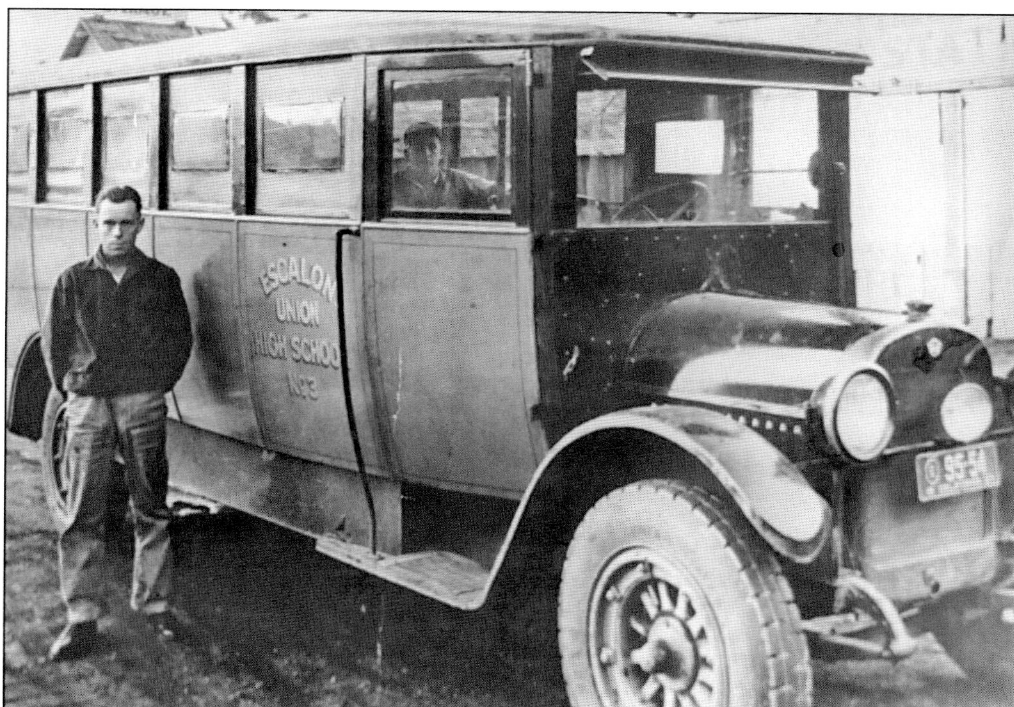


In this 1927 photograph, Ted Pehl stands alongside the Escalon Union High School No. 3 bus. The vehicle is an REO Speed Wagon.

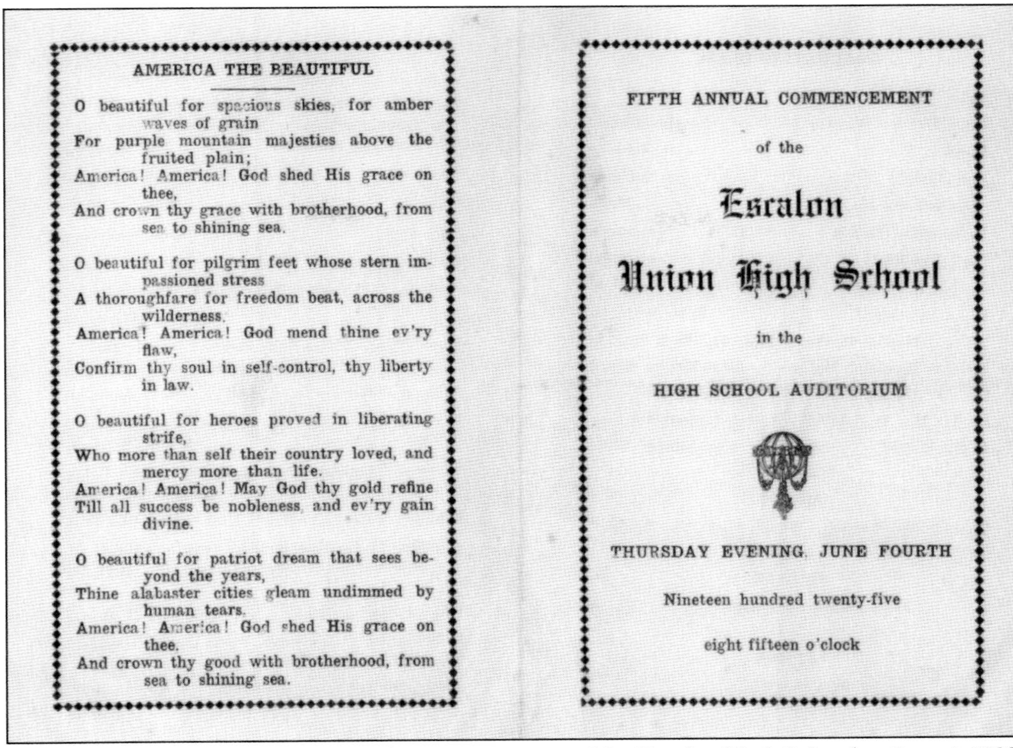

**AMERICA THE BEAUTIFUL**

O beautiful for spacious skies, for amber waves of grain
For purple mountain majesties above the fruited plain;
America! America! God shed His grace on thee,
And crown thy grace with brotherhood, from sea to shining sea.

O beautiful for pilgrim feet whose stern impassioned stress
A thoroughfare for freedom beat, across the wilderness.
America! America! God mend thine ev'ry flaw,
Confirm thy soul in self-control, thy liberty in law.

O beautiful for heroes proved in liberating strife,
Who more than self their country loved, and mercy more than life.
America! America! May God thy gold refine
Till all success be nobleness, and ev'ry gain divine.

O beautiful for patriot dream that sees beyond the years,
Thine alabaster cities gleam undimmed by human tears.
America! America! God shed His grace on thee.
And crown thy good with brotherhood, from sea to shining sea.

FIFTH ANNUAL COMMENCEMENT

of the

**Escalon**

**Union High School**

in the

HIGH SCHOOL AUDITORIUM

THURSDAY EVENING, JUNE FOURTH

Nineteen hundred twenty-five

eight fifteen o'clock

This program is from the fifth annual commencement of the Escalon High School on June 4, 1925. This year, 26 students graduated. Note the start time of "eight fifteen o'clock." School colors then were blue and white.

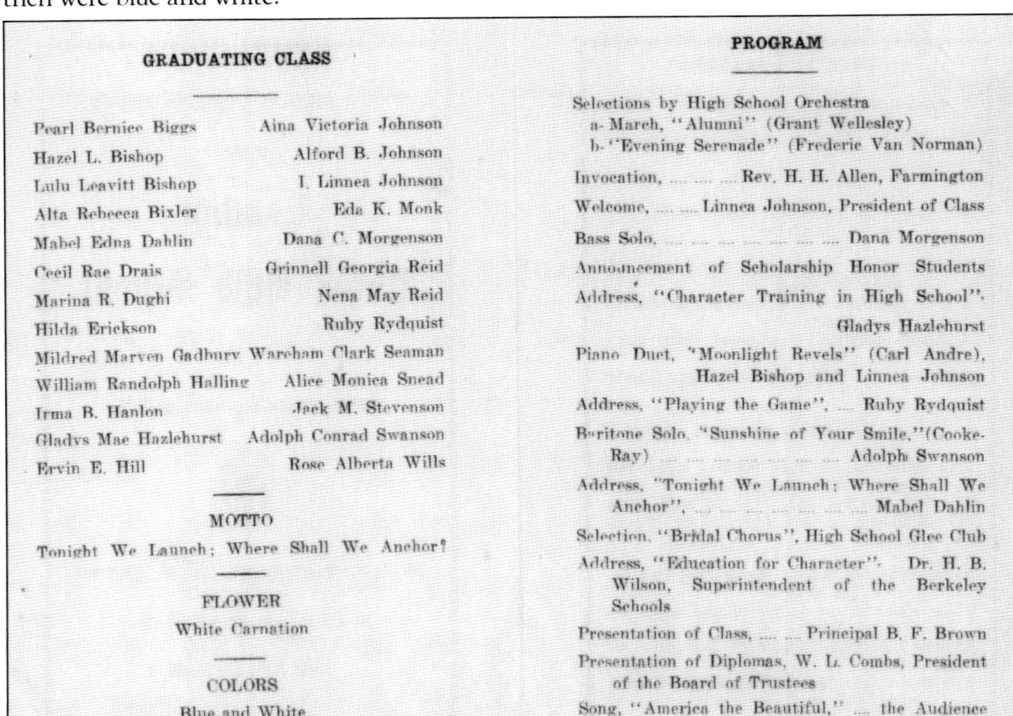

**GRADUATING CLASS**

| | |
|---|---|
| Pearl Bernice Biggs | Aina Victoria Johnson |
| Hazel L. Bishop | Alford B. Johnson |
| Lulu Leavitt Bishop | I. Linnea Johnson |
| Alta Rebecca Bixler | Eda K. Monk |
| Mabel Edna Dahlin | Dana C. Morgenson |
| Cecil Rae Drais | Grinnell Georgia Reid |
| Marina R. Dughi | Nena May Reid |
| Hilda Erickson | Ruby Rydquist |
| Mildred Marven Gadbury | Wareham Clark Seaman |
| William Randolph Halling | Alice Monica Snead |
| Irma B. Hanlon | Jack M. Stevenson |
| Gladys Mae Hazlehurst | Adolph Conrad Swanson |
| Ervin E. Hill | Rose Alberta Wills |

MOTTO

Tonight We Launch; Where Shall We Anchor?

FLOWER

White Carnation

COLORS

Blue and White

**PROGRAM**

Selections by High School Orchestra
- a- March, "Alumni" (Grant Wellesley)
- b- "Evening Serenade" (Frederic Van Norman)

Invocation, ........ Rev. H. H. Allen, Farmington

Welcome, ...... Linnea Johnson, President of Class

Bass Solo, ........................ Dana Morgenson

Announcement of Scholarship Honor Students

Address, "Character Training in High School", Gladys Hazlehurst

Piano Duet, "Moonlight Revels" (Carl Andre), Hazel Bishop and Linnea Johnson

Address, "Playing the Game", .... Ruby Rydquist

Baritone Solo, "Sunshine of Your Smile," (Cooke-Ray) ............ Adolph Swanson

Address, "Tonight We Launch: Where Shall We Anchor", ..................... Mabel Dahlin

Selection, "Bridal Chorus", High School Glee Club

Address, "Education for Character", Dr. H. B. Wilson, Superintendent of the Berkeley Schools

Presentation of Class, ...... Principal B. F. Brown

Presentation of Diplomas, W. L. Combs, President of the Board of Trustees

Song, "America the Beautiful," .... the Audience

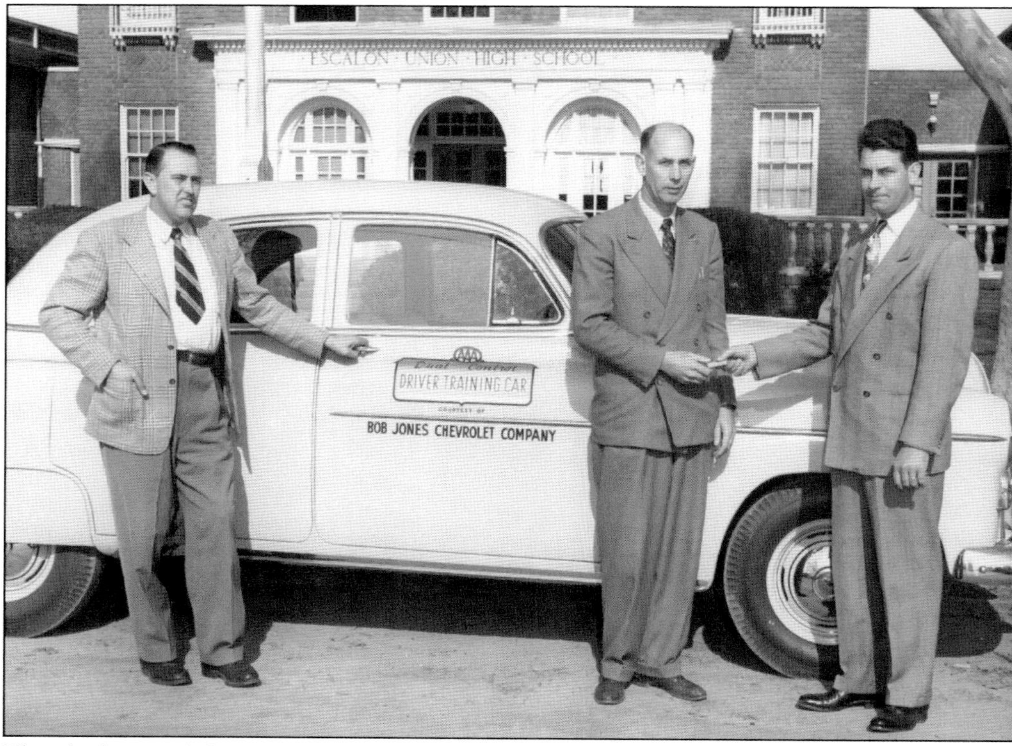


This dual-control driver-training car was donated by local businessman Bob Jones of the Bob Jones Chevrolet Company. From left to right are instructor Perley Skiles, high school principal Harold Whitlock, and Bob Jones.

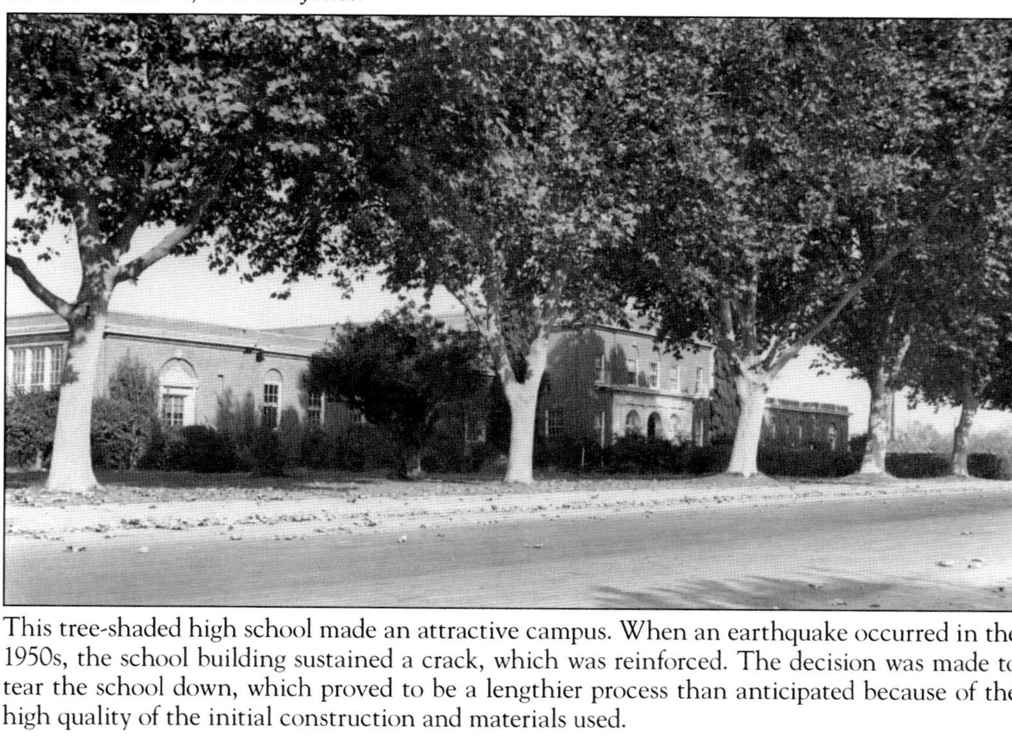

This tree-shaded high school made an attractive campus. When an earthquake occurred in the 1950s, the school building sustained a crack, which was reinforced. The decision was made to tear the school down, which proved to be a lengthier process than anticipated because of the high quality of the initial construction and materials used.

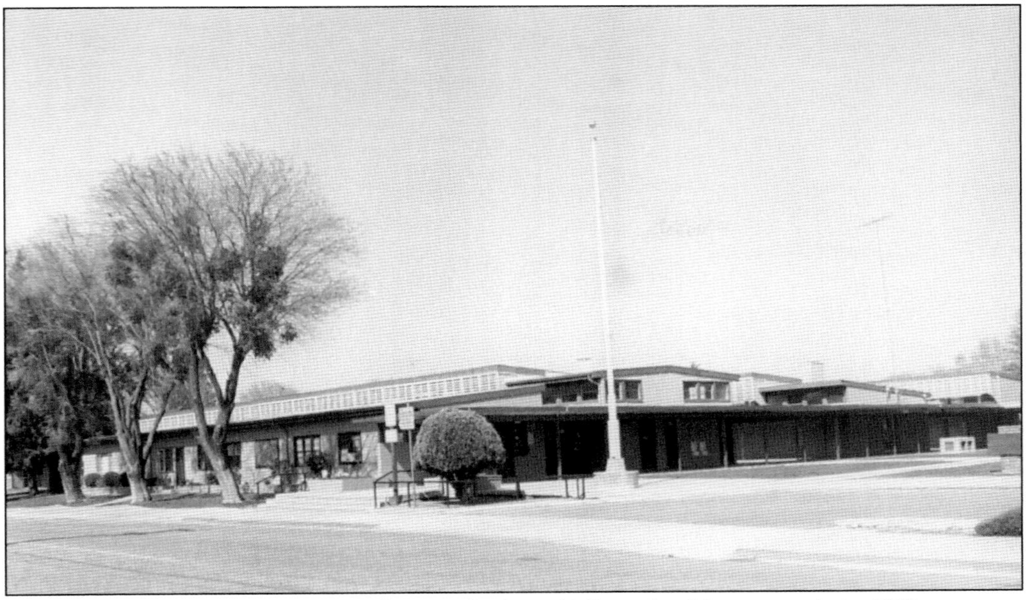

Dent Elementary School, in use today, was built in 1949, with additions made in 1958.

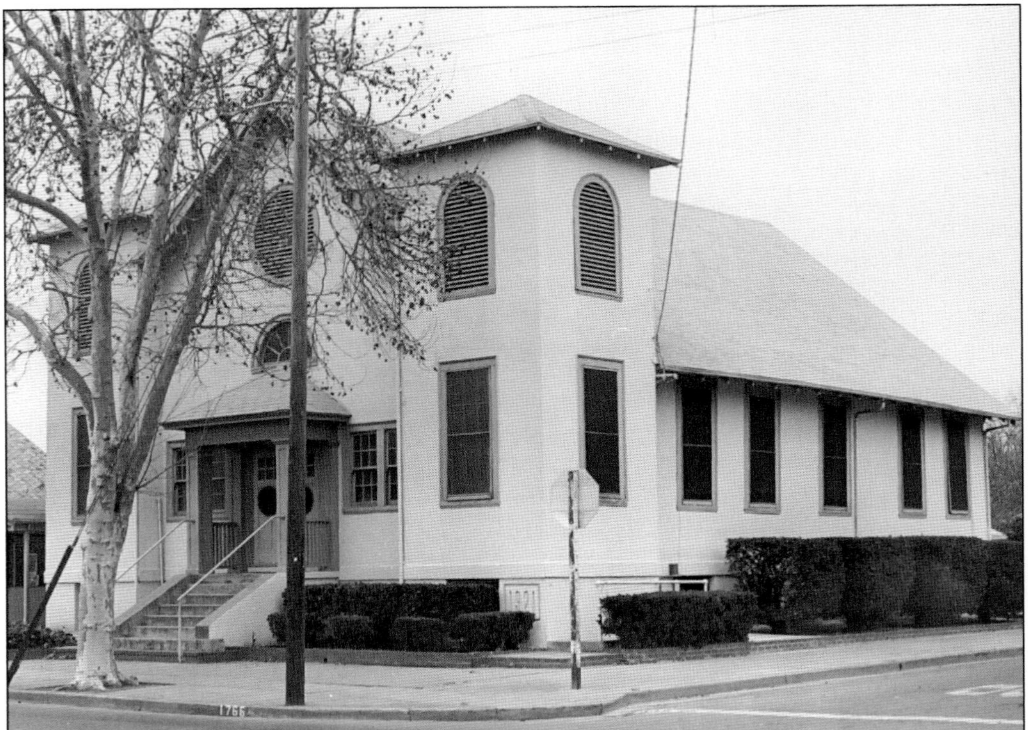

This was the Mission Covenant Church of Escalon, located at the corner of Second Street and Jackson Avenue. The church had begun in 1919 with meetings in people's homes before moving to the Presbyterian and Methodist churches. The first service and the dedication of this building were held in 1921. Initially, services were conducted in Swedish, but gradually, English became the predominant language of its congregation and services. The church now has a new building on Escalon Avenue.

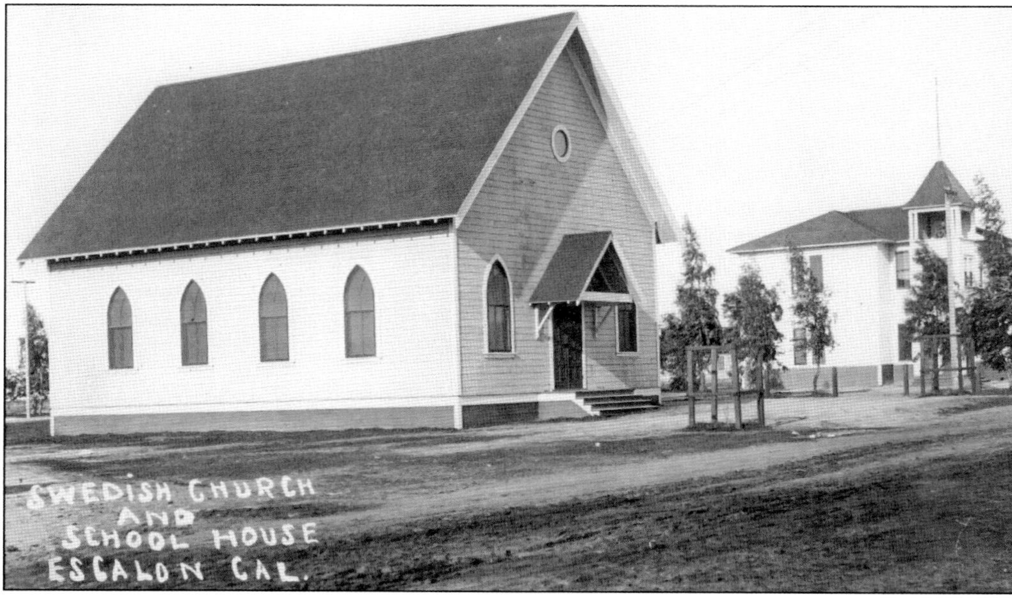


The Swedish Lutheran Church, organized in 1913, was located west of the Escalon Elementary School on First Street. Before the construction of the church building, services were held in the homes of its members and were conducted in Swedish, the language spoken by the majority of the congregation. In the 1930s, services began to be conducted in English. Neither building pictured stands today.

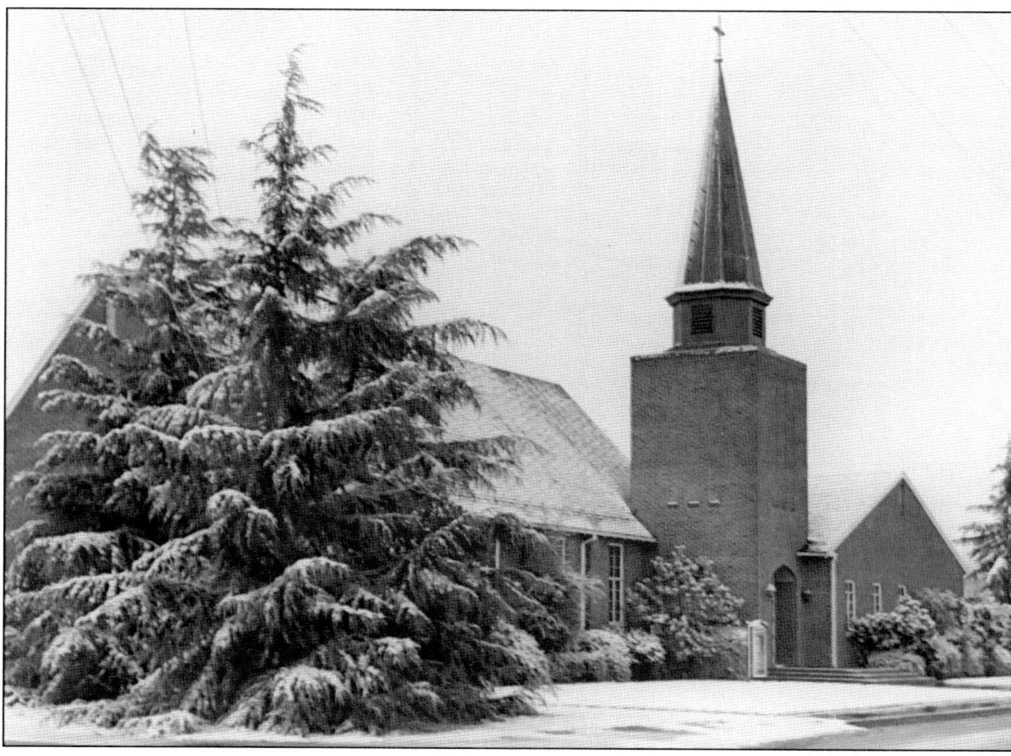

This newer building for the Saron Lutheran Church was built in 1950 and was dedicated on April 8, 1951, in its current location on North Street. It remains in use today.

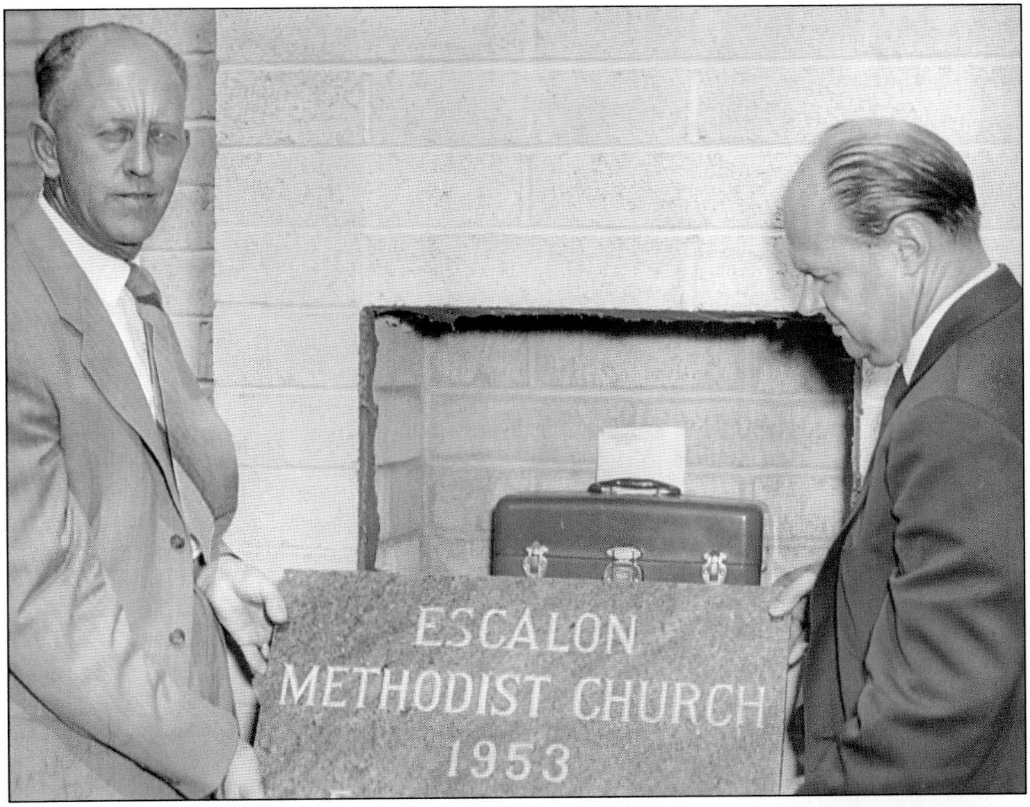


Rev. Albert W. Foster (left), pastor of the Methodist church, and Bishop Donald H. Tippet hold the plaque commemorating the consecration of the new Escalon Methodist Church. The church relocated to the corner of Brayton Avenue and Highway 120, its third location, after being on the corner of Third Street and Highway 120. This former location had been the church's home since 1910 and was shared in the final months with the First Baptist Church. The Methodist church is accorded the honor of being the first church in Escalon.

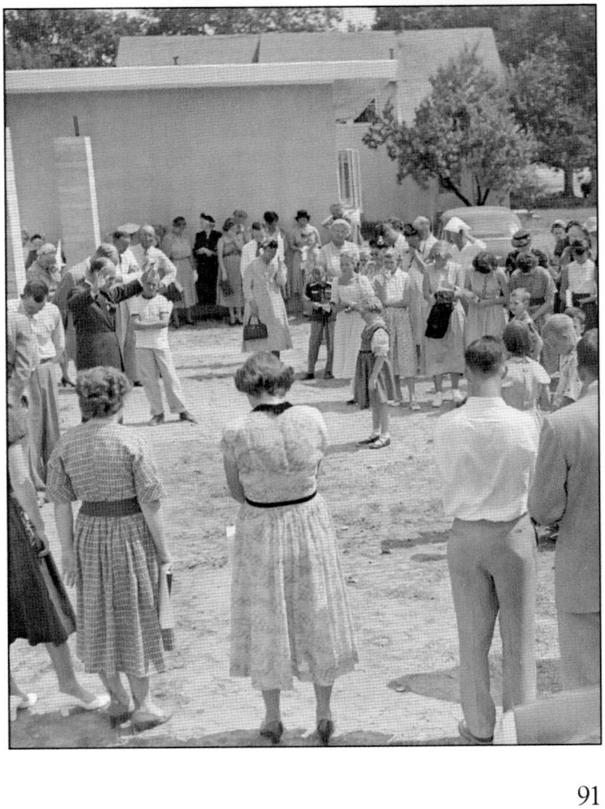

This was the consecration service for the new Escalon Methodist Church at the corner of Brayton Avenue and Highway 120, held in February 1954.

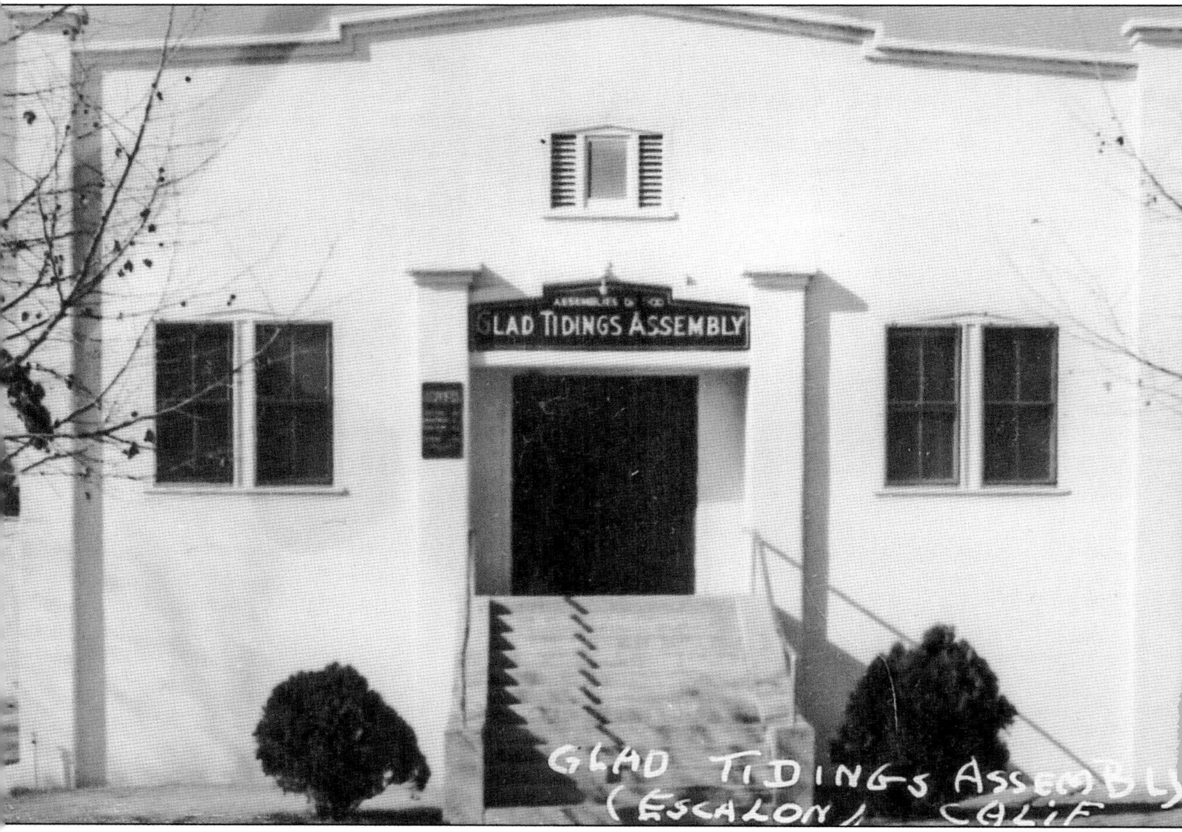


The Pentecostal Glad Tidings Assembly Church is pictured in the early 1900s. Members had been meeting in a storefront prior to the construction of this building at the corner of Second Street and Coley Avenue. In the 1950s, the congregation began meeting in the church's current location at the corner of California Street and Brayton Avenue and it became known as the Assembly of God church.

# *Nine*

# Business and Industry around the Town

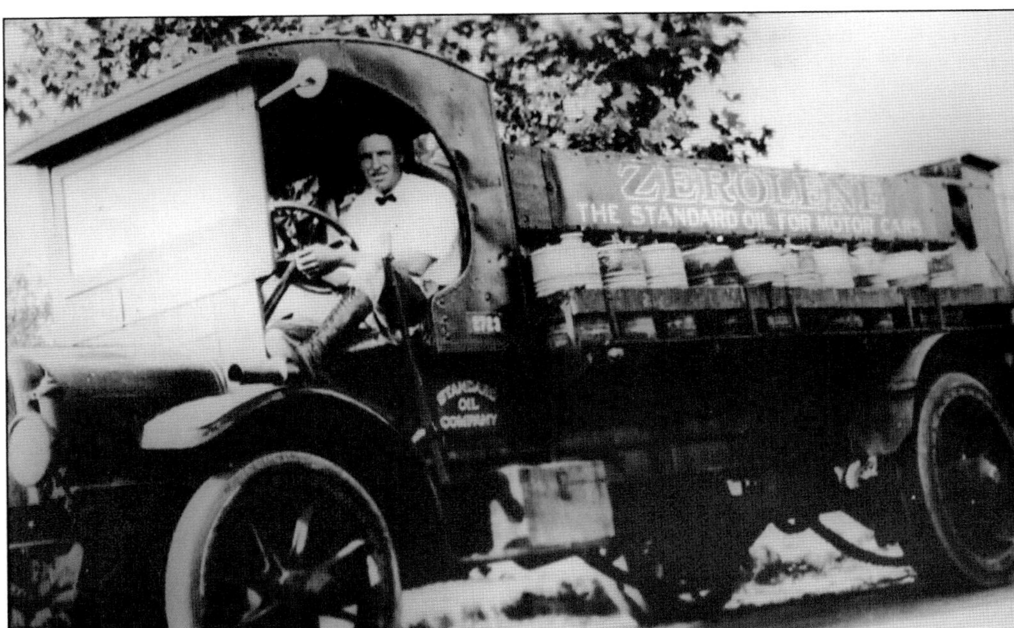


John Wright Sr., a Standard Oil dealer, is seen making deliveries in early 1923. His customers owned farms and dairies with tanks to be filled from these five-gallon cans. Eventually, Wright opened up the closed bulk plant in Escalon that had been built in 1919, where Wright's Petroleum stands now. Wright was honored as the Man of the Year in 1968 by the Escalon District Chamber of Commerce for his many years of service to the community. He also served as the grand marshal of the Park Fete parade in 1980. Three generations of Wrights (John's son Jack and Jack's son John and daughter Marianne) have all worked at this landmark business, making it the oldest family-owned business in Escalon.

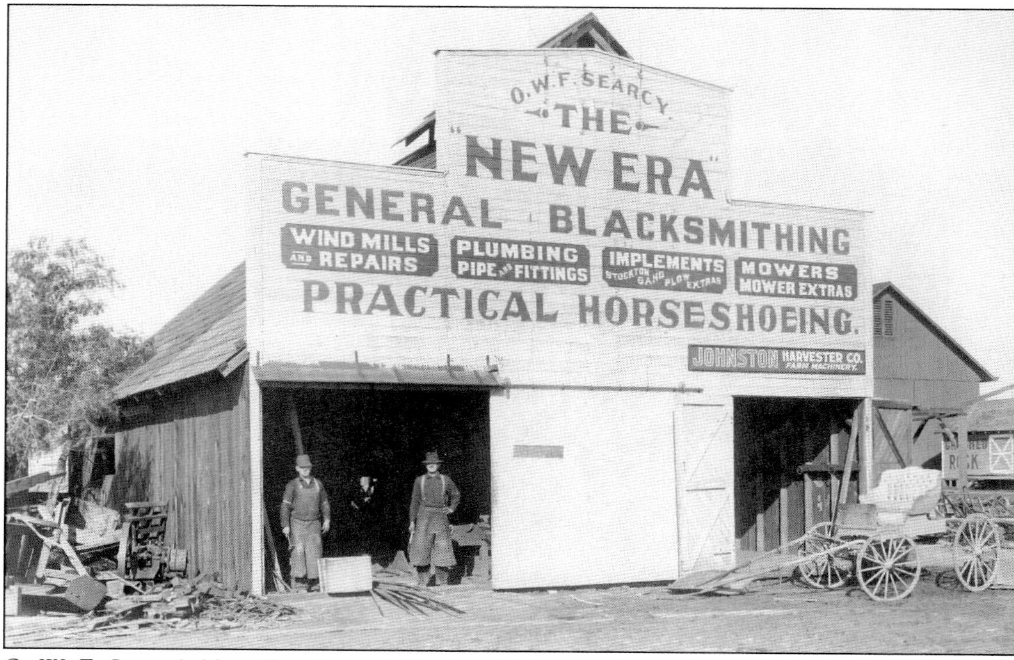


O. W. F. Searcy's New Era General Blacksmithing was located on what would become First Street, across from the lumberyard. It was here that Roy Adam Hetzler first came to work in 1911 before opening his own blacksmith shop a few blocks away. Based on the signs, this shop was the place for everything from horseshoeing to windmills and plenty in between.

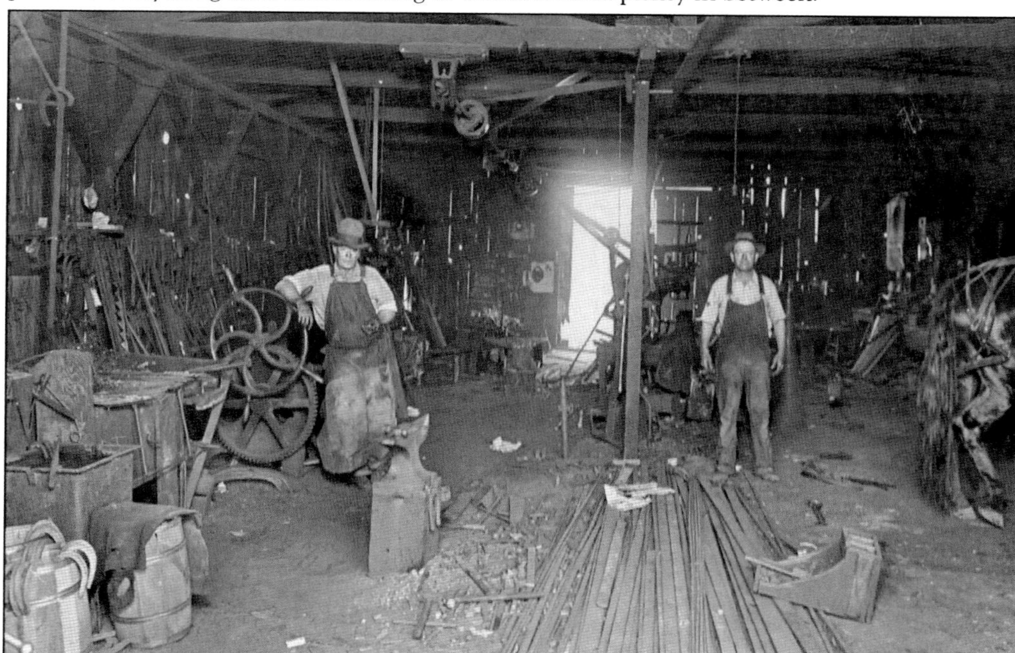

Inside a blacksmith shop, Roy Adam Hetzler (left) and an unidentified coworker are ready to take on the next job. Horseshoes, an anvil, and other miscellaneous tools and equipment are visible. Beneath the cog wheels on the left are runners for a Fresno scraper, an earthmoving tool ideally suited to the sandy soil in this area.

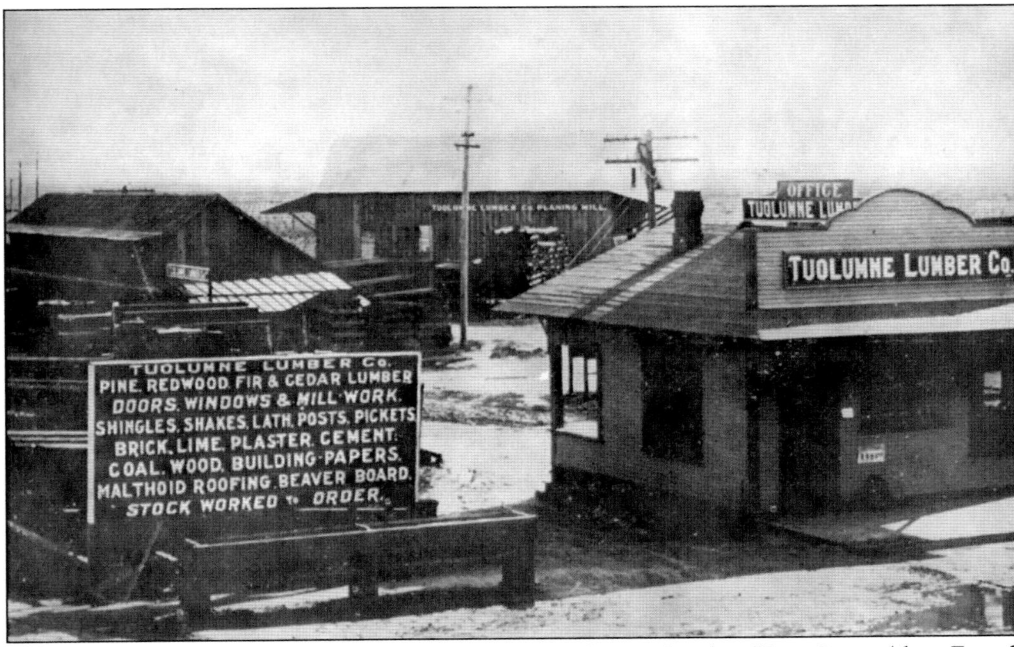


The office of Tuolumne Lumber was built in 1898 on the south side of First Street (then French Camp Road) just west of the Santa Fe Railroad tracks. Early on, the building was used as a store and post office for a short time. Though the building no longer exists, the cement pad that served as the office's foundation is used by the current business, Escalon Lumber and Hardware, as a holding place for bricks offered for sale. An outbuilding used by Tuolumne Lumber as a cabinet shop, believed to have been built in 1903, was destroyed by what is suspected to have been an arson fire in 2008.

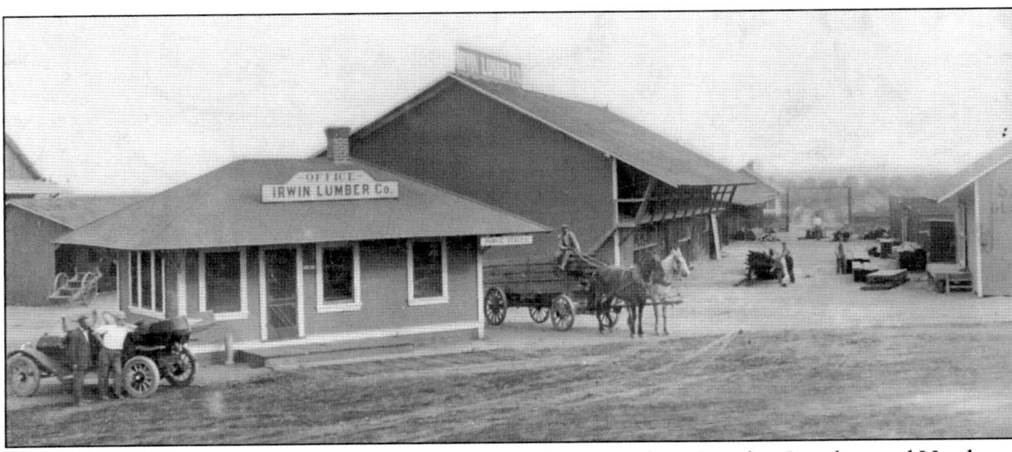


The Irwin Lumber Company at one time occupied the area where Escalon Lumber and Hardware has been for more than 40 years. In this 1912 photograph are (from left to right) Henry Barth, S. J. Irwin (the owner beginning in 1911), and Axel Gustafson. Some of the outbuildings pictured still stand today.

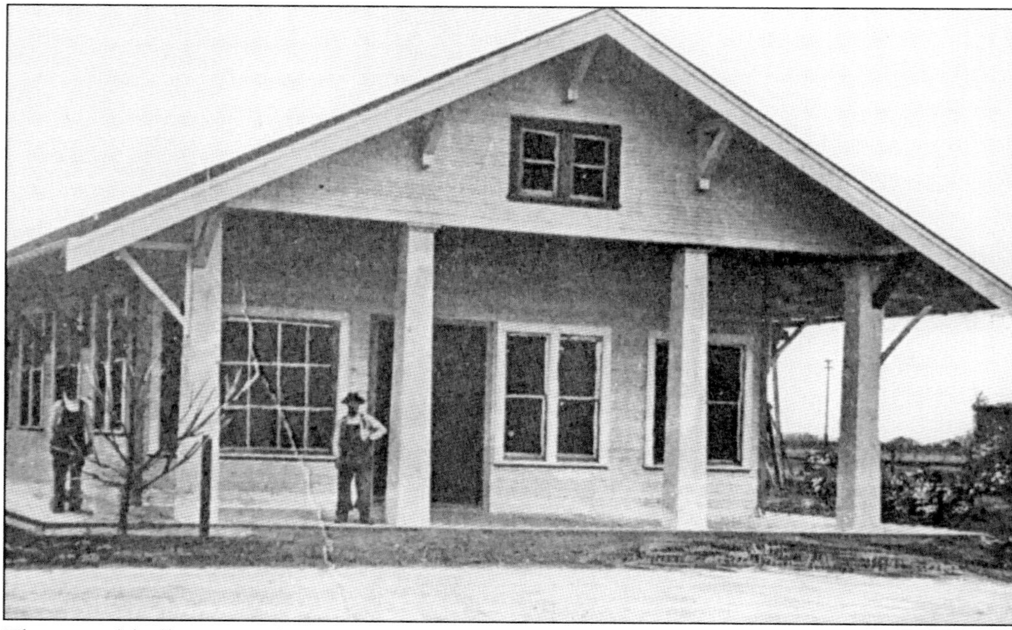

This social hall was on the north side of French Camp Road at the corner with Weiss Way, across from the lumberyard.

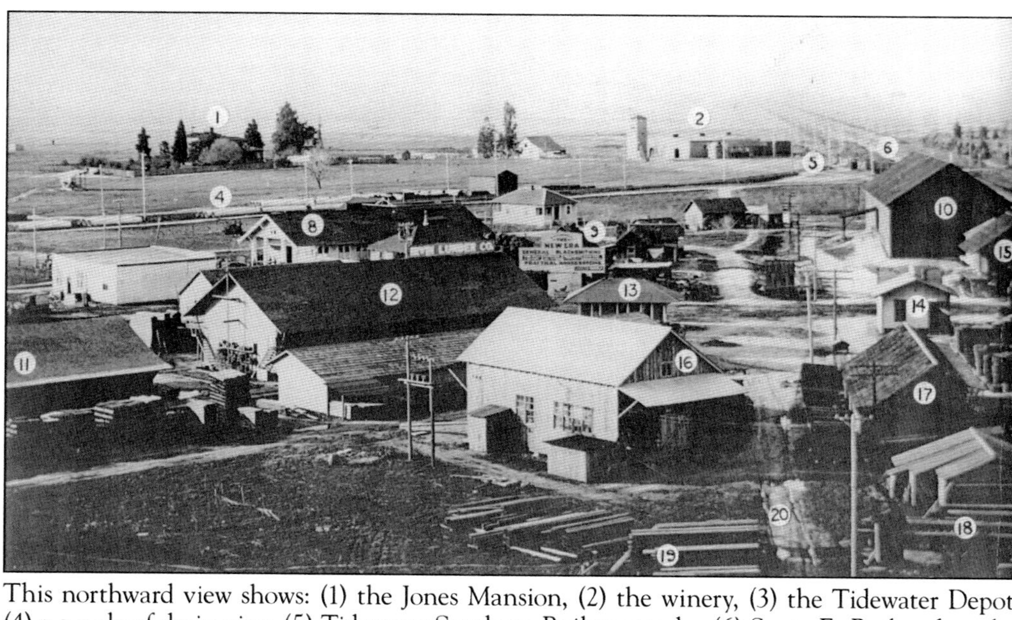


This northward view shows: (1) the Jones Mansion, (2) the winery, (3) the Tidewater Depot, (4) a supply of drain pipe, (5) Tidewater Southern Railway tracks, (6) Santa Fe Railroad tracks, (7) French Camp Road, (8) the social hall, (9) O. W. F. Searcy's New Era General Blacksmithing, (10) Humphrey's warehouse, (11) and (12) Irwin sheds, (13) Irwin Lumber Company, (14) Tuolumne Lumber, (15) a cement storage shed for Irwin Lumber, (16) lumber, (17) and (18) Tuolumne sheds, (19) the Irwin lumberyard, and (20) the roadway to P&L Concrete.

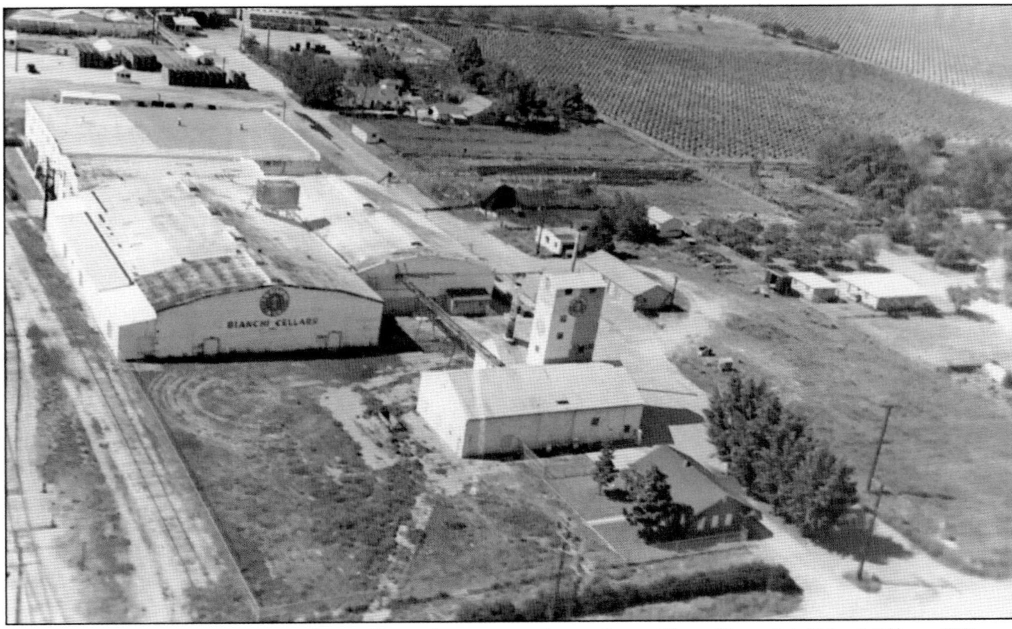


The Bianchi Winery is seen here. Brandy was made in the still at Bianchi. The Village Winery started Solera Cellars here in 1946. When Bianchi purchased the Village Winery in 1950, it became Bianchi Cellars. Bianchi then purchased Solera Cellars in 1951. Bianchi grew grapes near Escalon for its wines. This view is roughly southward.

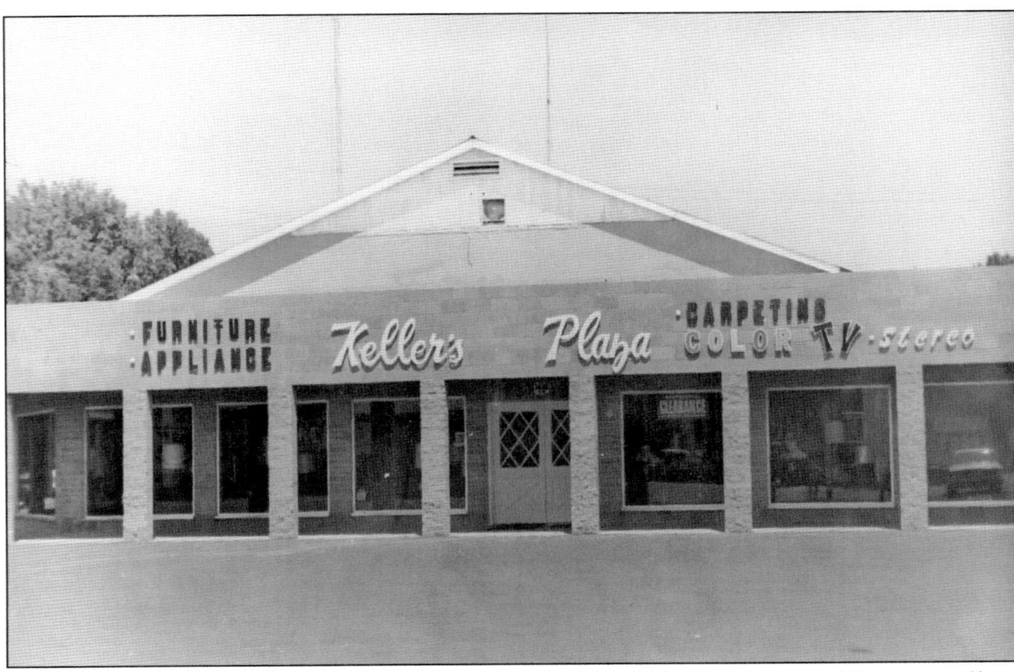


Keller's Plaza was located on Highway 120 where the True Value store is now. The store offered furniture, appliances, carpeting, televisions, and stereos. The quality of the furniture was so good that some items remain in Escalon homes today in nearly the same condition as when they were newly purchased some 40 years ago.

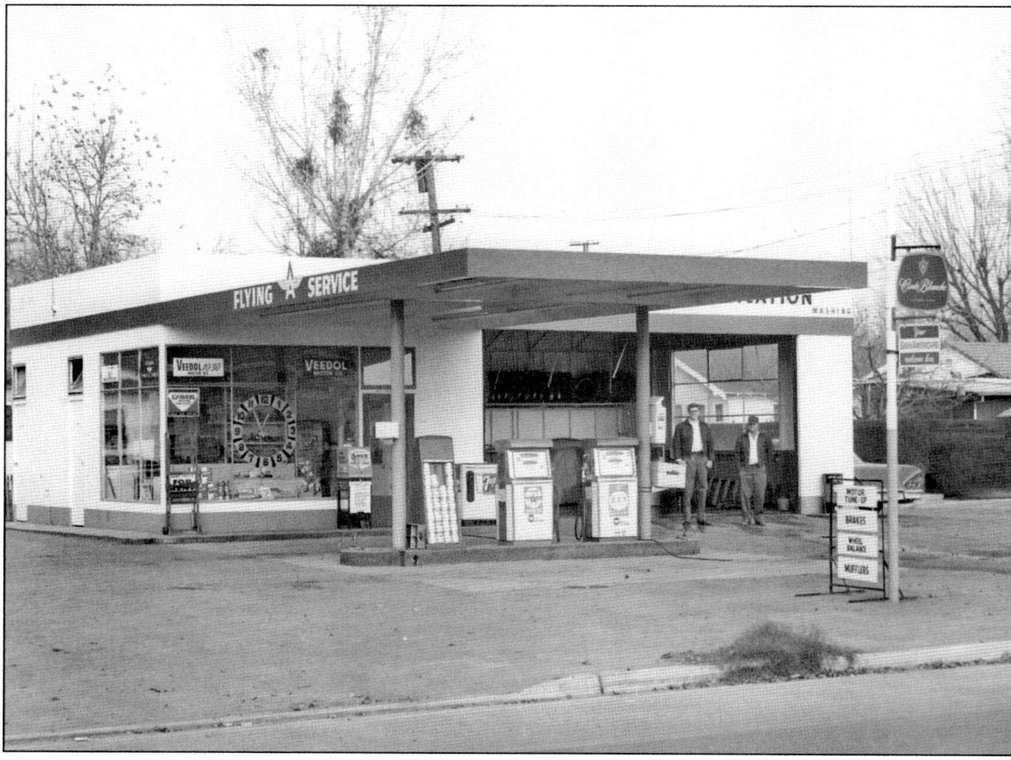


In 1961, the Flying A Service on Highway 120 at Kern Street was operated by Jack Thomas (left) and his father, Ed. Today the Century 21 real estate office is located here.

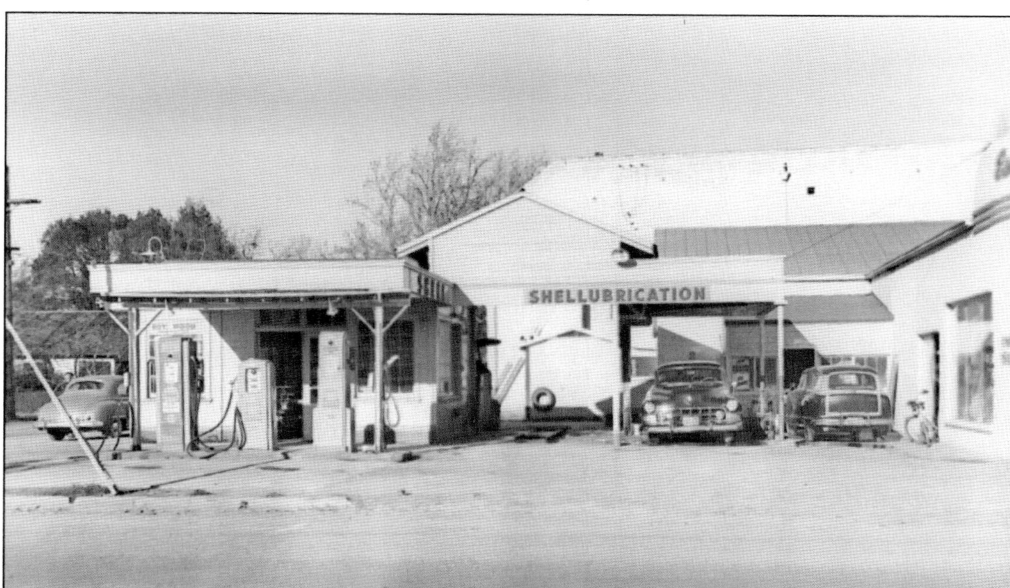


Roy Wood was the proprietor of this Shell service station next to Escalon Tire Supply on Main Street. Shaw's Market, on the other side of the tire shop, would eventually expand, using the tire shop area. The area this gas station stood on is now the parking lot for the current market.

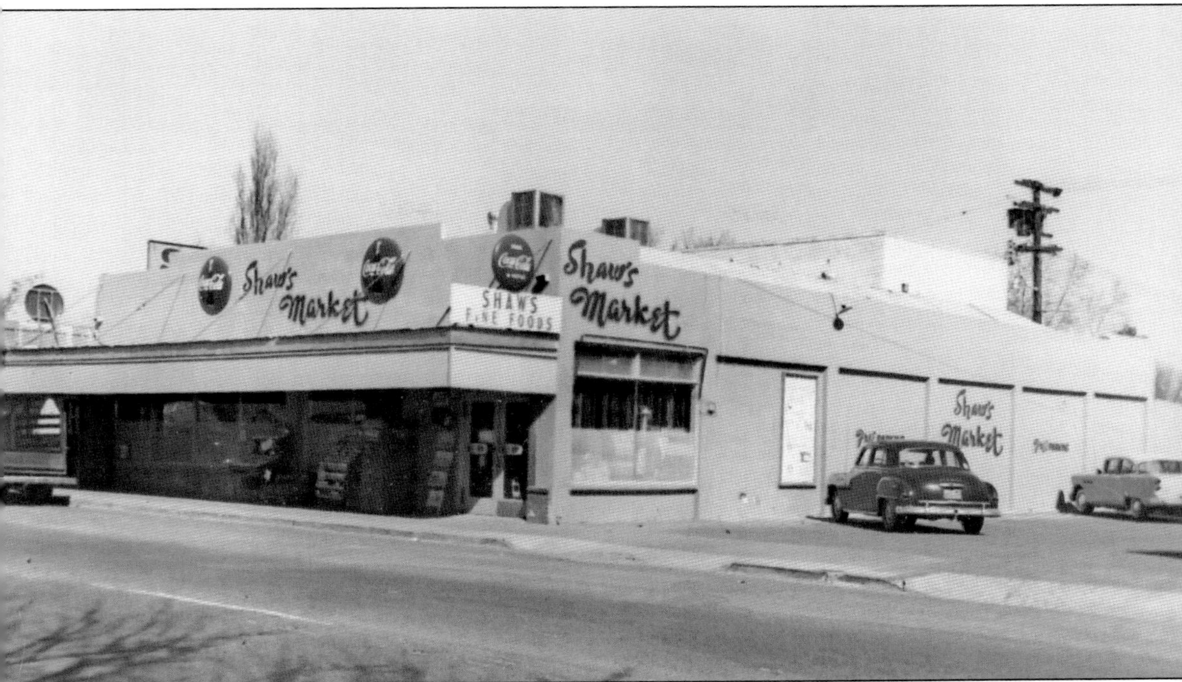


Fine foods could be purchased at Shaw's Market on Main Street in the 1940s. It sat next to the Shell service station and Escalon Tire Supply at the corner with Viking Street. When Leroy Shaw needed more space, he bought the gas station and tire store from Carl Peterson, leased out the gas station, and used the tire store to expand the square footage of his market. After this, the store's name was changed to Shaw's Shop and Save Market. Later it would become the Main Street Market. The current occupant of this building is Los Altenos Market. The current location for the Main Street Market is on McHenry Avenue.

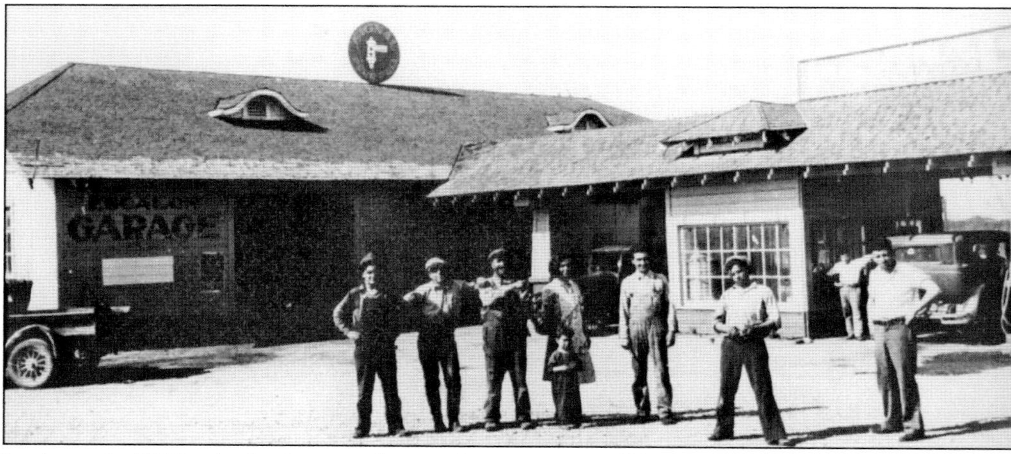


In the early 1900s, the business at the northwest corner of Yosemite and Escalon Avenues was a Signal Gasoline Station. Pictured here from left to right are Luis Dennis Jr., William Augusto, John Augusto, Mary Dennis, Luis Dennis Sr., Deno Macsenti, William Macsenti, and Tom Dugo. The business was owned by Luis Dennis Sr. until Dugo bought it in the late 1930s.

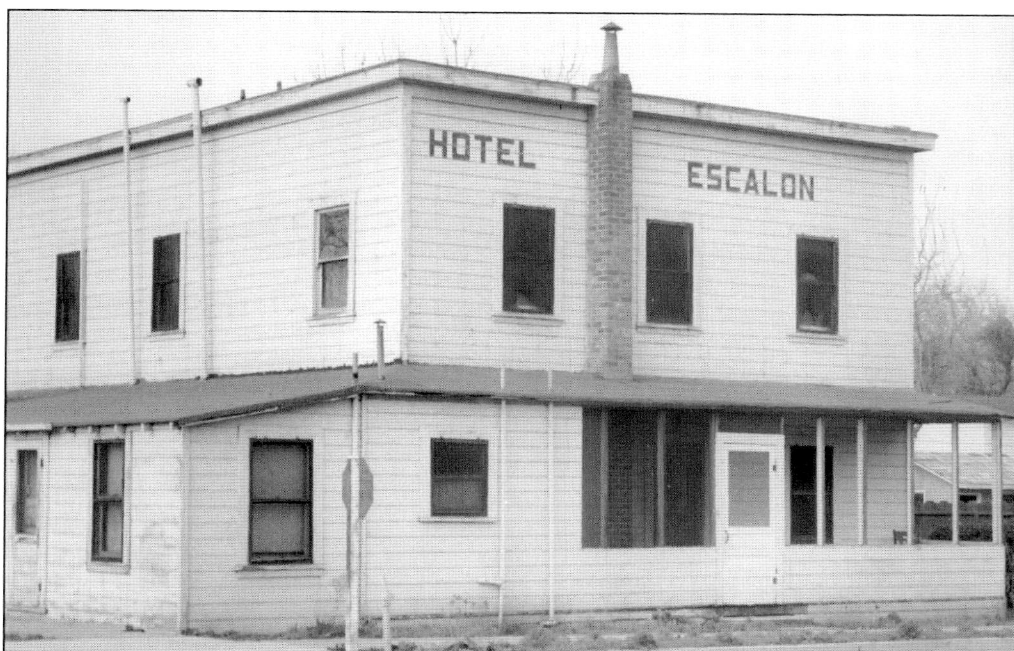


The Hotel Escalon, built about 1915 and pictured around 1940, was located at the corner of Third Street and Coley Avenue. The hotel was run by Lydia Stockel for many years and was eventually torn down in the 1970s to make room for a new city hall. This corner property is currently occupied by the Escalon Police and Planning Departments.

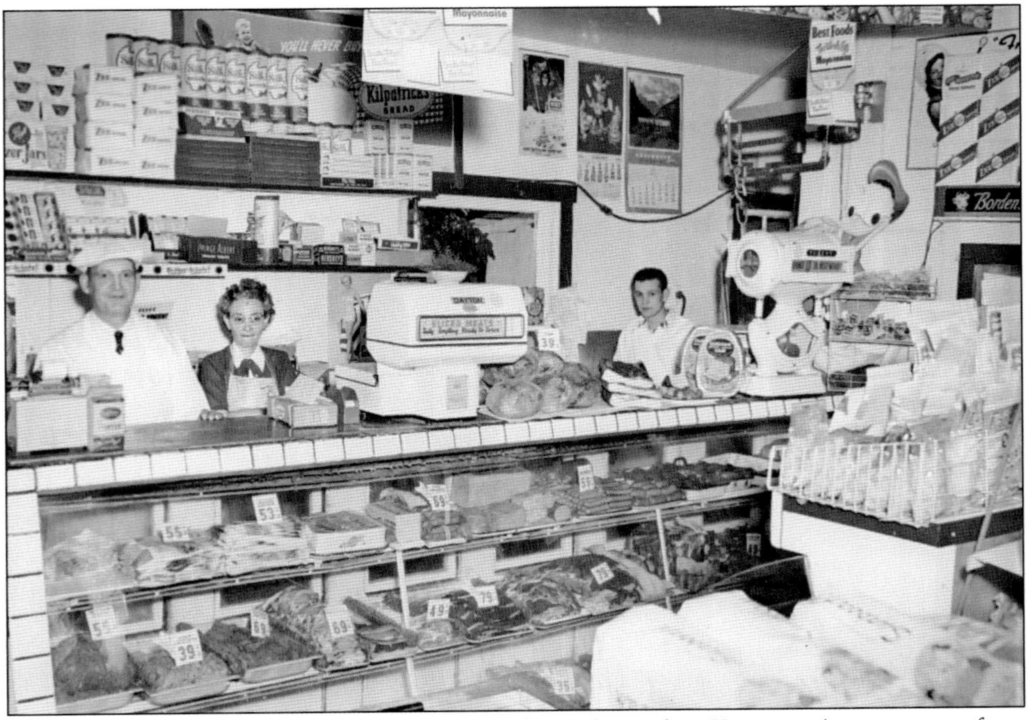


This is the interior of Fitch's Meat Market, which was located on Yosemite Avenue across from the high school in the 1940s. At the time of this photograph, sliced bacon sold for 53¢ a pound and hams for 39¢ a pound. For some students, the big attraction at Fitch's was fishing a huge dill pickle out of the standing pickle barrel.

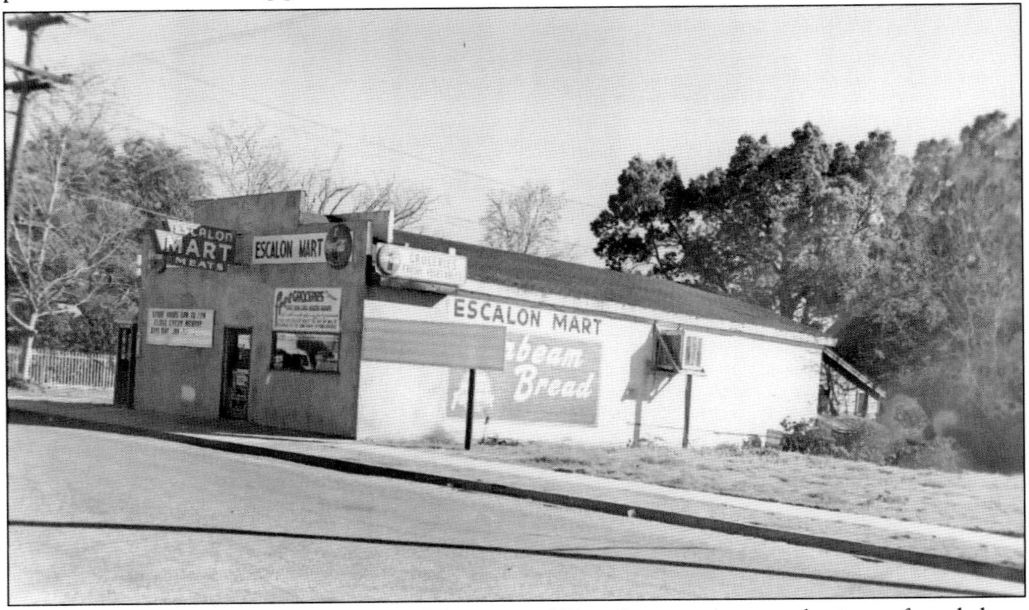


The Escalon Mart was at the corner of Center and First Streets. Among the items found there were meats, groceries, fresh vegetables, and Sunbeam bread. This building would later be home to a succession of different businesses, including a short run as a bicycle repair shop. It remains standing today.

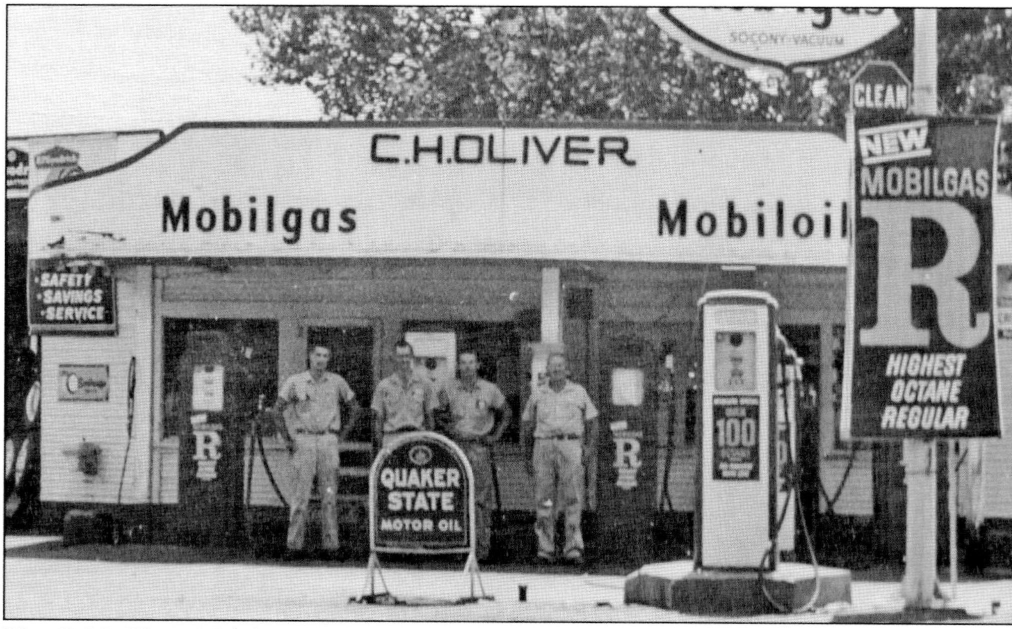


The C. H. Oliver Mobil gas station was owned by Cecil Oliver. It was located on the southeast corner of McHenry Avenue and Highway 120. Pictured in the 1950s are (from left to right) Larry Clark, Doug Beckwith, Tom Largent, and Cecil Oliver. One hazard of being located alongside a road with quickly moving traffic as the increased potential for an accident. One day in the early 1950s, a truck loaded down with bales of hay took this corner a little too rapidly for its load and ended up on its side next to the gas pumps. The ties holding down the hay bales broke, releasing bales of hay in several directions. Fortunately, no one was hurt.

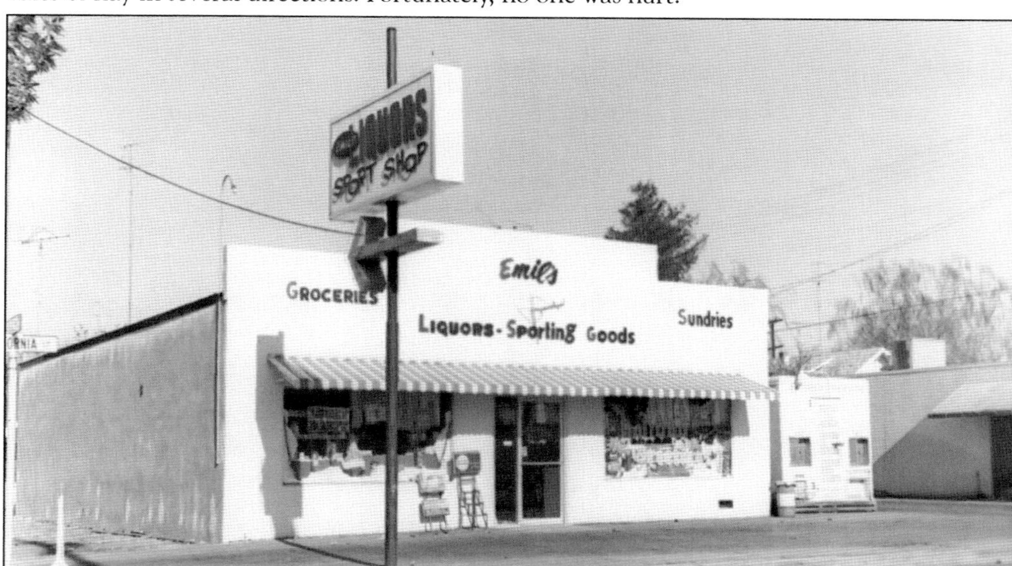


Emil Cabral once owned Emil's Liquors and Sport Shop, selling groceries and sundries from this building on the north side of Highway 120. The building later was home to Irene's House of Cheese, the House of Cheese, Calizo's Deli, and now Groppetti's Deli. Emil's Liquors is now Emil's Food Mart and is currently located across the highway from its former location at the intersection with Main Street.

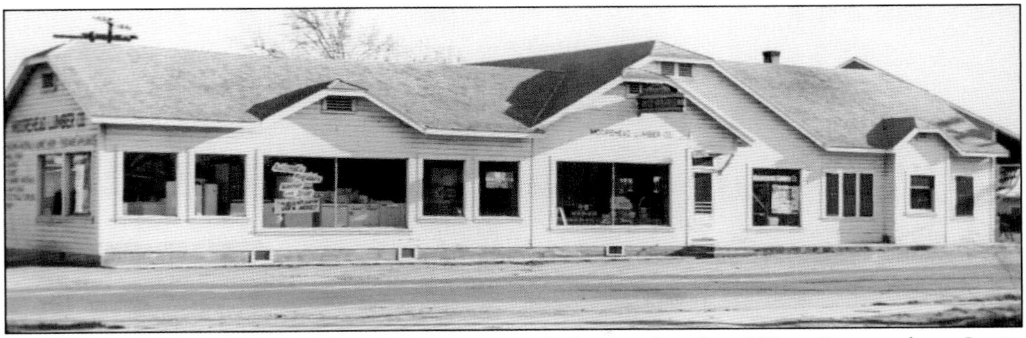

The Moorehead Lumber Company once occupied the south side of First Street where Irwin Lumber had been and where Escalon Lumber and Hardware is now. Charles Moorehead had been a longtime employee of Irwin Lumber before he purchased the business. Marv Schmidt began working there in 1947 and purchased the business in 1965. It became M&J Lumber and then Escalon Lumber and Hardware.

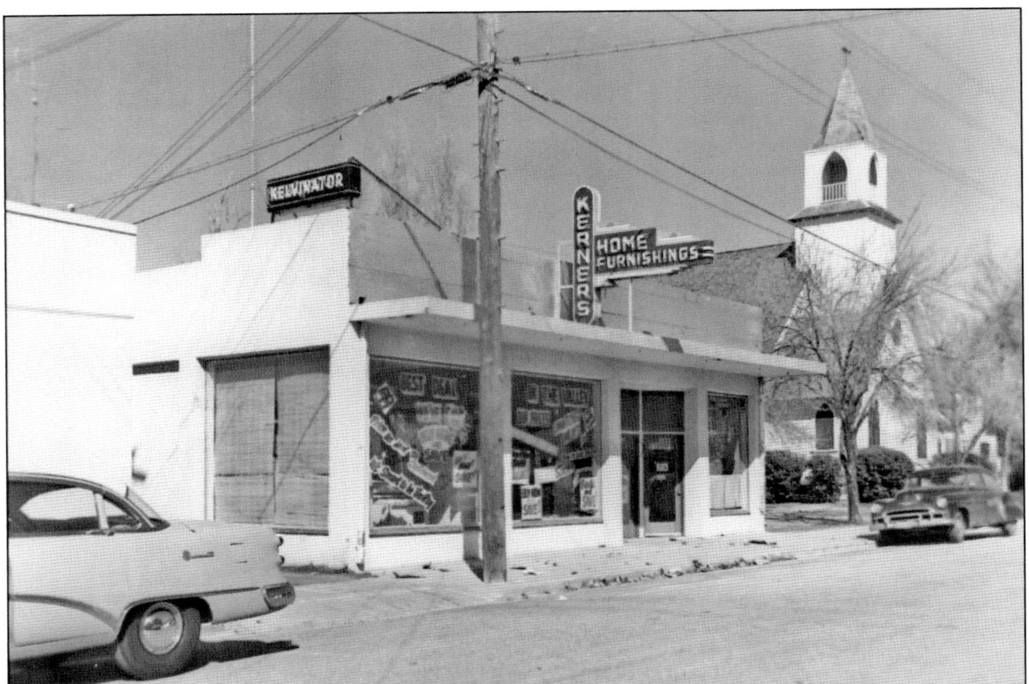


Kerner's Home Furnishings, pictured around 1948, was owned by Monroe Kerner on the north side of First Street between Main Street and Highway 120. The building would later house Carl and Virginia Cova's grocery store and Vern's Shoe Repair. It is now the engineering offices of Hogan Manufacturing, Inc. Beyond the store, the former Swedish Lutheran Church is visible.

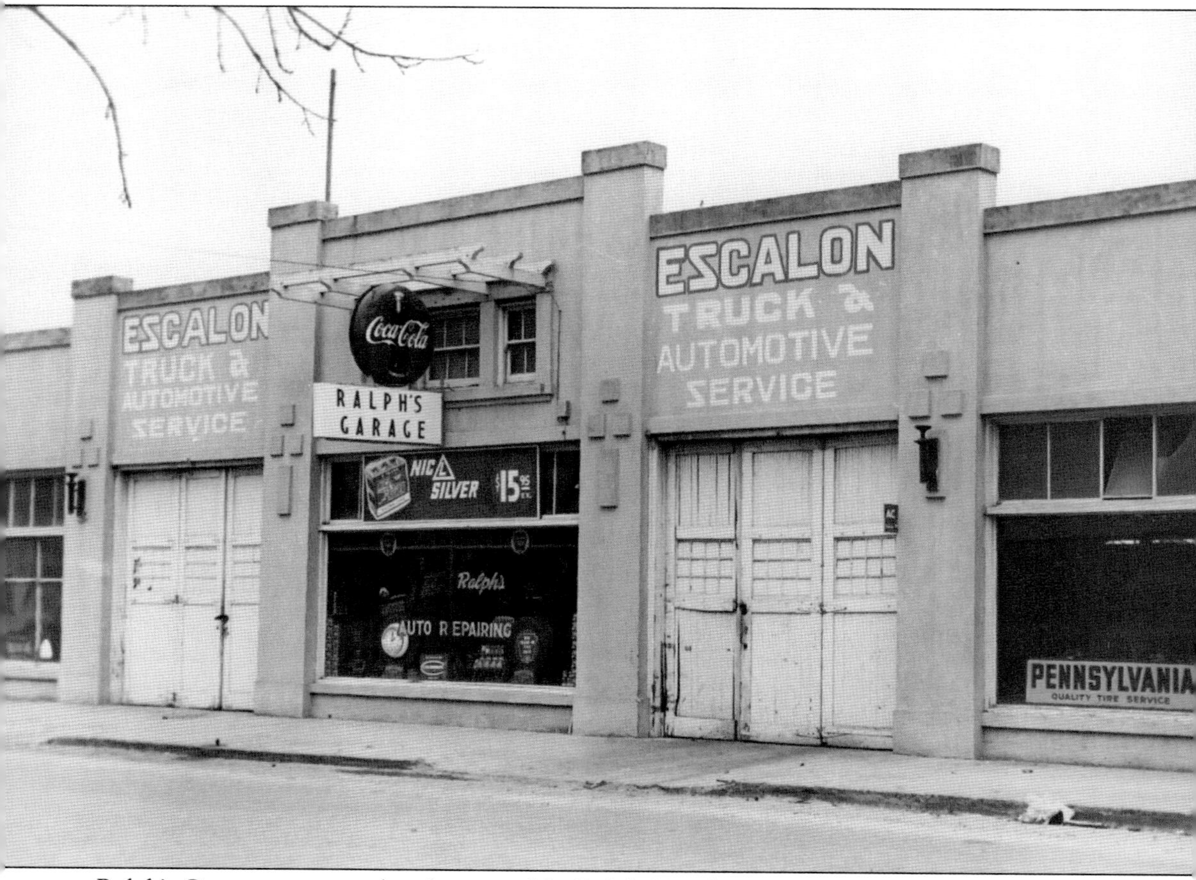


Ralph's Garage was owned and operated by Ralph Verschoor on the south side of First Street between Center and Main Streets, next to the lumberyard. Ralph had returned to Escalon after wartime military service and purchased this auto shop in 1952 with a partner, Louis Cinpianelli. The building had been built in 1919 by S. J. Irwin, owner of the lumberyard, and was at one time a Chevrolet dealership, showcasing two models made in Oakland. In the 1920s, it was the Star Garage, and from 1948 until 1952, it was a retail business for used furniture. This building is now home to Escalon Transmission.

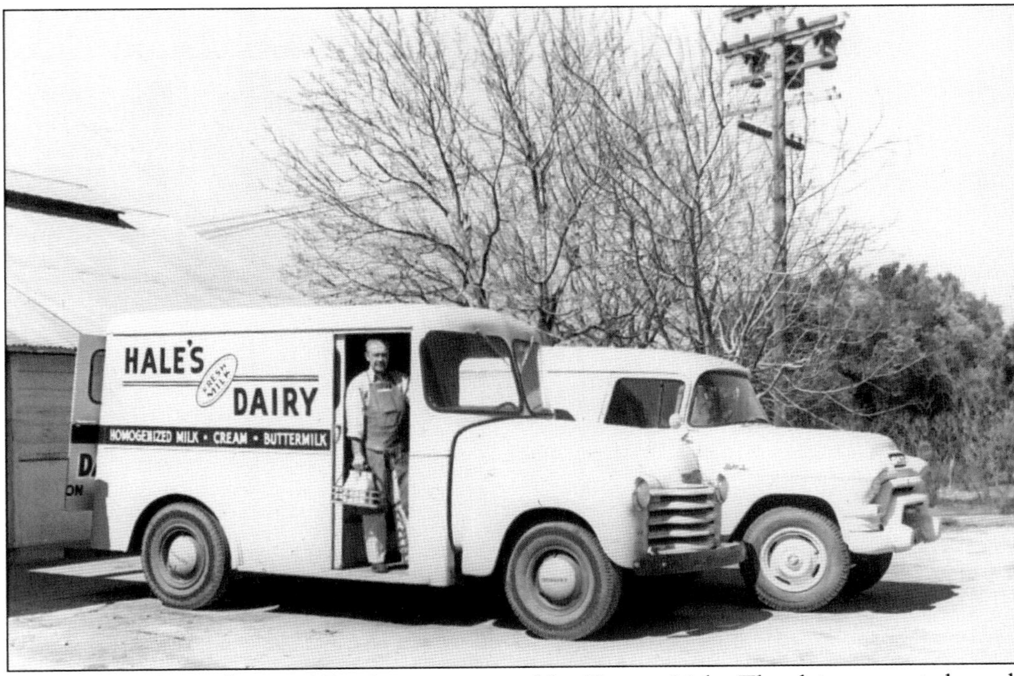


Hale's Dairy, located east of Escalon, was owned by Harvey Hale. The dairy occupied nearly 200 acres and had about 200 head of dairy cattle. It offered home milk delivery in the 1940s. Several milk bottles and other memorabilia from this business are on display in the Escalon Historical Museum. Muriel Hale, Harvey's wife, was a fourth-grade teacher. One of her former students recalls working at a local bank years later and waiting on Harvey Hale. He complimented her on her penmanship, and she credited his wife with excellent instruction.

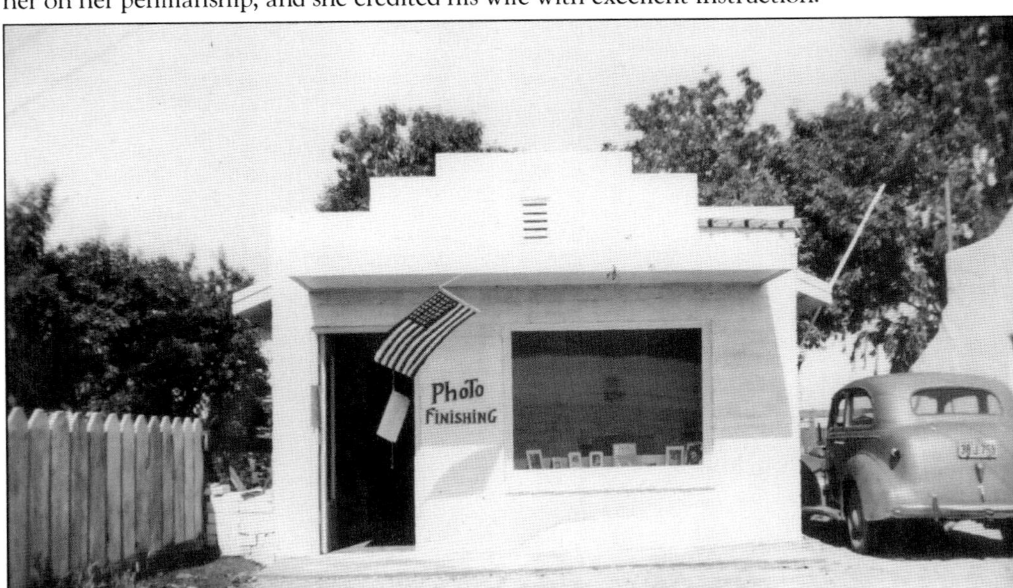


This building on Escalon Avenue was built by Tom and Angelo Dugo, and served as the first location for Dugo's Photo Finishing Studio. Later it became the Escalon Veterinary Hospital for veterinarian Tom Hagan. Dugo's Photo Studio was later located on Main Street for several years, until the studio was sold to David Marshall.

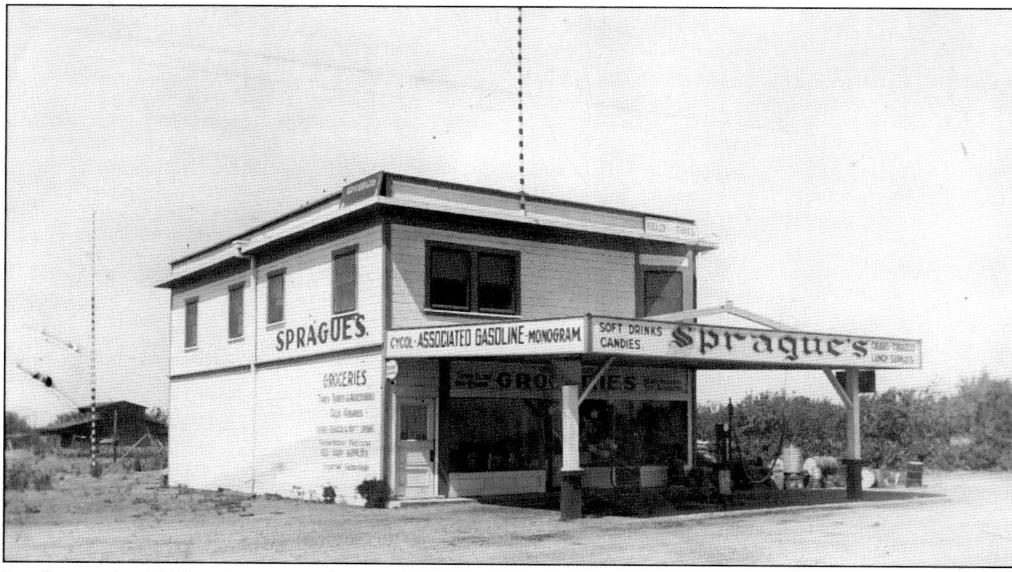


In the early 1900s, Spragues, located west of Escalon at Simms Station, offered gasoline and groceries; tires, tubes and accessories; oils and greases; cigars, tobacco, and soft drinks; candies, notions, and medicines; feed and dairy supplies; and imported Italian goods. This photograph is from around 1928. The store had been located in Atlanta, but when that town died, Merle Sprague moved to this spot on Highway 120. This building later burned to the ground.

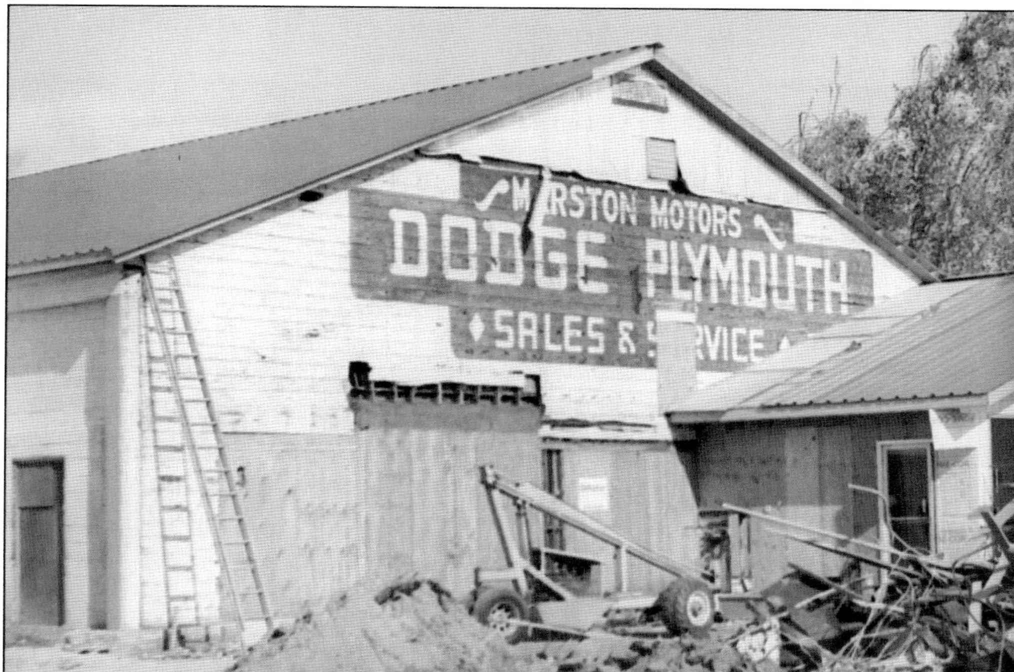


When the True Value hardware store was being remodeled in November 1998, the sign for Marston Motors Dodge Plymouth Sales and Service was revealed, indicating the building's earlier life. Cecil Oliver had constructed the building in 1947 to house the Dodge Plymouth dealership and sold it to the Marstons. Over the years, the building was home to Reid Motors, an army reserve armored tank unit, Keller's Plaza, Mid-State Surge, and finally, True Value.

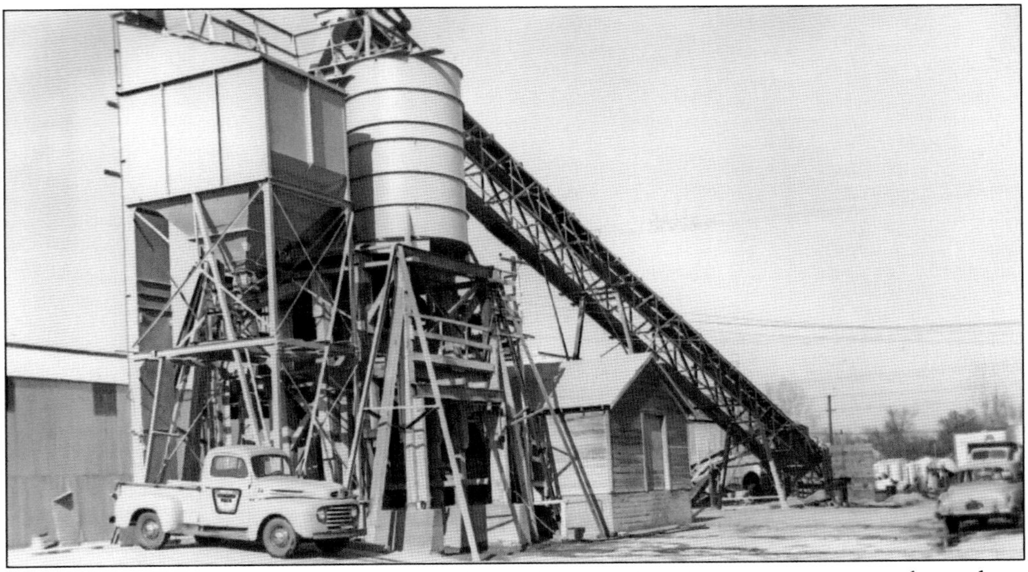

Standard Rock/Standard Materials was located on Coley Avenue approximately midway between First and Second Streets, where Hogan Manufacturing, Inc., now has one of its plants. It supplied ready-mix concrete for construction, asphalt, hot road oil, rock, cement, grading, and excavating.

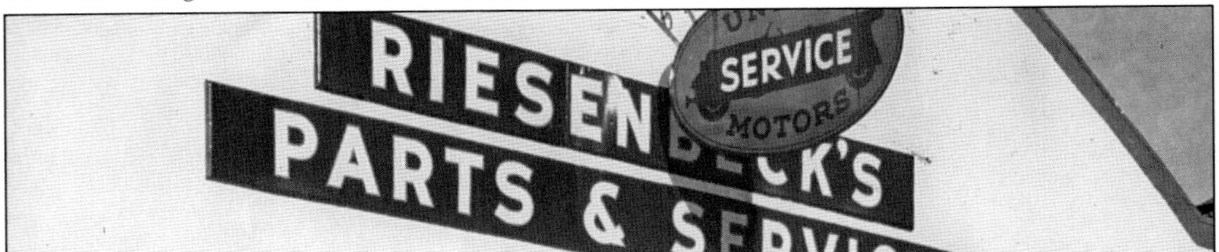


Riesenbeck's Parts and Service was located at the corner of Main and California Streets, where Emil's Food Mart is now. Jack Riesenbeck stands second from the right in this picture. The garage opened in 1925. In 1937, gas pumps were added. The business operated as a Standard Oil station from 1941 to 1949.

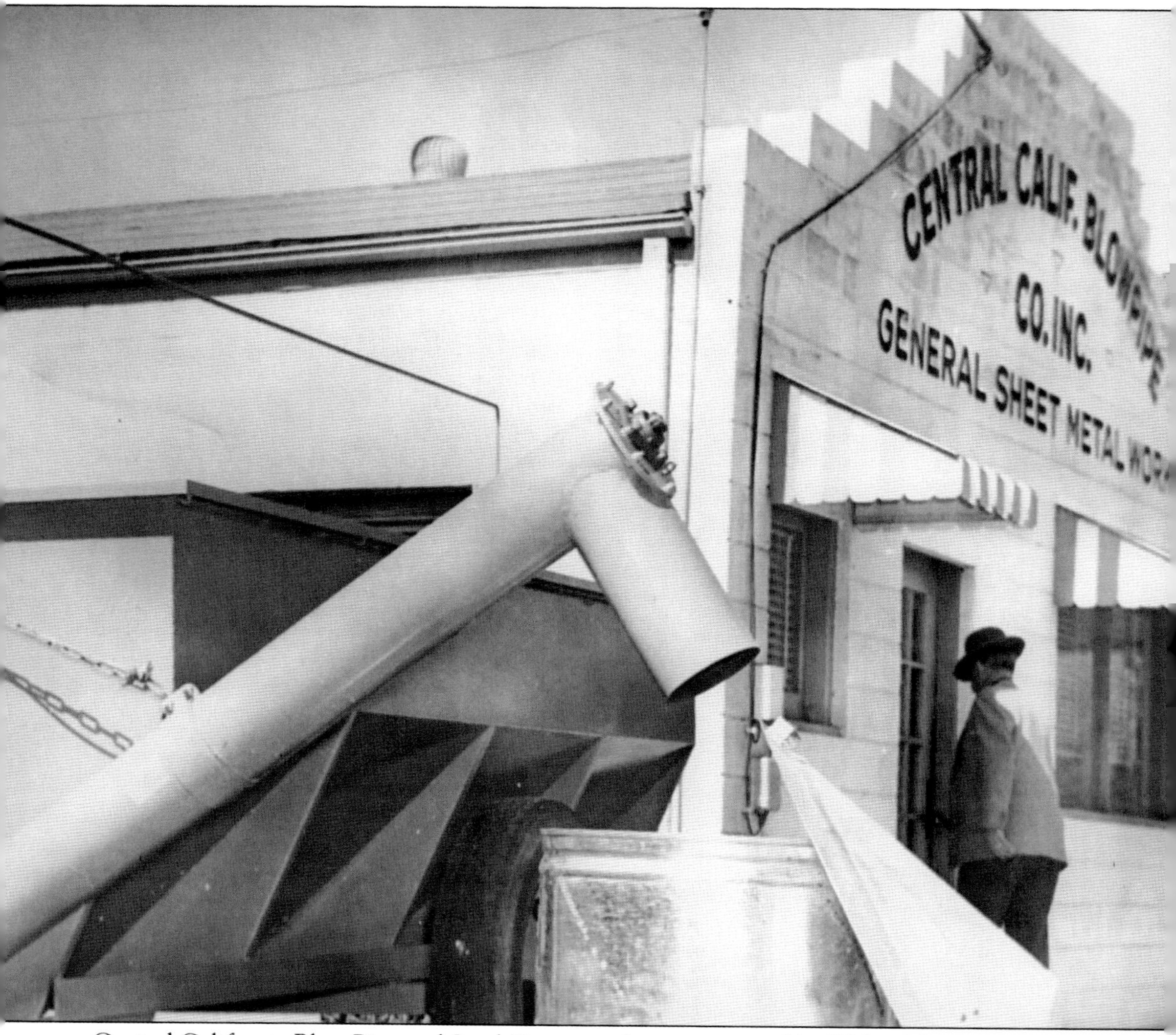


Central California Blow Pipe and Steel Company, Inc., was started by Walter Hogan in 1944. It began as a small blacksmith shop specializing in sheet-metal fabrication. Over the years, there have been several acquisitions and mergers, and some changes to product lines. The company at one time manufactured steel beams for commercial buildings. After one merger in 1971, the company took on the name of Hogan Manufacturing, Inc. Now grown into multiple plant and office locations, the company manufactures wheelchair lifts, among other items. The generosity and civic-mindedness of Walter Hogan is evident in the community of Escalon in scholarships for graduating students and Hogan Park, which is named in his honor.

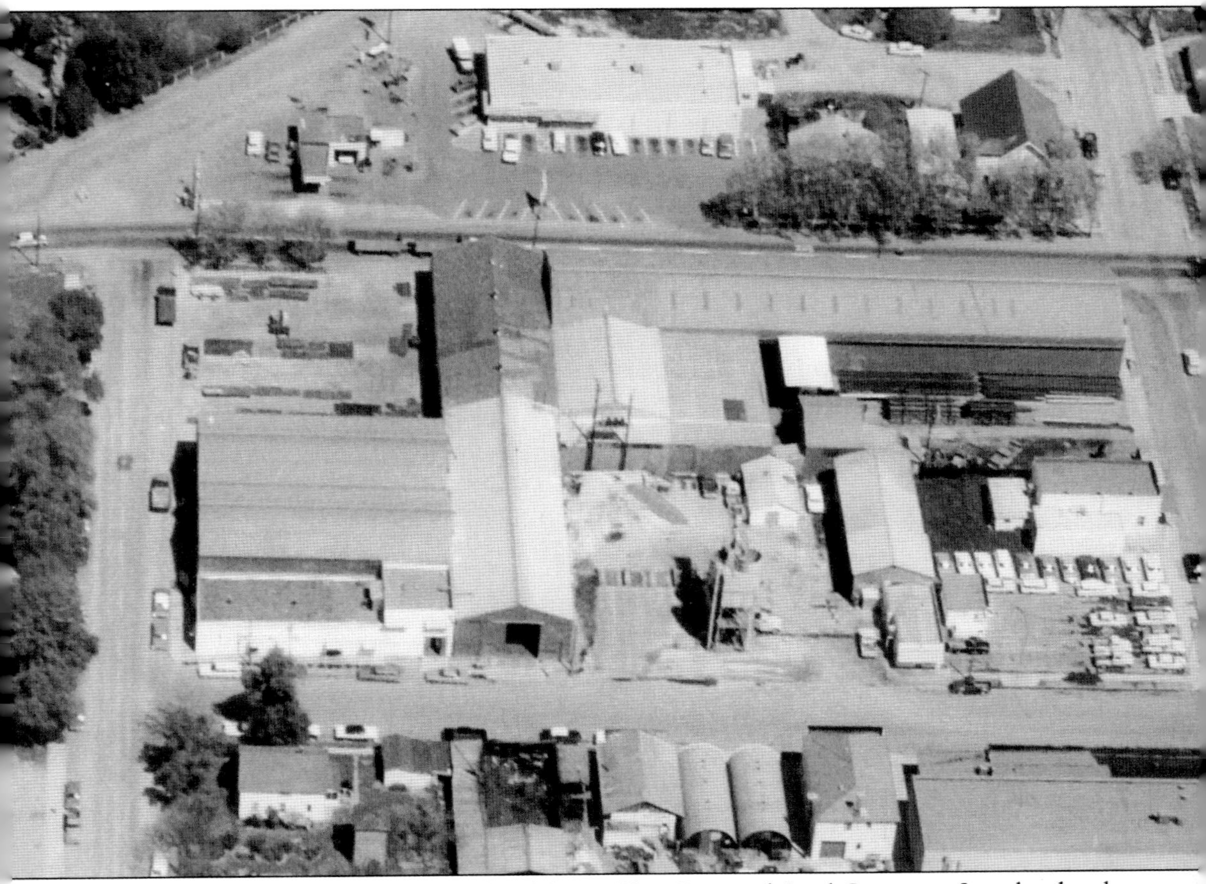

This is an aerial view of the Central California Blow Pipe and Steel Company, Inc., bordered by Jackson Avenue/Highway 120, Second Street, Coley Avenue, and First Street. The company did not yet occupy the entire block, as it does now. Visible in the block are the batch plant that had belonged to Standard Rock, the jail and courthouse building, and the J. M. Souza Ford dealership lot. On the near side of Coley Avenue, a residence is where the Union Safe Deposit Bank would eventually stand. To the right is Solari's Blacksmith Shop, Sutton and Borquist Pump, and two Quonset huts (one containing the Tip Top Cleaners) where the parking lots are now. The theater and hardware store are on the corner currently occupied by the Escalon Branch Library. The site of the Presbyterian church to the left on First Street is obscured by vegetation. Across the highway is the first location for Escalon's Big Boy Market, then named Bi and Bi Supermarket, placing this photograph in the early 1960s.

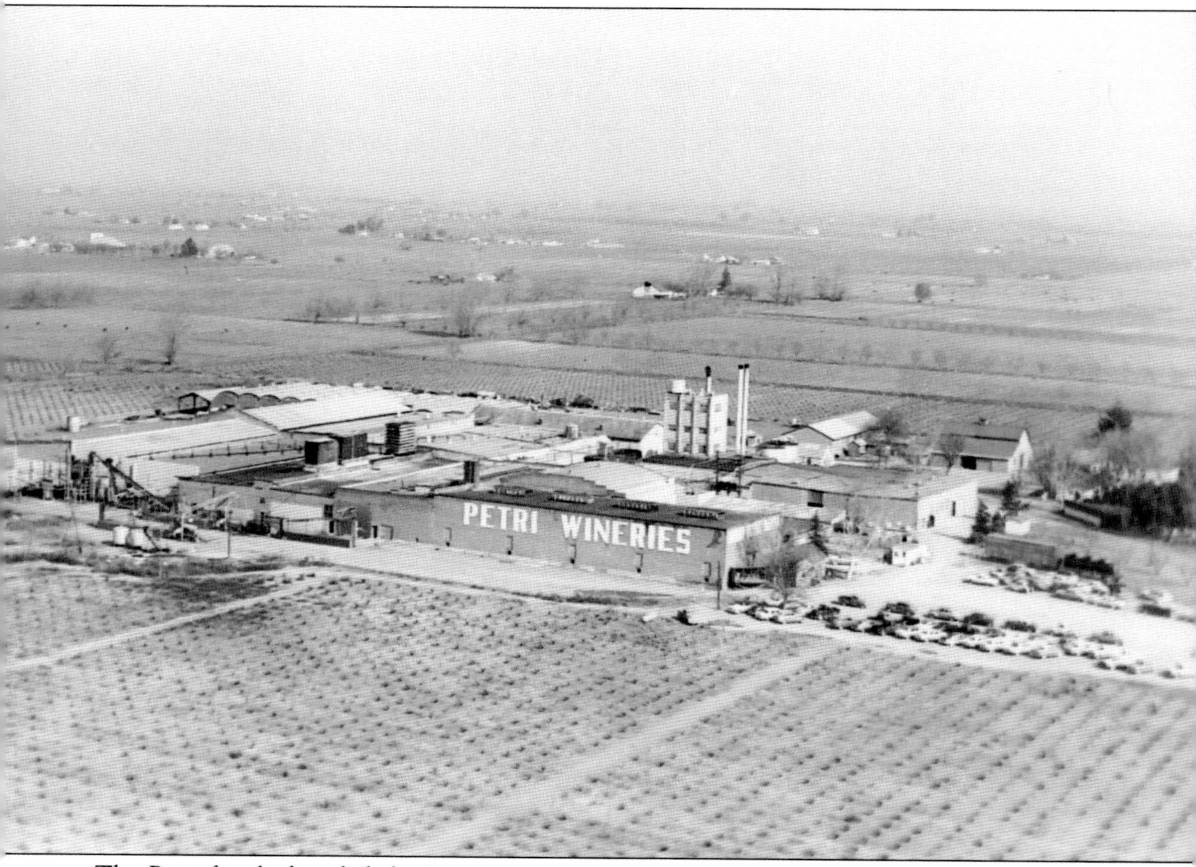


The Petri family founded the Petri Winery west of Escalon on Highway 120 and owned and operated it for many years. Along with the winery, the family acquired a few vineyards. During Prohibition, they sold sacramental wine for religious purposes and also sold grapes. After Prohibition, the wine business flourished. Heublein took over the winery in the late 1960s and was in turn bought out by Canandaigua in the 1990s. Over the years, many Escalon residents were employed by the wineries in a variety of capacities, and a few lived in the houses on the property.

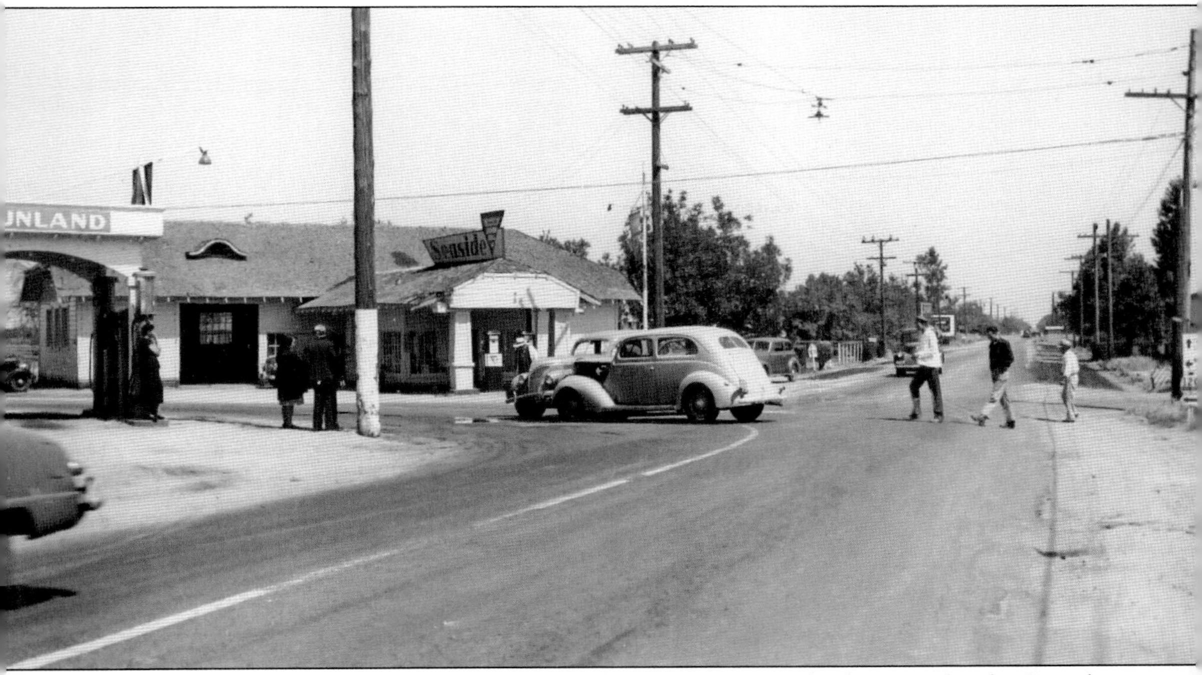

Around 1940, the corner of Yosemite and Escalon Avenues was the location for the Seaside service station on the northwest and the Sunland service station on the southwest. On the right is the pump house for the first Escalon swimming pool. Succeeding businesses on the northwest corner would include the restaurants Pump House, Don Angelo's, El Senor Frogs, Franco's, Pierre's, and currently, Cancun. Later occupants of the southwest corner would include Troy's Trading Post.

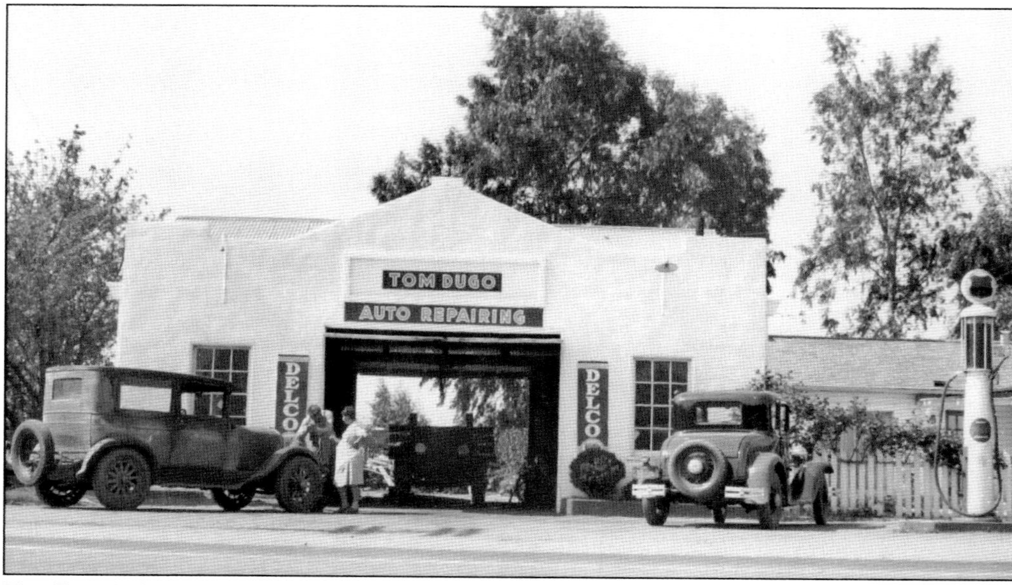


Tom Dugo's Auto Repairing was located on the west side of Escalon Avenue north of Highway 120. The building is now the location for Dugo Signs. The residence on the right is still there today. Note the Model A automobile on the right.

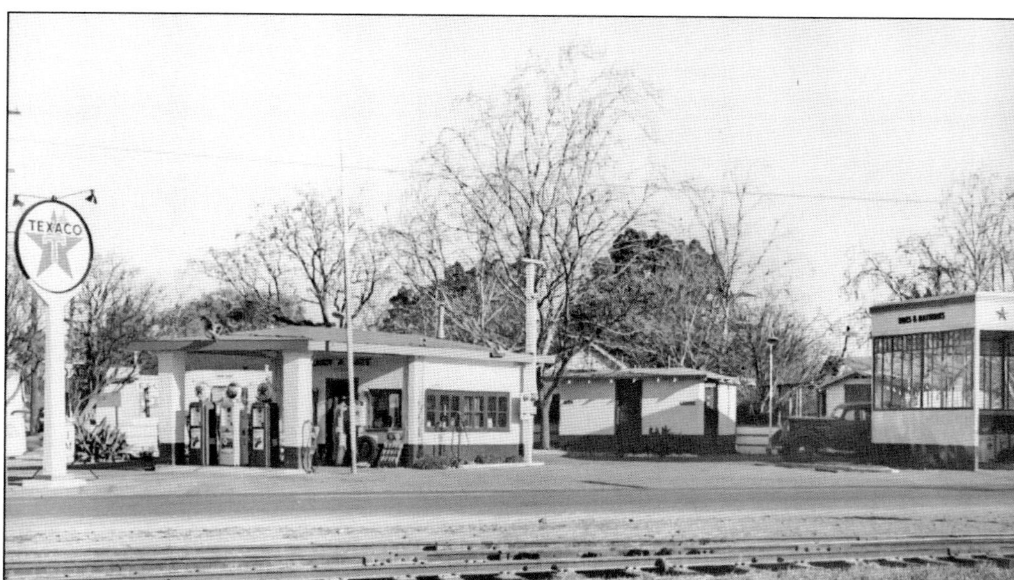


Casey's Texaco station, owned by Casey Matt, was at the corner of McHenry Avenue and First Street. Casey purchased the station in 1948 and operated it until it was shut down in 1975. The businesses now occupying these buildings are Country Cutts Barber Shop and the Aquatic Discount Scuba dive shop.

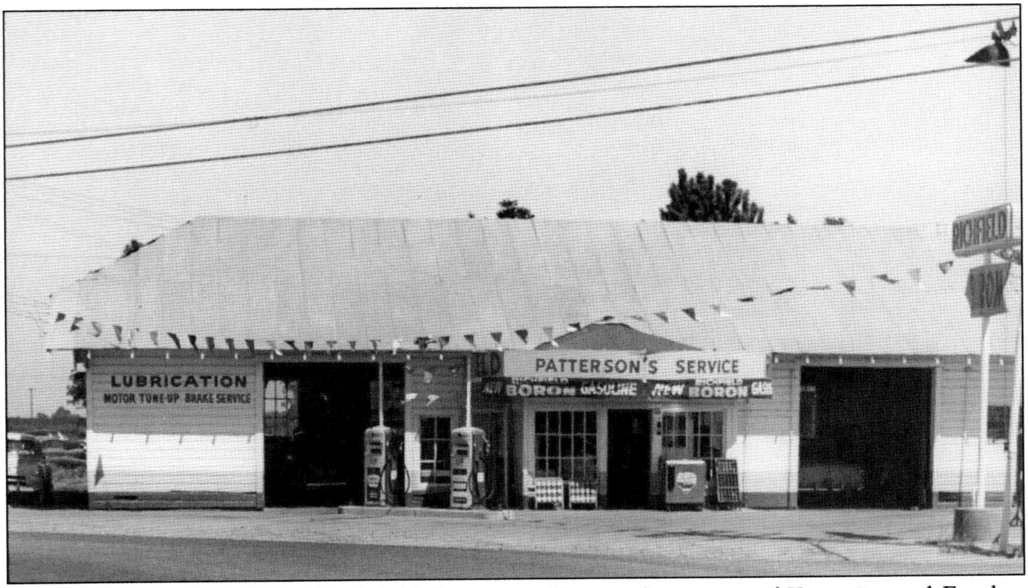


Patterson's Service provided Richfield Boron gasoline at the corner of Yosemite and Escalon Avenues around 1950. Other businesses previously occupying this same structure were Signal gasoline and Seaside service station. Some things stand out in a small community. There are those who have said over the years that Escalon has had a disproportionately large number of gasoline stations and churches.

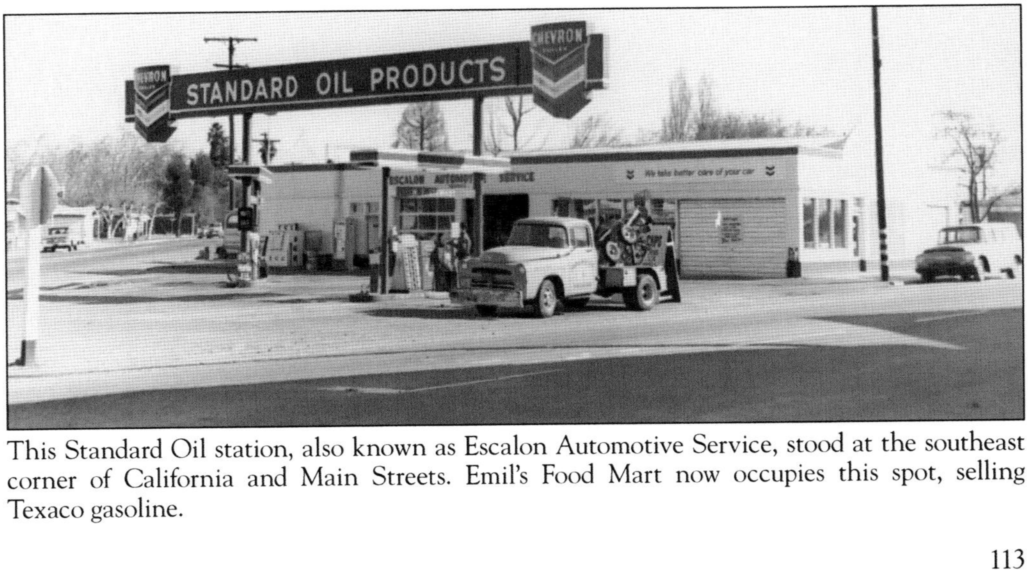


This Standard Oil station, also known as Escalon Automotive Service, stood at the southeast corner of California and Main Streets. Emil's Food Mart now occupies this spot, selling Texaco gasoline.

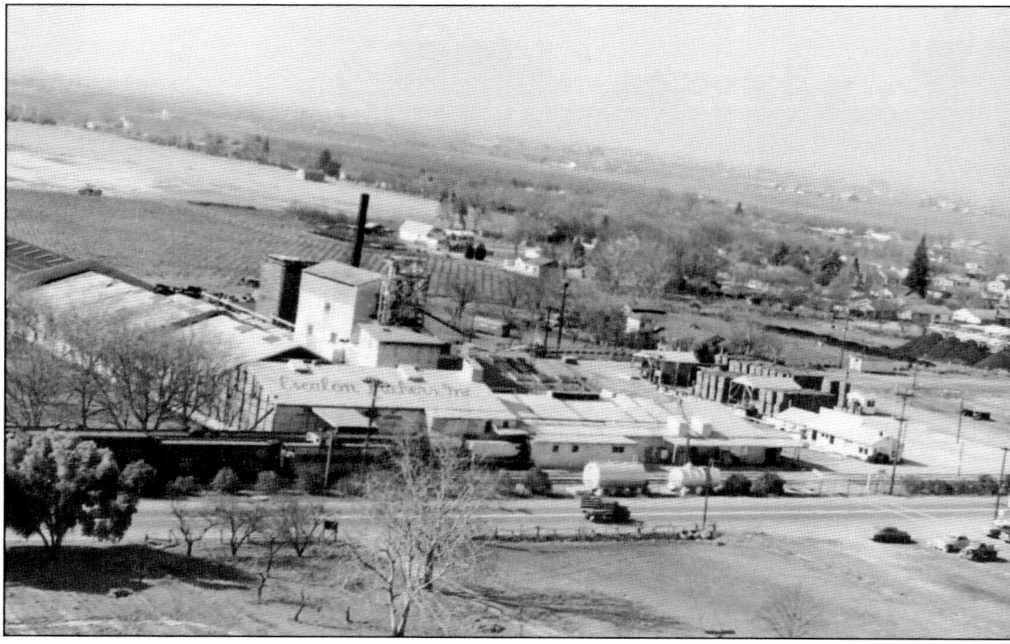

The building that housed Escalon Packers was built in 1936 and has been in operation since 1937 under various names and owners. Foods processed over the years have included tomatoes, cherries, peaches, apricots, prunes, and garbanzo beans. Today the business is known as Escalon Premier Brands, a subsidiary of the H. J. Heinz Company, and is a specialty processor of tomato products. At the time of this photograph—the 1950s, judging by the automobiles—the entrance to the plant was on McHenry Avenue, and employees parked across the street.

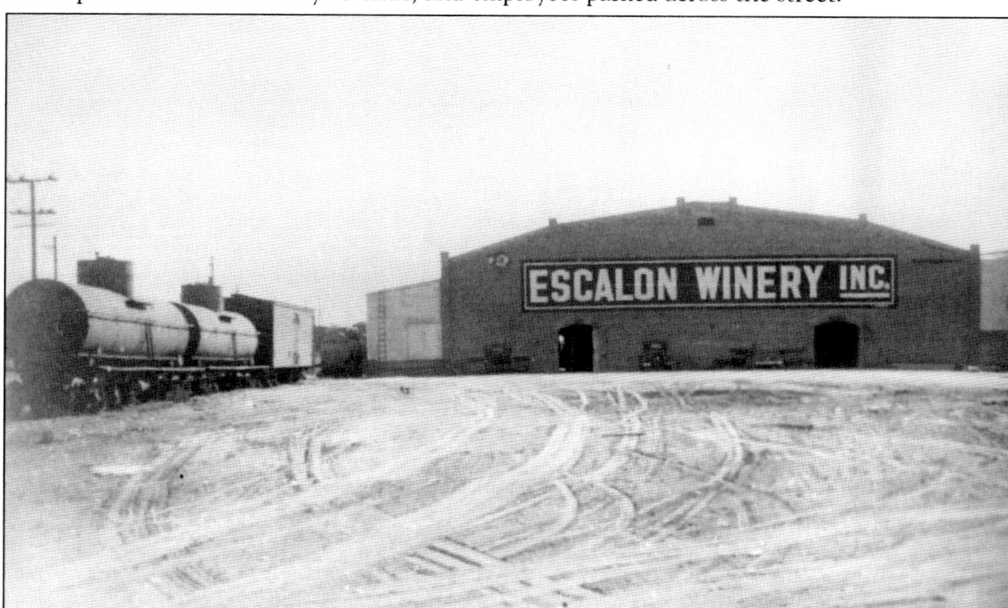


The Escalon Winery was built in 1913 to the west of the Tidewater Southern Railway tracks, south of First Street. Later it would be known as the Village Winery, Solera Cellars, Bianchi Cellars, Bianchi Winery, and finally, the Old Winery, when it contained shops and a restaurant, before being torn down.

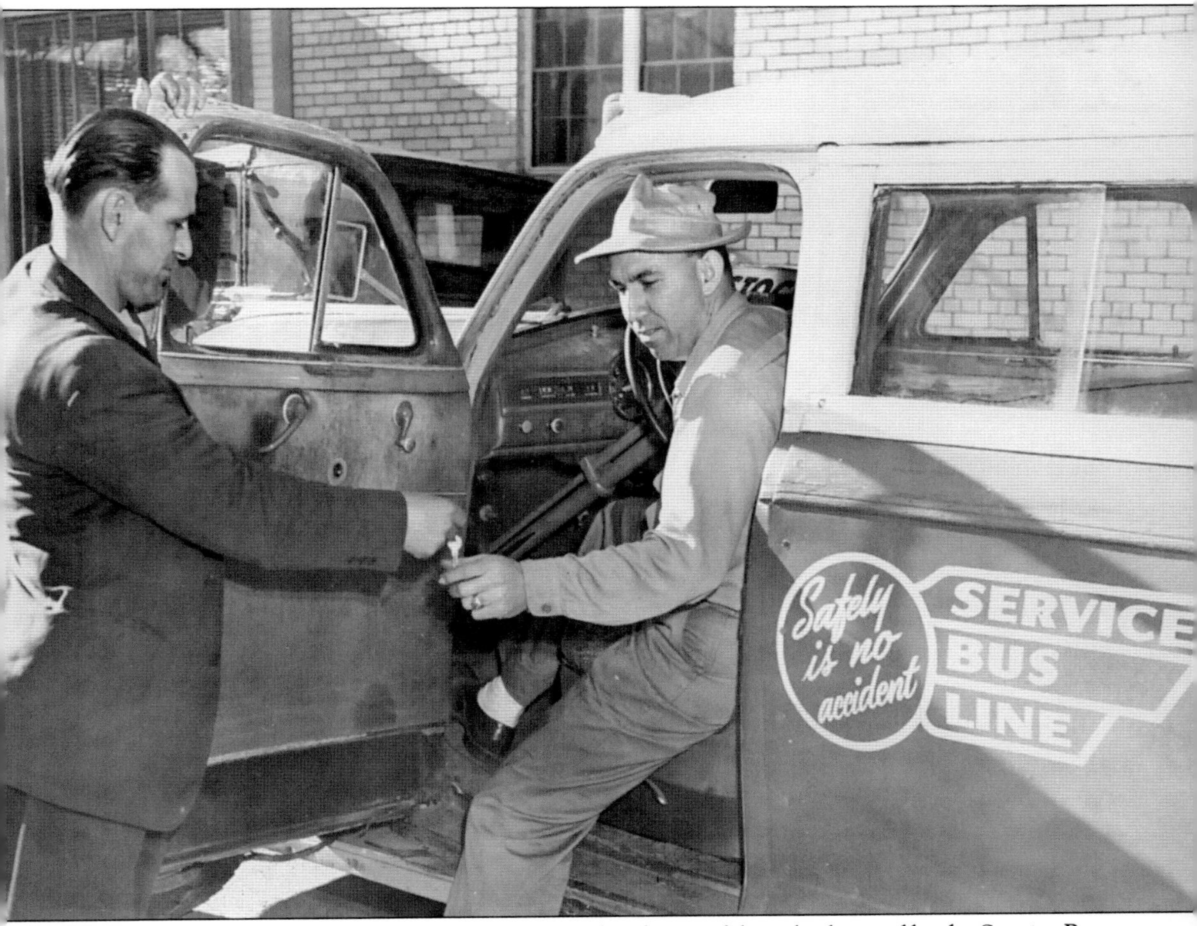


Angelo Bonzi (left) and Angelo Dugo are pictured with one of the vehicles used by the Service Bus Line, a taxi service. Station stops were in Farmington, Bellota, Linden, Peters, Escalon, Modesto, Empire, Waterford, Hickman, Hughson, and Glenwood. Service was provided daily except on Sundays and holidays. In addition to passengers, commodities were transported weighing up to 100 pounds. For weights of up to 20 pounds, the charge was 75¢; for 21 to 40 pounds, 85¢; for 41 to 60 pounds, 95¢; for 61 to 80 pounds, \$1.05; and for 81 to 100 pounds, \$1.25.

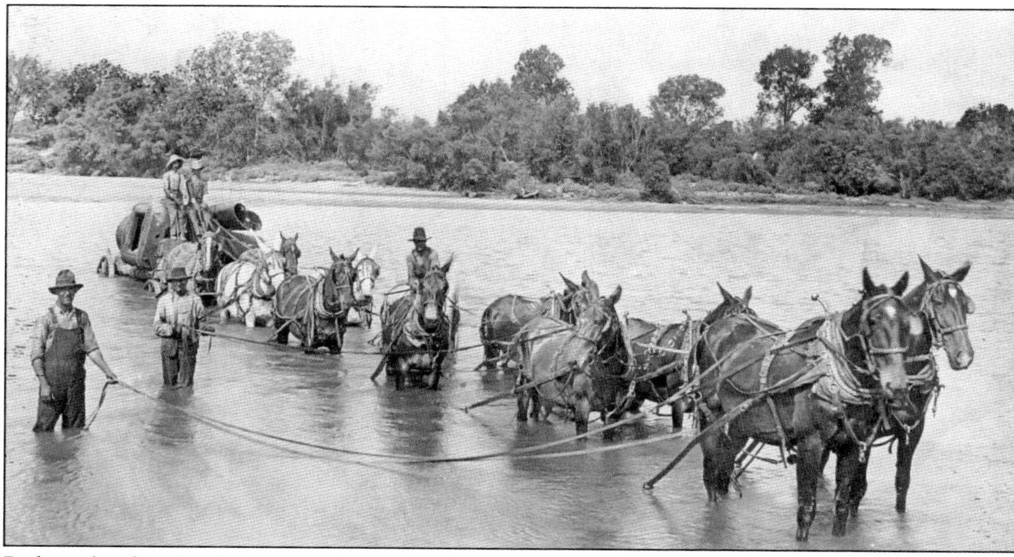

Before the first bridge was built across the Stanislaus River, ferry systems were put in place. This wagon with a locomotive firebox and collapsed boiler pipe is being pulled by a horse-and-mule team. A second team of three horses and one mule helped while crossing the river. This photograph was donated to the Escalon Historical Museum by Freeman Reid.

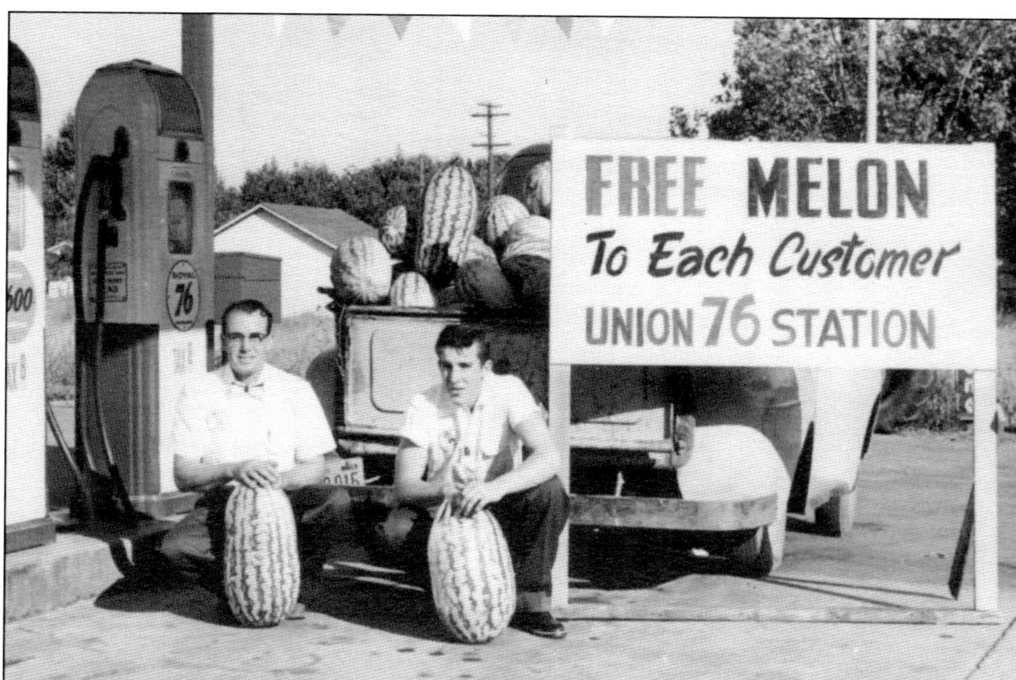


A free melon was offered to each customer at this Union 76 station on Highway 120. Pictured are the owners, Arvy Coburn and his son, A. C.

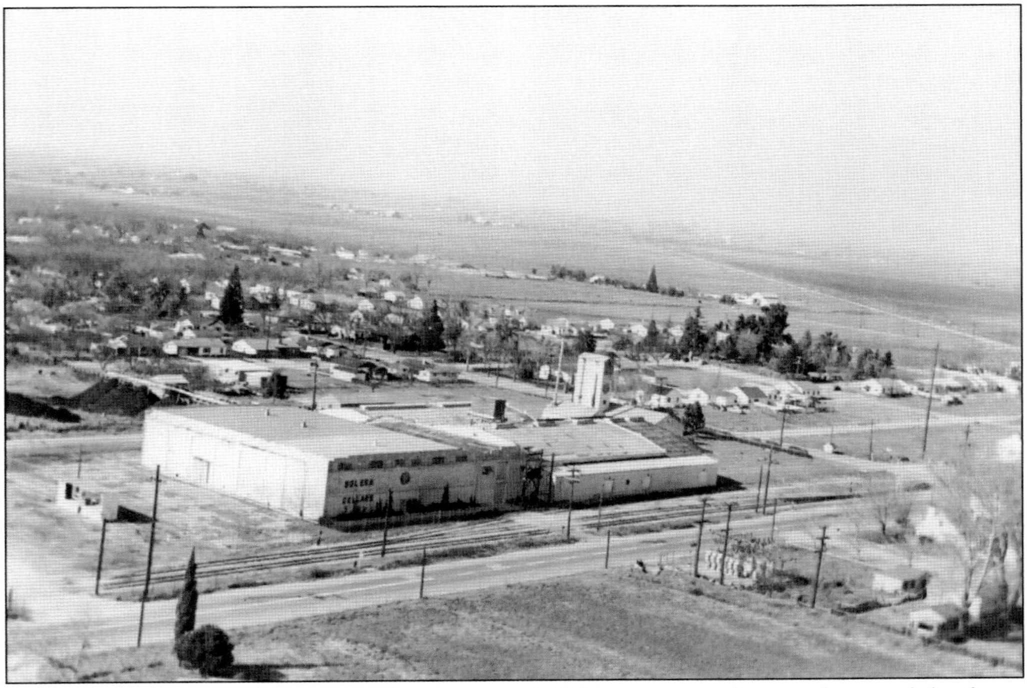


Solera Cellars, pictured in an aerial view around 1948, were touted as producers of the finest Solera wines and other fine wines. To the right of center is the Jones Mansion, surrounded by palm and evergreen trees. This view is toward the northwest.

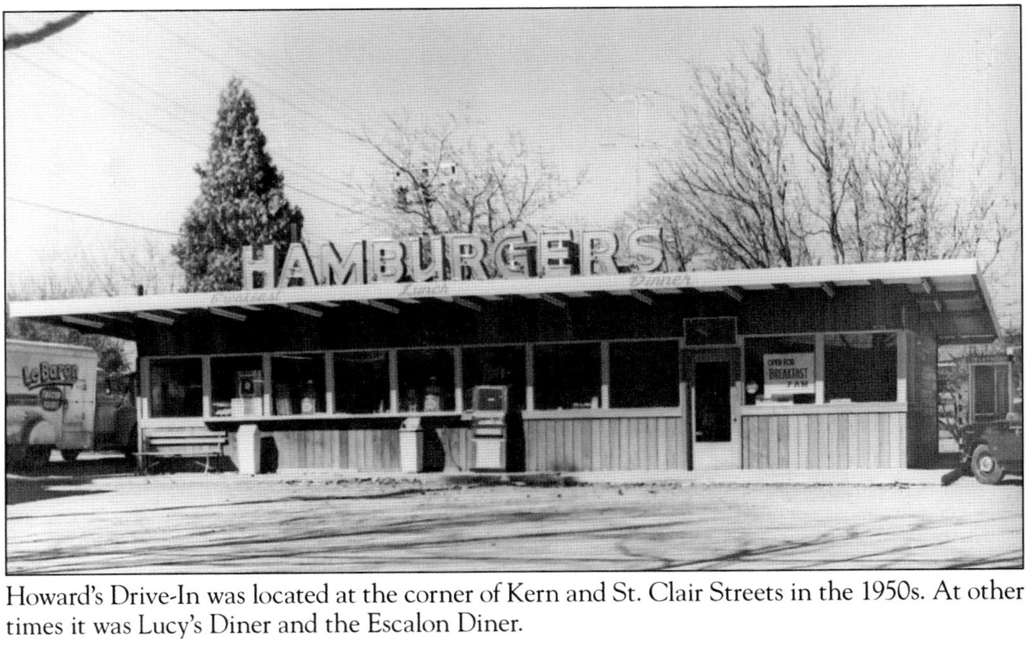


Howard's Drive-In was located at the corner of Kern and St. Clair Streets in the 1950s. At other times it was Lucy's Diner and the Escalon Diner.

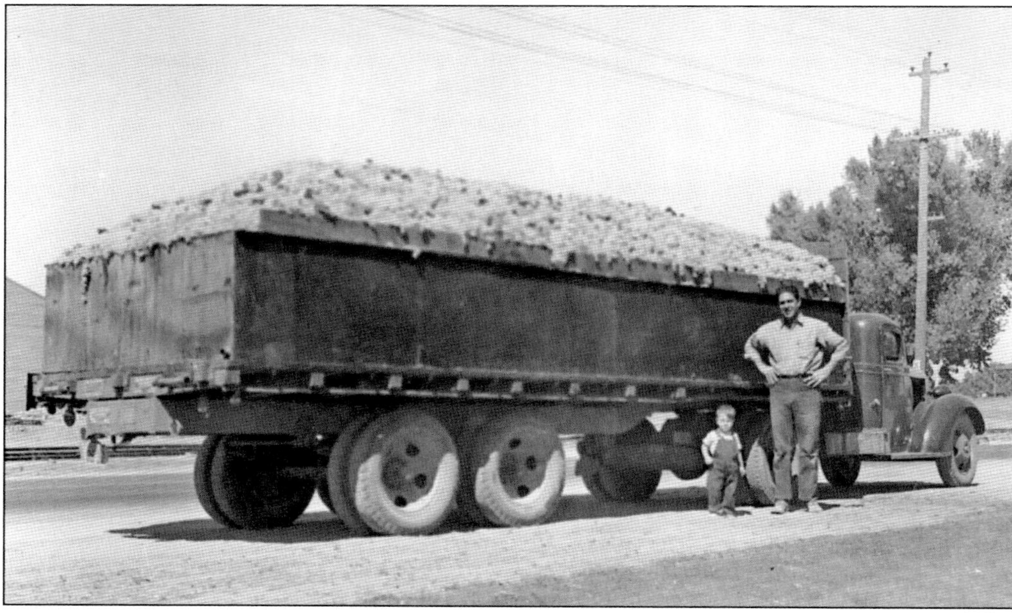

Tony Gonzales and his nephew, Bill, transport a truckload of grapes in 1947. Tony and his brother, Vic, operated a trucking company in Escalon. In addition to grapes, they hauled lumber, peaches, and just about whatever needed to be transported. The company existed for quite a few years in the late 1930s and 1940s.

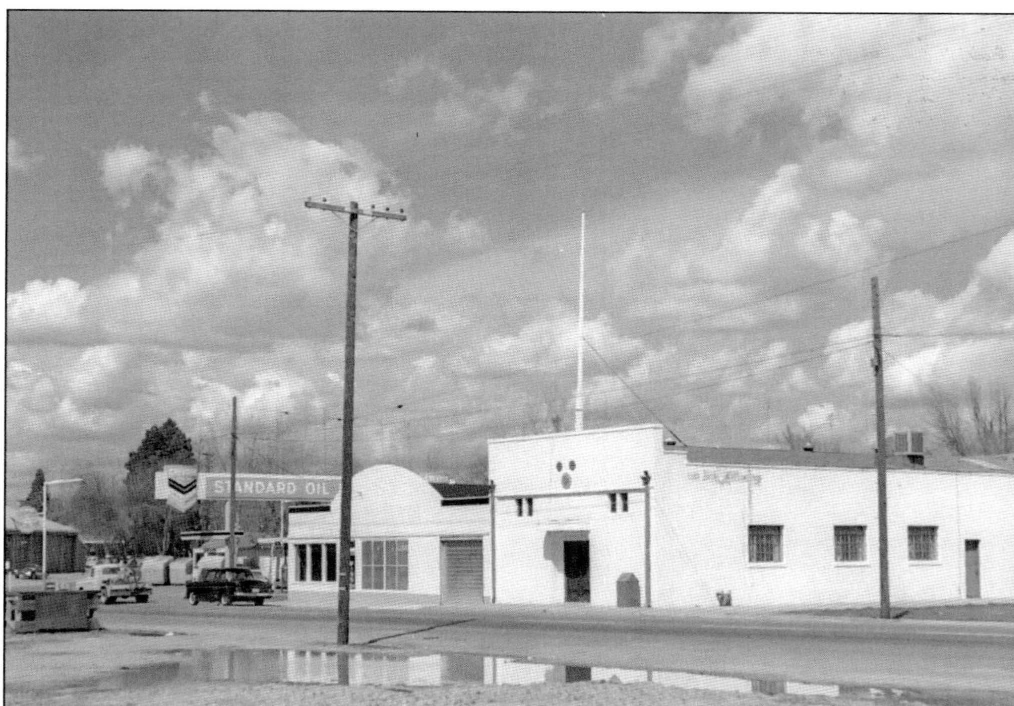


On the left is the Standard Oil station at the corner of Main Street and Highway 120. On the right, facing Main Street, is the former location of the American Legion Hall. Many dances and much imbibing of alcohol took place in the hall.

# *Ten*

# IN SERVICE TO THE COMMUNITY

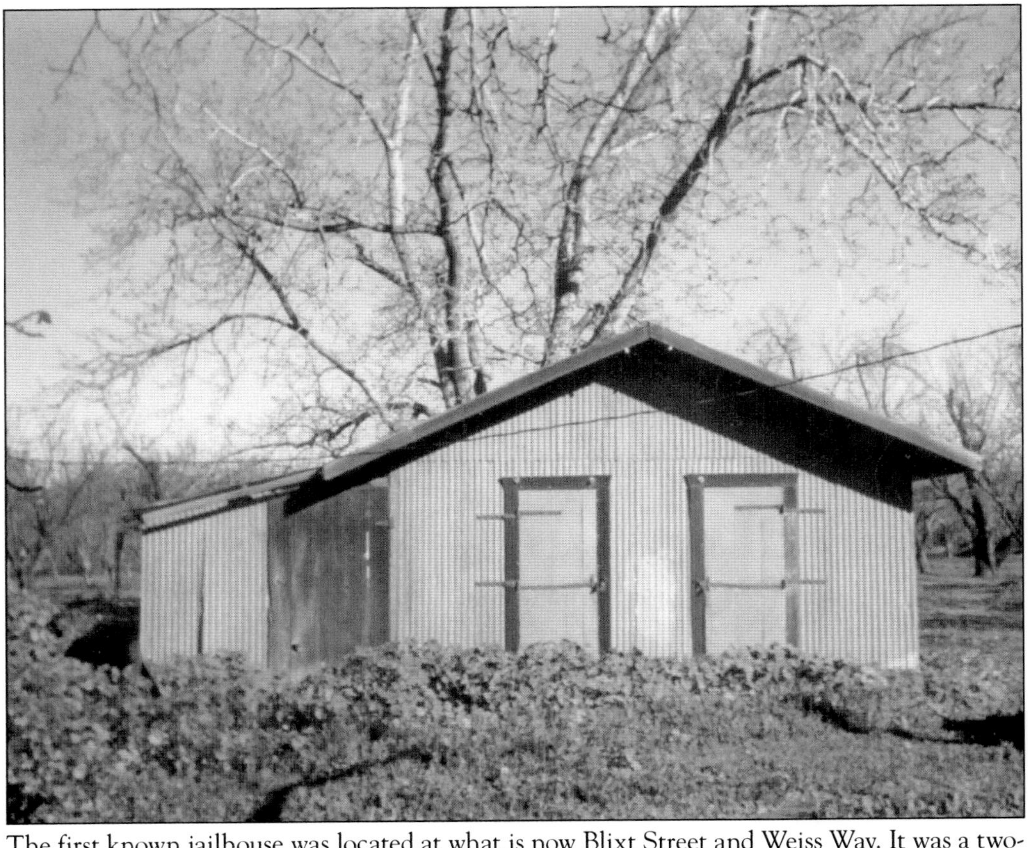

The first known jailhouse was located at what is now Blixt Street and Weiss Way. It was a two-part building. The first part was the jailhouse, and the second was a barn for Al Landon's horse during the time he served as the constable of Dent Township from 1914 to 1946. It is reported that the building was erected in 1917 and was moved to Campbell Road in the 1930s.

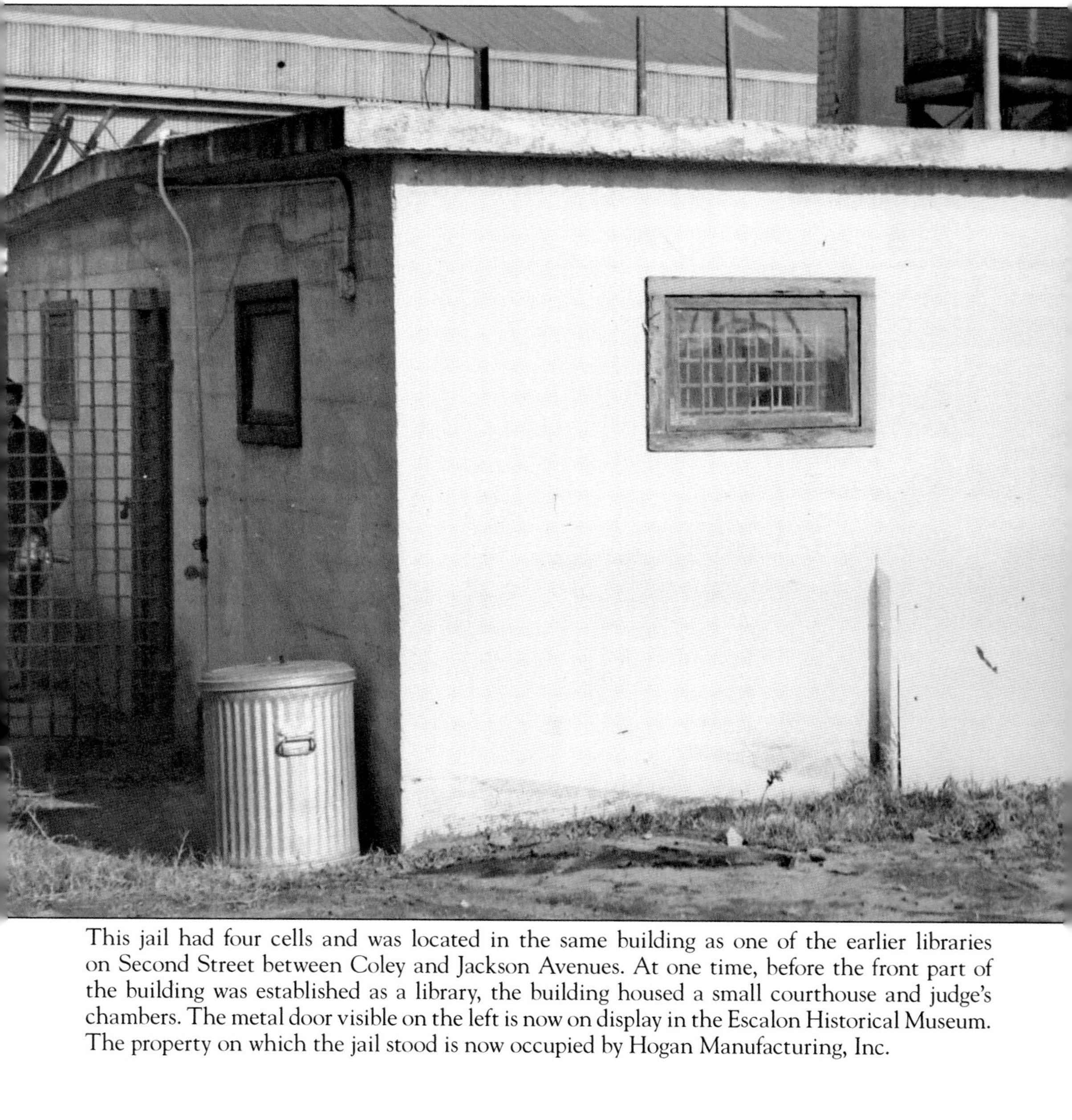

This jail had four cells and was located in the same building as one of the earlier libraries on Second Street between Coley and Jackson Avenues. At one time, before the front part of the building was established as a library, the building housed a small courthouse and judge's chambers. The metal door visible on the left is now on display in the Escalon Historical Museum. The property on which the jail stood is now occupied by Hogan Manufacturing, Inc.

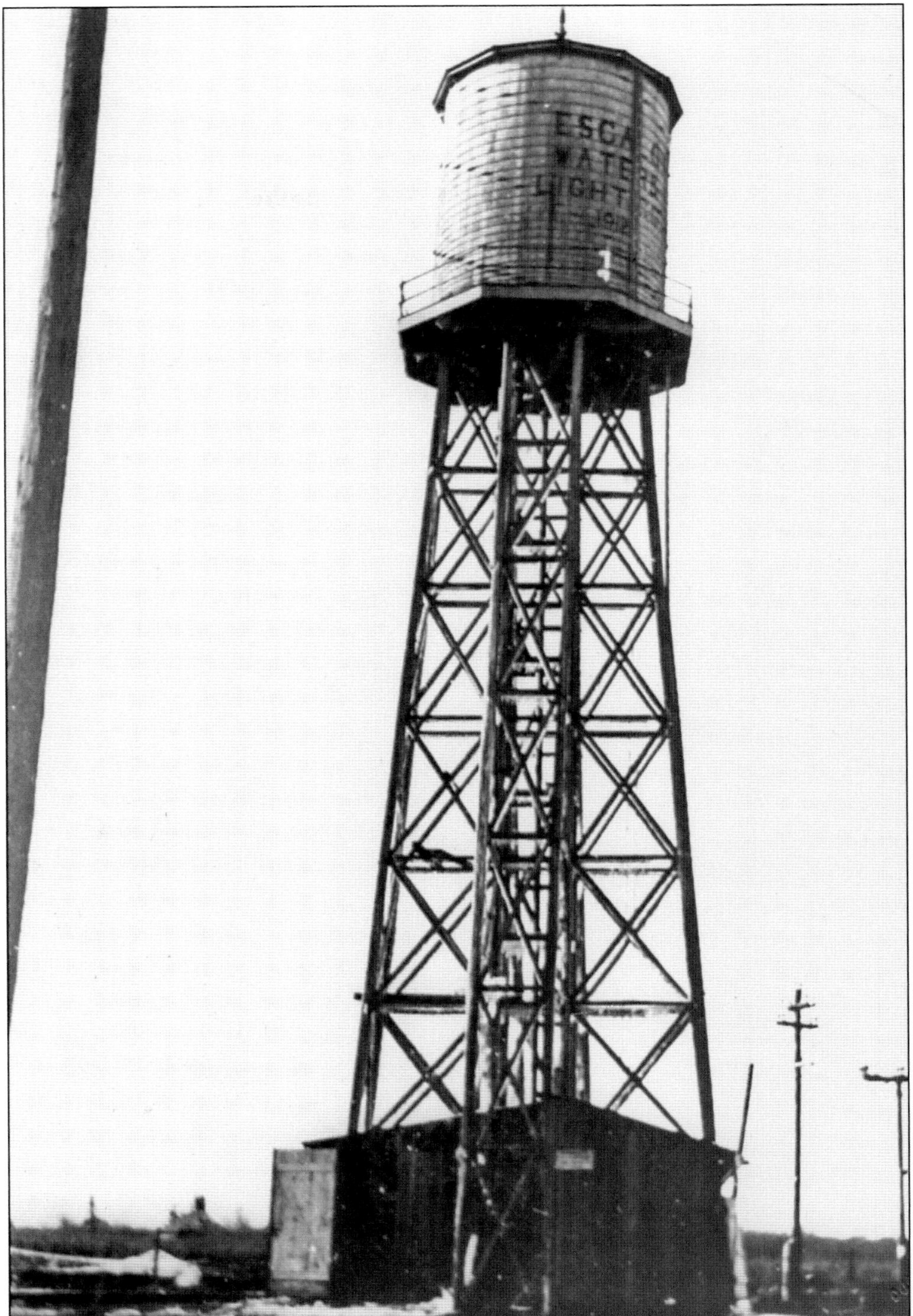

The Escalon Water and Light Company provided the first public water supply to the community when this water tower was built in 1912. Before this service, all water to businesses and residences was supplied by wells and windmills.

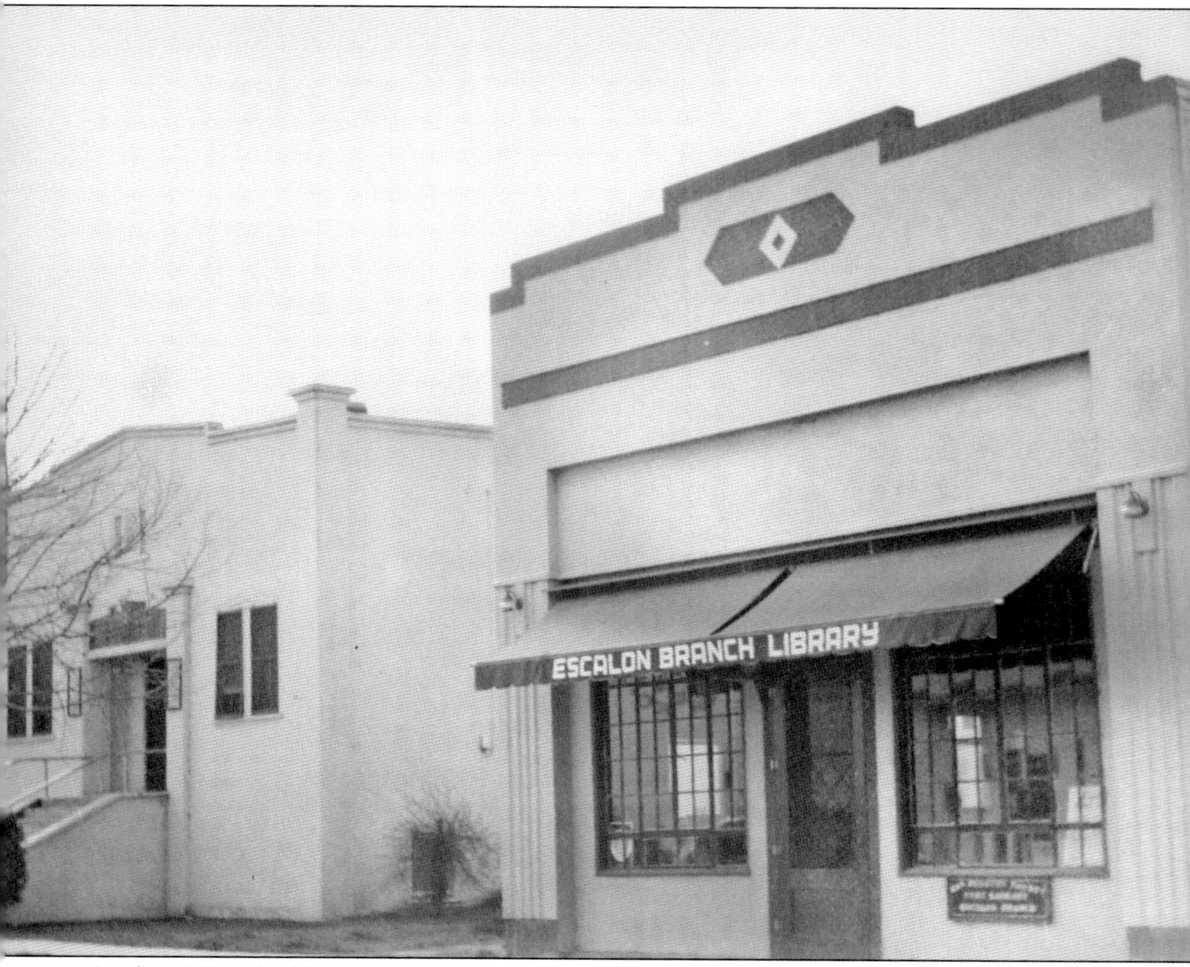


In the 1940s, the library in Escalon was located next to the Glad Tidings Assembly Church, which stood at the corner of Coley Avenue and Second Street. Earlier the library had been run out of Escalon Drug by E. W. Bidwell, the grammar school, and the courthouse before combining with the county library system in 1920 and gaining its own building.

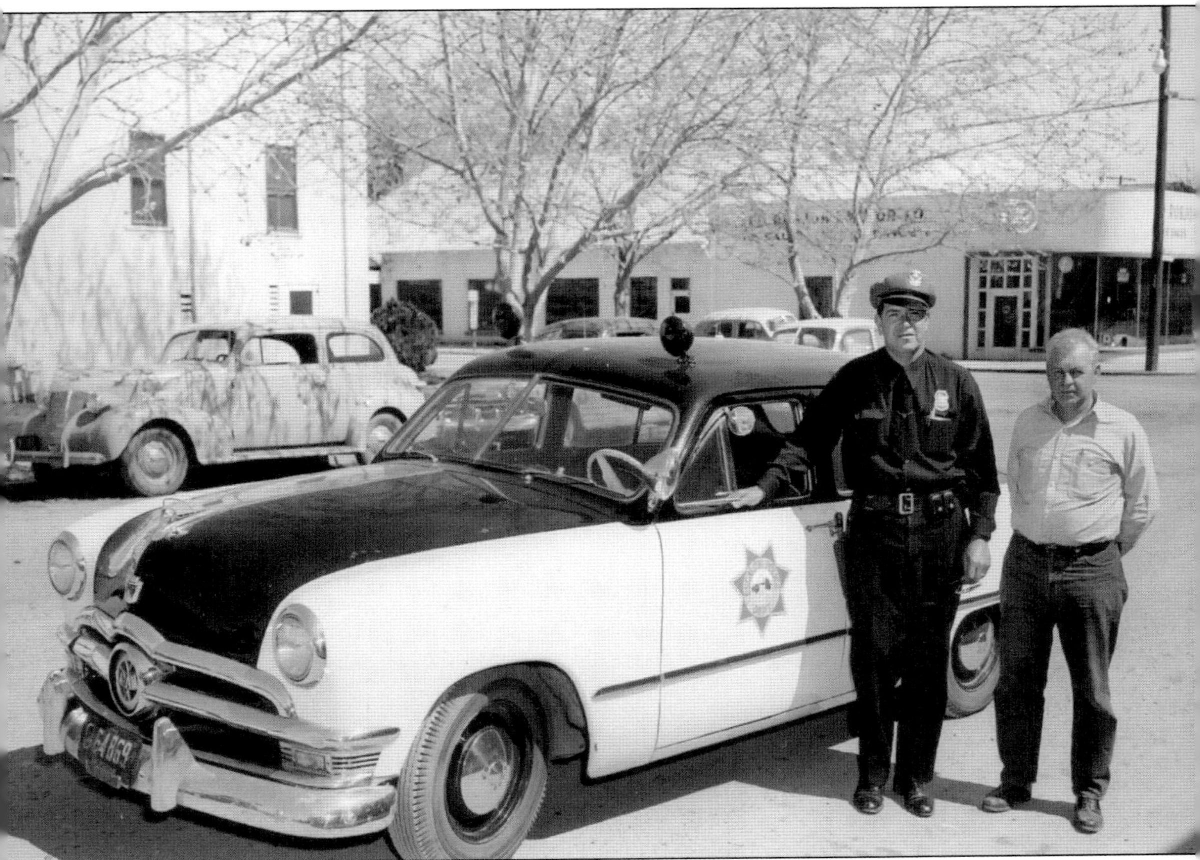

Constable Tony Gonzales (left) and Merral Clark, a local businessman and Escalon's first fire chief, are pictured on Coley Avenue. The corner building was built and occupied by Blixt Automotive Service in 1936. In 1947, the corner building became the showroom and parts department for Blixt and Eliason Ford. In 1950, the dealership was sold to R. C. Stevens Ford, then Ed Robjohn Ford (pictured), and then Joe Souza Ford. The car dealership was home to the Escalon Historical Society's museum in the 1990s.

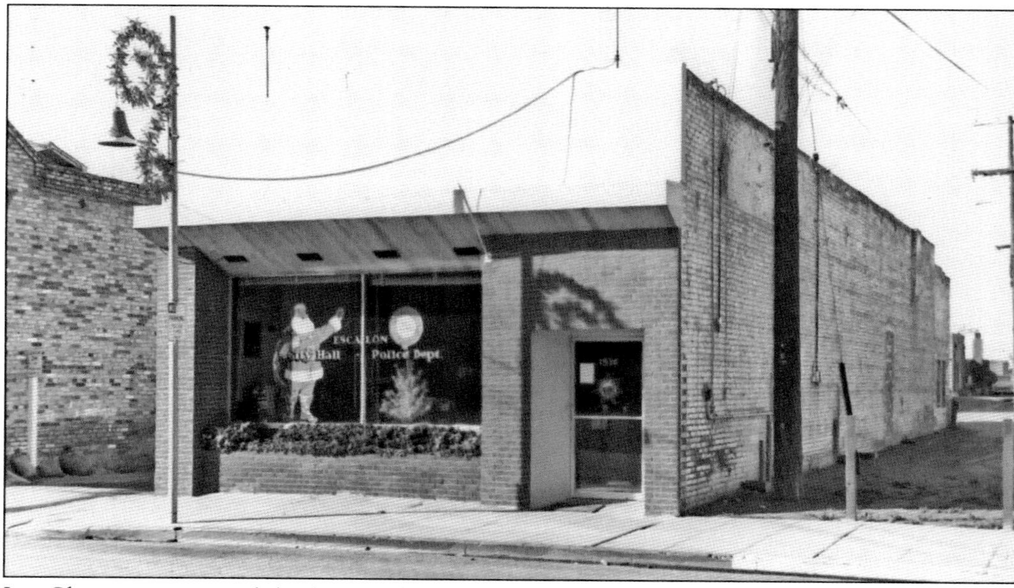

It is Christmastime, and the first city hall/police department, located in this building on Second Street between Main Street and Coley Avenue, is duly decorated. The Escalon Branch Library now has its parking lot in this spot. City hall's next location was at the corner of Coley Avenue and Third Street, where the police and planning departments are located. Currently in its third location at Main and Fourth Streets, city hall will be relocated to McHenry Avenue.

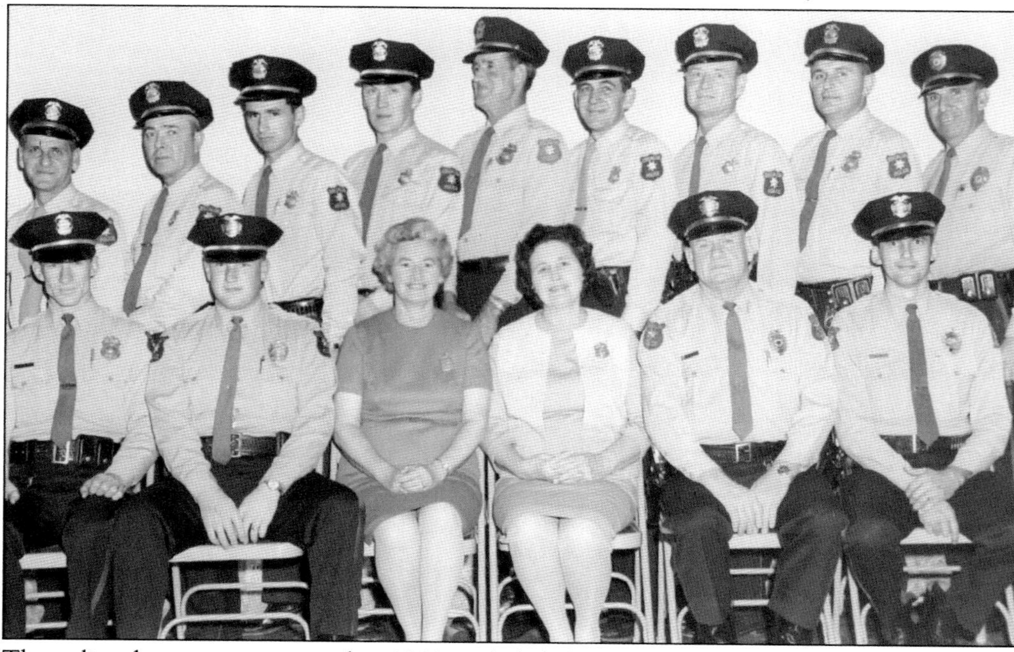

The police department, pictured in 1964, included, from left to right, (first row) patrol officers Dave Beary and Bill Johnson, city secretary Edna Ihrig, matron Mary Dugo, Chief Jim Black, and patrol officer Jim Payne; (second row) reserve officers Angelo Bonzi, Ralph Abernathy, Dan Lowry, George Johnstad, Harvey Capps, Al Paddack, John Ennis, and Les Prater, and Sgt. Angelo Dugo. At this time, the police department was located on Second Street between Main Street and Coley Avenue.

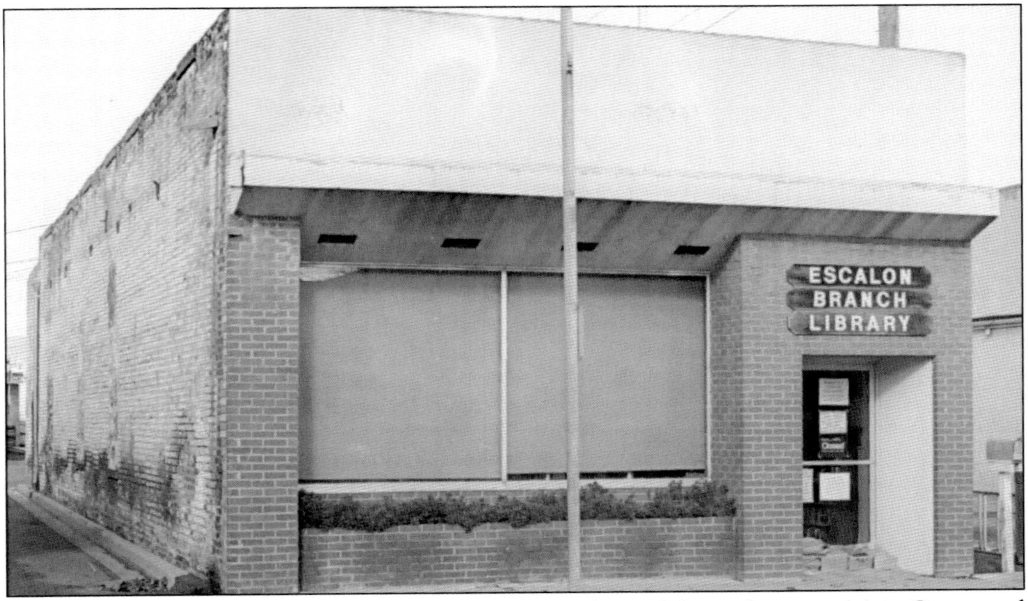


This location for the Escalon Branch Library was on Second Street between Main Street and Coley Avenue, where the parking lot is for the current library building. At one time, Bender's Bakery occupied this spot, and later the Escalon Police Department and City Hall occupied this building. The building was demolished in the early 1990s. The sign above the door is now displayed in the Escalon Historical Museum.

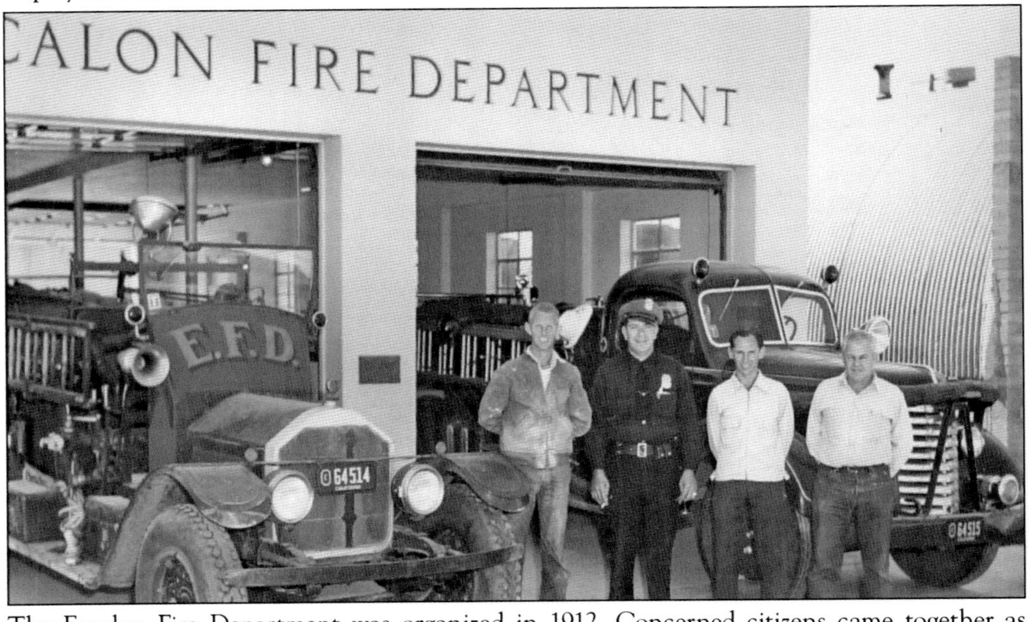


The Escalon Fire Department was organized in 1912. Concerned citizens came together as volunteers in order to prevent the devastation wrought by fire. The original crews included members with surnames figuring elsewhere in the history and business community of Escalon—names such as Haines, Leighton, Ridley, McPherson, Gustafson, Searcy, Herzinger, Irwin, Hetzler, and Fisk. The first portion of the firehouse, as seen in this picture, was built in 1950. Pictured from left to right are volunteer Curtis Maxfield, constable Tony Gonzales, volunteer Harry Lafayette, and Chief Merral Clark.

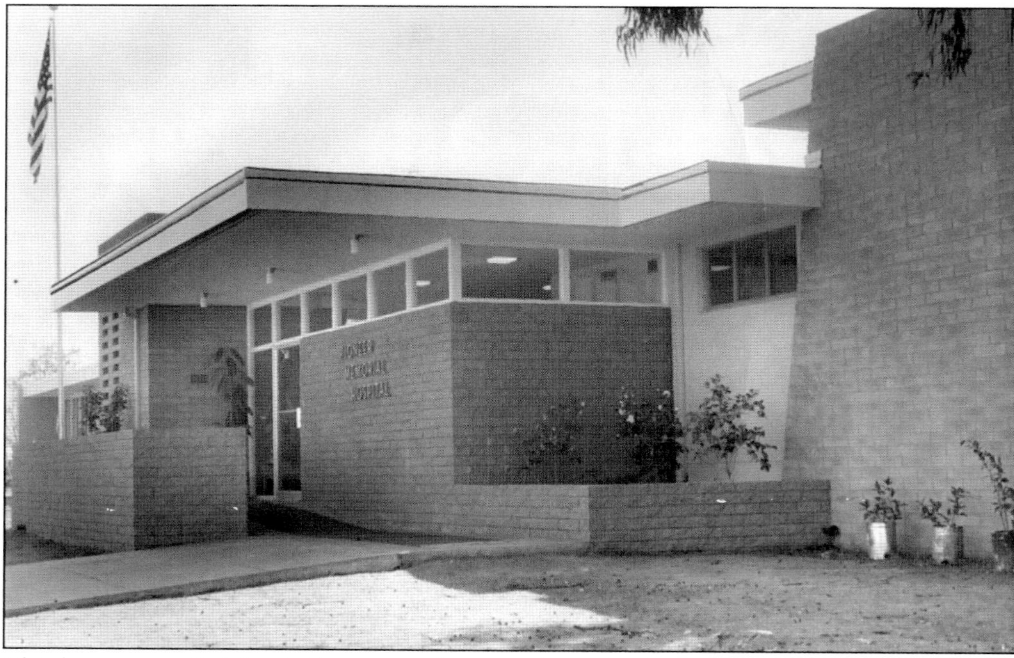

This location on California Street was the second one for the Pioneer Memorial Hospital and came into use after construction was completed in 1960. This hospital operated for a total of 30 years at the two locations. This building is now home to the Golden Acres Home and Care.

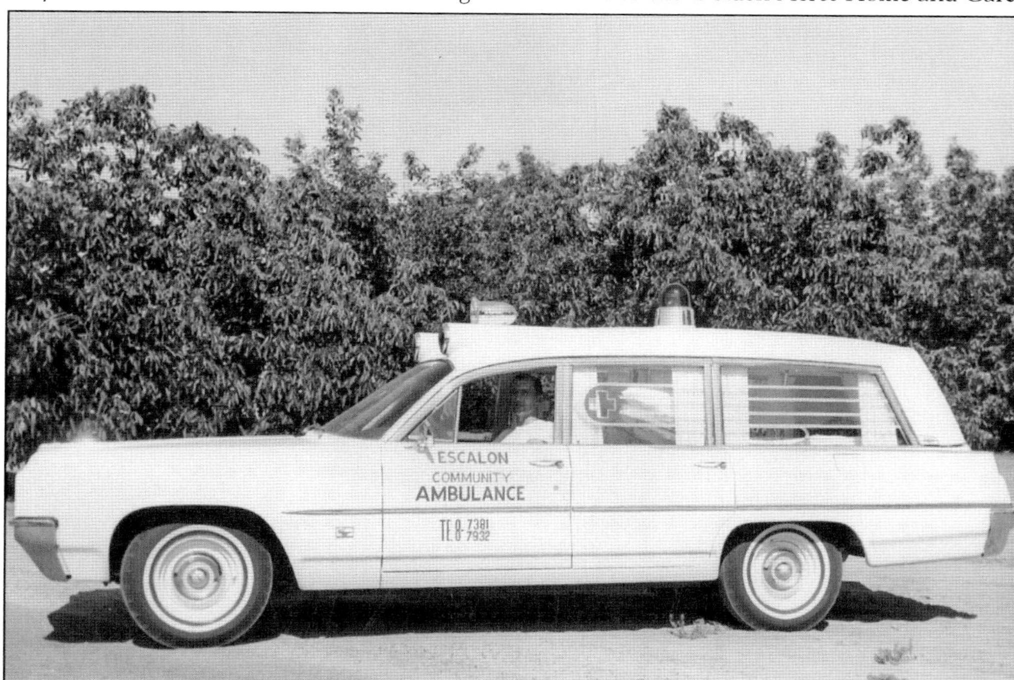


The Escalon Community Ambulance Association purchased the first new ambulance for the Escalon community in 1963 and ran it with volunteers. Delivery of the ambulance was taken in Blythville, Arkansas, and it was driven to Escalon by police officer Jim Payne (pictured). The ambulance was housed at the hospital.